Giuliana Cavallini

St. Martin de Porres

APOSTLE OF CHARITY

Cross and Crown Series of Spirituality

LITERARY EDITOR

Reverend Jordan Aumann, O.P., S.T.D.

NUMBER 26

Giuliana Cavallini

St. Martin de Porres

APOSTLE OF CHARITY

TRANSLATED

BY CAROLINE HOLLAND

TAN BOOKS AND PUBLISHERS, INC.
Rockford, Illinois 61105

This volume is a translation of
I Fioretti del Beato Martino by Giuliana Cavallini,
published by Edizioni Cateriniane in Rome in 1957

IMPRIMATUR ✝ Cletus F. O'Donnell, J.C.D.
Vicar General, September 19, 1963

Printed and bound in the United States of America

TAN BOOKS AND PUBLISHERS, INC.
P.O. Box 424
Rockford, Illinois 61105

1979

OFFICIAL APPROBATION OF THE
DOMINICAN ORDER

This interesting and inspiring biography of St. Martin de Porres was originally entitled I FIORETTI DEL BEATO MARTINO and was presented to the public in 1957. In that same year the Master General of the Dominican Order, now Michael Cardinal Browne, O.P., wrote a letter of commendation to the author, Giuliana Cavallini.

At the time of the canonization of St. Martin de Porres the biography was published in a new edition by the Office of the Dominican Postulator General, under the title, VITA DI SAN MARTINO. At the same time, the English version was prepared for the *Cross and Crown Series of Spirituality* of the B. Herder Book Company by Caroline Holland of Chicago. New material was added to the original volume in order to make this biography as definitive as possible.

I am very pleased that Father Jordan Aumann, O.P., General Editor of the *Cross and Crown Series of Spirituality*, has selected this biography for American distribution. I am certain that through the medium of this excellent English translation the life of St. Martin de Porres will be made known to many more readers and those who are already devoted to him will gain a more intimate knowledge of his holy life.

I am also happy to state that by the authority of the Most Reverend Aniceto Fernández, O.P., Master General of the Dominican Order, this volume is recognized and presented as an official biography of St. Martin de Porres.

May God, through the intercession of St. Martin, bless this volume with every success.

Father Tarcisius Piccari, O.P.

POSTULATOR GENERAL

Santa Sabina
Rome, Italy

PREFACE

In the summer of 1955, when I finished this biography of Martin de Porres, I wrote a Preface as an explanation of the title I had given the work: *"I Fioretti del Beato Martino"* (*The Little Flowers of Blessed Martin*).

Now, after Martin's canonization and with the publication of these *"fioretti"* in English, I find nothing to be changed in the original Preface, although the title of the book cannot remain as it was in the Italian edition. A translation of the original title into English would have little meaning.

☆

These *"fioretti"* are neither a chronological nor a critical story of the life of Martin de Porres. They are episodes taken from the testimony given during the process of his beatification. The persons who gave the testimony had known Martin during his lifetime and they were asked to state under oath what they knew about him. It is certain, therefore, that these witnesses faithfully presented the facts as they knew them. The events were too extraordinary to be forgotten, especially since so little time had elapsed since they happened.

The sole justification for the presentation of these extraordinary details of the life of Martin de Porres—inexplicable from any natural point of view—is the person who emerges from the sworn testimony of the witnesses. The inclusion of such details is natural and even necessary, for no portrait of the Saint would be complete if these exterior manifestations of his sanctity were omitted.

We can accept, and even enjoy, these amazing details, knowing that the authentic sanctity of the Dominican Brother of Lima rests on another basis: the constant and heroic practice of the virtues, and principally that of charity, the virtue which unquestionably marked his whole life.

Many lives of Martin de Porres have been written in the last hundred years, especially in the United States, where devotion to him has grown in a remarkable manner ever since 1866. In that year Father Felice Barotti erected a chapel in Washington as a center for the Negroes to whom he had dedicated his apostolate. The chapel was placed under the patronage of the holy Negro Brother whom Father Barotti proposed as a model and a symbol of hope for the suffering victims of racial prejudice.

Martin de Porres, whose sanctity was so rich and varied in its aspects, attracts and comforts. A true son of St. Dominic, faithful to the severest traditions of his Order, Martin had a mind and heart open and ready to respond to all the needs of his fellow men. And while he planned and carried out magnificent projects in what we today would call the social apostolate, he did not disdain at the same time to exercise his skills and even his gift of healing in the service of animals and plants.

Among the numerous books written about Martin, many of them of great importance, these *"fioretti"* blossom in all humility. They bloom as a result of the spiritual development of that "tree of love" which was the soul of Martin de Porres, to use an expression of St. Catherine of Siena. In her allegory of the tree planted in the soil of humility and nourished by prayer, she states that such a tree blossoms in charity, to the praise of God and the benefit of men.

☆

I add to the original Preface only the hope that these *"fioretti,"* crossing the frontiers of the land where they blossomed, may carry to the vast world the sweet odor of the sanctity of Martin de Porres and inspire in souls a love for the beauty of a holy life. May they also contribute in their own small way to that revitalization of the Mystical Body of Christ which Pope John XXIII earnestly desired as a result of the Ecumenical Council, as he stated in his solemn address at the canonization of Martin de Porres.

Giuliana Cavallini

MISSIONARY OF THE SCHOOLS

≻ 1 ≺

*Her ways are beautiful ways: and
all her paths are peaceable* (Prov. 3:17).

St. Martin de Porres was born in Lima, Peru, on December 9, 1579.

There is no need to describe Lima nor to outline its history. Those who are uncertain of its geographical position need only consult a map of South America. If one follows the outline of the western coast from north to south, Lima will be found about one-third the way down the length of the continent, near its port, Callao.

The story of the first decade of the Spanish conquest is such a mixture of daring and cruelty that admiration for these intrepid pioneers is cut short by horror at their inhumanity. The first white men to arrive on the shores of the New World were, it is true, fearless in facing and overcoming the thousand unknown dangers presented by a deadly climate and a savage land infested with wild animals and with insects even more dangerous than the beasts. But at the same time, thirst for gold made them masters of cruelty, contrasting strangely with that character of heralds of the Gospel, in which they gloried, and probably with sincere intentions.

It is almost a miracle that the Catholic faith was established among the Indians in spite of the brutality practiced by the conquistadors.

When Hatuey, chief of Cuba, was offered baptism at the very moment that the invaders, dissatisfied with the gold he had offered to sate their cupidity, were preparing to burn him alive, he asked the missionary priest, "Will the white Christians also enter into paradise?" Receiving an affirmative reply, he is said to have retorted, "Then I prefer to do without it!" [1]

But the Indians soon found staunch defenders. In 1510, twelve Friars Preachers founded a monastery on the island of Santo Domingo, and on a Sunday of the same year, one of them, Father Anthony de Montesino, denounced the cruelty of the Spaniards from the pulpit: "Because of the cruelty and tyranny you have inflicted upon an innocent and peaceful people, you are farther from salvation than the Moslems who deny the name of our Lord Jesus Christ!" And he declared that neither he nor his fellow priests would give absolution to those who mistreated the natives.

Indifferent to all protests and threats, Father Montesino continued to preach constantly on the same theme until the day he embarked upon a ship leaving for Spain so that he could plead the cause of the Indians before the King. It was not easy to gain an audience with King Ferdinand; all those interested in the unlimited plundering of the land across the sea impeded him. It seems that finally Father Anthony (a man whose courageous heart was matched by his athlete's physique) gained entrance to the King's presence by sheer force, throwing aside an attendant stationed at the door to prevent his entering. The first laws for the protection of the rights of the Indians, known as the Laws of Burgos of 1514, resulted from his audience with the King.

But the preaching of Father Anthony had an even greater effect. It aroused the interest of Bartholomew de Las Casas, then a diocesan priest, but later to become a Dominican and a bishop. He would dedicate his whole life to the cause of the Indians and would become a model for all defenders of the natives against the tyranny of the whites.[2]

The new laws, which were to crown the efforts of Las

Casas in 1542, were not yet promulgated when Pizzaro and Almagro, with few men but great daring, came down from Panama in a small boat, journeying southward towards the fabled land of the Incas. It is sad, but not surprising, that the conquest of Peru was marked by the same scenes of horror that had been staged in regions conquered in the preceding years. The inhabitants of Peru had reached a high degree of culture and their system of government was perfectly organized. The contrast between the brutal methods of conquest and the customs of a population far from primitive was therefore all the more striking. In fact, in some respects the Peruvians were more civilized than the Europeans who used violent means to substitute their authority for that of the Incas.[3]

In a few years the whole country was conquered for the Spanish. On the feast of the Epiphany, 1535, Pizarro laid the foundation of the new capital, destined to replace the old capital of Cuzco, which was situated in the mountains and too far from the seaport. This new capital was at first called "City of the Kings," in memory of the day of its foundation, but later the commemoration of the Three Kings was supplanted by the vivid and sonorous presence of the river which passes through the city, the Rimac. And from "Rimac" the name "Lima" was derived.[4]

The first years of the history of Lima were tormented ones, filled with the struggle not only between the Spaniards and the natives, but between the Spaniards themselves. The thirst for power and wealth, which made the conquerors capable of any cruelty that could open the door to treasure, led them to fight against one another in order to attain the posts of honor and profit. The city was not yet seven years old when Pizarro was murdered in his own palace, victim of a plot headed by

[3]

the son of the same James de Almagro who had been Pizarro's companion in the conquest of Peru, and of whose death Pizarro cannot be held innocent.

Nevertheless, with the rapidity with which every seed brought from the Old World seemed to develop in the New, Lima swiftly acquired enough calm to become a center of culture as well as the political and commercial capital. In 1551 the Dominicans founded a university there, the University of St. Mark, the first to be established in all the territory of the two Americas. Lima had been founded only sixteen years previously.

The sons of St. Dominic were the first to preach the Gospel in the land of the Incas. They had shared the perils of the Peruvian adventure with Pizarro in the same boat in which he and his men sailed south through the Pacific. Missionaries of many other orders followed them: Franciscans, Augustinians, Mercedarians, Jesuits. But Divine Providence reserved for the first missionary workers the finest fruits of the seed of the Gospel sown between the seacoast and the forbidding heights of the Andes.

The first bishop was a Dominican, Vincent de Valverde. The first center of culture was Dominican, the University of St. Mark. And, far more important than all else, the first saint was a Dominican, St. Rose of Lima.

But even before the waters of baptism had infused, together with sanctifying grace, the seed of sanctity into the soul of little Rose of Santa María—in fact, seven years before—another privileged soul, destined to reach the heights of perfection in the Order of Friars Preachers, received the gift of supernatural life at the same baptismal font in the church of St. Sebastian in Lima.

Martin was the son of John de Porres, a noble Spanish gentleman and Knight of the Order of Alcántara, and of Anna Velázquez a free Negress. When the father saw that the infant's skin was black, he did not wish to acknowledge the baby as his son. The baptismal registry carries the entry, "Martin, son of an unknown father." But later, John repented and legally acknowledged Martin and Joan, the daughter born two years later.[5]

Martin's first years were spent with his mother and little sister. Since he was quick-witted, Anna sometimes sent him to do the shopping. Martin left with the money and the empty basket. Often—but not always—he returned without any money and the basket still empty. There were so many poor in Lima, and Martin could not refuse those who asked for charity.

And how much time he took to go to the market! He could spend half the morning disposing of a few pennies. Not because he stopped along the way to play with other lads his age, but because if he came across a church, he went in to greet his heavenly Father, who had made him His son, while his own earthly father had repudiated him. He passed from the light of the street to the mysterious and prayerful shadows of the church, and going the length of the spacious nave with the light step of a tiny Negro boy, he knelt before the altar. There he stayed, absorbed in prayer, his huge eyes, wide open and showing very white in his black face, fixed on the crucifix or on a picture of the Virgin, wrapped in the silence of the soaring arches and in the profound peace so different from the noisy squalor of his own home.

But at home he had to settle accounts with his mother, who, having very little money, could not approve the generosity of her little son. "See, it's your fault that today we have nothing to eat; not only you, but also your little sister and myself!"

Martin took his punishment in silence. If he wept, it was over his mother's difficulties. And at the first opportunity, he repeated the offense.[6]

In the meantime, the little circle of acquaintance of Anna Velázquez began to notice the child, so intelligent and so good. There were perhaps those who shook their heads and criticized John de Porres who, rich though he was, left the mother and children to live in misery.

At that period John de Porres did not live in Lima, but in Guayaquil, Ecuador, where he had a government post. He went to Lima only from time to time. After one of these visits to Lima, he returned to Guayaquil with the two children and kept them with him, treating them as a father should treat his own children. In addition to engaging competent teachers for them, he himself completed their education by daily contact, spending with them whatever free hours he could spare from his official duties.

Thus it happened that on one occasion, when taking a walk with Martin and Joan, John de Porres met one of his uncles, James de Miranda, who asked him who the two children were. He answered frankly, "They are my children, and those of Anna Velázquez. I have them with me here, and I am seeing to their education."[7]

Martin was then eight years old, Joan six.

This serene interlude did not last long, perhaps not more than four years. It was interrupted and ended when John de Porres left Ecuador to govern Panama. Joan was entrusted to the care of the uncle, James de Miranda, and John took Martin back to Lima to his mother. He wanted the boy to be confirmed before his own departure for Panama. Before leaving Lima, John gave Anna sufficient funds to permit Martin to complete his education and to learn a trade, and also enough money to ensure their being freed from privation.

[6]

≻ 2 ≺

The wisdom of a discreet man is to understand his way (Prov. 14:8).

AT THE AGE of twelve or a little more, Martin had to make his first important decision, the choice of a trade which would help him earn a living for himself and his mother, since his little sister was being provided for by their great-uncle, James de Miranda.

It is possible that he made his decision with the affectionate approval of his father before the latter left Lima, weighing with him the factors for and against the various possibilities. But it does not appear that John de Porres imposed his paternal authority upon the will of his son; it seems rather that Martin made his choice freely, in accordance with his own inclinations and desires.

As a consequence of this free choice, Martin went to the shop of Marcel de Rivero to learn to be a barber, which in those days meant not only cutting hair and beards, but also letting blood, treating wounds and fractures, and even prescribing medicine for the more ordinary cases of illness. A *"barbero"* or *"cirujano"* was, in fact, at the same time a barber, surgeon, doctor and pharmacist.

Martin applied himself arduously to the study of his profession. Perhaps he foresaw how useful it would be in helping the poor. Along with much good will, a degree of intelligence above the ordinary began to be apparent in him. Soon Marcel de Rivero had not much more to teach him, and several times when he had to be absent from the shop, he left Martin in charge of the "first aid" room.

On one of these occasions, Martin saw three or four men coming into the consulting room, carrying an Indian who had been badly beaten and was bleeding from numerous wounds received in a street brawl. Upon learning that the doctor was not there, their faces fell. Entrust a man in that condition to a mere boy, an apprentice? But all their misgivings vanished when they saw Martin set to work with assurance and skill. Martin washed the wounds and bound them up skillfully, then refreshed the man, who was exhausted from the loss of blood, with a glass of good wine. They were still more satisfied when, after a few days, the Indian returned to his work, as well and as strong as before.[1]

Because of this and other similar incidents, the fame of the young native student began to spread throughout Lima, as he showed he possessed an ability not inferior to that of his teacher from overseas. And such was the skill of the student that, little by little, the clients came to prefer his eye and his hand to the eye and hand of the professor.

Martin could have earned a great deal of money and lived in comfort with his mother. But the same charity which drove him, as a small child, to give to the poor the money his mother had entrusted to him to buy their daily bread, now moved him to devote himself to the poor. He refused money almost with horror. It does not seem, however, that his professional disinterestedness aroused the same indignation in his mother as the thoughtless charity of his childhood had done. Since John de Porres had assumed responsibility for the little family, they were no longer in need, and Anna Velázquez, who, like her son, had a good heart, was not a woman to wish for superfluities when she had the necessities.[2]

Nor did she object to the habit Martin had acquired when very young of visiting the churches along his way. It is true, of course, that Martin as a boy and a student knew better than he did as a child; so now, instead of coming home later, he left earlier. He set out at daybreak, and along the way between his home in Calle Malambo and the shop of Marcel de Rivero, he stopped a long time in the church of St. Lazarus, serving as many Masses as he could. But he was always on time at the shop.

Then, after having spent the whole day in the effort to perfect himself in his profession and use it to help the poor, he shut himself up in his room to feed his soul with spiritual reading and prayer. But because he did not accept money from his patients, and perhaps because he did not wish his mother to know about his long vigils, he begged the owner of the house, Ventura de Luna, to give him the candle stubs too small for her own use. She gave them to him willingly. However, her curiosity was aroused by this continuous request for candle stubs, and one evening Ventura decided to find out what Martin was doing at night. She went to his door, put her ear against it, and listened. She thought she heard sighs and stifled groans. She bent down to peer through the keyhole. On his knees, motionless, his face bathed in tears, his arms outstretched in the form of a cross, his eyes fixed on the crucifix, Martin seemed to have concentrated his whole being in that gaze and that posture which reflected the object of his contemplation.

Ventura watched him, holding her breath, and then went softly away. Since her discovery had made a deep impression on her and she could not get it out of her mind, she felt impelled to talk about it with her friends.

She did even more; she invited them to come and share in her discovery. Night after night the friends of Ventura de Luna peered into the keyhole at the secret of the mysterious exchange of love between Christ crucified and Martin, while he remained blissfully unaware of their indiscretion.³

It was at this period of Martin's life that God gave the first indication—or one among the first—of the prodigies He would perform later through Martin. The boy had planted a lemon in the courtyard of the house in which he lived. In a short time a small lemon tree flourished there and bore fruit in all seasons of the year. Many years after his death "the lemon tree of Brother Martin" was still growing and giving fruit the year round.⁴

CHAPTER

⊱ 3 ⊰

Come, follow Me (Matt. 19:21).

ONE MORNING the patients of Marcel de Rivero—those who went to his shop to have their hair cut, their beards trimmed; those who wanted to be bled, who had a sore to be treated, or who wanted some herbs for a poultice; all of the clients of Rivero who now could be said to be rather the clients of Martin; the young and the old, white, mulatto and black—all were thrown into a state of consternation upon learning that Martin was retiring from his profession.

But why? To enter a monastery.

If only he had let them know something of his plans a few days earlier, they would have tried to dissuade him. They would have made him see that it was folly, a mad illusion arising from egotism, or perhaps from pride, to think of abandoning a life spent helping the poor in order to withdraw from society and think only of himself. The glory of God?

There was plenty to do for the glory of God here in ordinary daily life, where the poor suffered and the powerful abused their power, proclaiming themselves Catholics and messengers of the faith while they were more often living denials of the Gospel.

But there was more to be said than that. In this society, still so far removed from a just and peaceful order, did not the colored race—the disinherited Indians and the Negroes bound to their land and relegated to the last place—have a right to look up to him as a liberator? His life was an unanswerable reply to those who, not so long ago, had seriously asked if the Negroes had a soul like that of the whites and could therefore be baptized.

Why withdraw the comfort of his luminous example, of his life spent entirely in the exercise of the purest charity, at a time when darkness seemed to extinguish the light? Why abandon the poor? No one could take his place among them.

Martin must have felt these objections arising in his own heart. But the life he had led up to this moment, even though it was a life of work and prayer, was no longer sufficient for him.

There are those who set themselves an objective, and once it is attained, go happily on their way for the rest of their lives. And there are those who, each time they have reached a goal, look up still higher at the goals yet to be attained, and they never find peace until they have reached the plentitude of their desires, longing to rest "there, where it is best to be, upon the pure and limpid heights." [1]

Martin was one of the latter group. He had that thirst for perfection and the full gift of self which is an exigency of charity, of that charity which had grown in him during his long nocturnal meditations, during which he had tasted to the full the words of St. Paul: "Christ humbled Himself, becoming obedient to death, even to death on a cross," and "loved me and gave Himself up for me" (Phil. 2:8; Gal. 2:20).

The cry of Christ dying on the cross, "I thirst," had aroused in Martin a thirst for the honor of God through the salvation of souls, and he felt an irresistible desire to respond to the cry of Christ with all the ardor of his soul. "O sweet and good Jesus," wrote St. Catherine of Siena, "at one and the same time You cry out 'I thirst' and ask to be given to drink. And when do You ask the soul to give You to drink? When You show Your charity and Your love. Thus it is right that He who loves should be loved. Then the soul gives its Creator to drink, when it returns Him love for love." [2]

To accept this imperious invitation, Martin had ceased to work with Rivero and presented himself to the Friars Preachers of the monastery of the Holy Rosary. There, he requested the humblest post in the monastery, which even by its very title, expressed his desire to give himself. He asked for the habit of a *"donado,"* a lay helper or lay coadjutor. The *donados* were members of the Third Order who offered their services to a monastery and lived there permanently, receiving food and lodging as compensation for their work. They took upon themselves the heaviest tasks and were considered as ranking below the lay brothers. Their habit was a white tunic and a black cape, but without the scapular and capuce.

Martin felt that receiving this habit, the mark of the lowest rank in religious dignity, was worth more than his freedom, his profession, his apostolate in the world. In utter simplicity of heart, he offered all these things to obtain it. He was then fifteen or sixteen years old.

When Martin presented himself to the monastery of the Holy Rosary and asked to be admitted to the family of St. Dominic, it is possible he was not unknown there. The friars may have noticed him praying in their church, or some of them may have heard praises of his efforts to help the poor and of his life so filled with good works. It is not altogether improbable that he had already found a spiritual director among the Dominicans.

Moreover, such a humble request did not require great recommendations. The prior of the monastery of the Holy Rosary spoke to the Father Provincial, and both of them—Father John de Lorenzana, the provincial, and Father Francis Vega, the prior—agreed to open the doors of the monastery and of the Dominican Order to Martin.

They acted wisely in doing so. Through them, the Order offered to Martin the secure life of its constitutions, the consolation of a tradition strengthened by the experience of several centuries, and a spirituality whose fecundity was already proven by the lives of numerous Dominican saints. All this was good from Martin's point of view.

But on his part, Martin brought to the Order a will set upon following the path laid out, always and everywhere, without any intention of turning back. His was the kind of will that produces saints. And this was good from the point of view of the Order which, in him, would see the number of its saints increased.

Many years later, when everyone knew of Martin's sanctity and he was sought out as an advisor by the most prominent ecclesiastics and laymen, a fellow religious one day said to him point blank: "Brother Martin, would it not be better for you to remain in the palace of His Excellency the archbishop of Mexico, rather than to stay here, cleaning the toilets of the monastery?"

Without hesitation Martin replied, using the words of the Psalmist: "I have chosen to be an abject in the house of my God" (Ps. 83:11).

At the moment he entered religious life it is probable that

Martin could not quote the words of the psalms. But the meaning of that verse was already engraved in his soul, and he knew how to express it by his actions. He expressed it clearly when he had to defend his firm decision against the strong objections of his father.

To John de Porres, it seemed that Martin had gone too far. He did not object to his son's wishing to become a member of that illustrious Order of Preachers which had sprung from the heart and genius of a great Spaniard, and was already renowned in Spain and in other lands because of its apostolate and its glorious saints. But he could neither conceive of nor tolerate the idea that his son should wish to enter the Order as a lay helper, to spend his whole life on the level of a servant. John de Porres used all his influence and brought pressure to bear upon the Father Provincial to induce him to receive Martin at least as a lay brother, if not as a cleric. An impediment might prevent Martin's being admitted to the rank of a cleric, but nothing stood in the way of his being received as a lay brother.

To satisfy John de Porres, Father Lorenzana tried to persuade the young man to "take the capuce." He found him firm in his decision, hard as a rock: "I have chosen to be an abject." And nothing could make him change his mind.[3] Examples of this firmness occurred several times in Martin's life. Since he was truly and deeply humble, as well as profoundly and completely obedient, we must conclude that he refused because of higher motives.

Father Lorenzana understood those motives and he therefore made John de Porres see that he must not insist upon his viewpoint. And John de Porres, so accustomed to seeing others bow to his will, had to bow to the will of his own son. But perhaps he did so without bitterness. It was his own son, and no stranger, who was opposing him; and by that very opposition the son showed himself to be worthy of his father. The son showed that his soul was as noble as that of his noble ancestors: the soul of a knight, responsible to the call of an ideal and ready to fight to his last breath to attain that ideal.

John's good Christian sense may have made him guess that Martin, through this determined desire to be abject, would bestow on the name of the Porres family its greatest and purest glory.

CHAPTER

➤ 4 ➤

The patient man is better than the valiant;
and he that ruleth his spirit,
than he that taketh cities (Prov. 16:32).

WHEN Martin entered the monastery, he did not cease to work. It meant working as before, and even more. He was given the task of sweeping the cloisters and the corridors, and of cleaning the toilets. Martin applied himself to this disagreeable work with simplicity and ardor and did not think it unusual. He had sought the humble position of a lay helper, and it was logical that the least agreeable work should be assigned to him.

So many times we are illogical because we are inconstant; our generosity is exhausted in its initial venture. Profound souls—the saints—are consistent to the end, and when in the light of faith they have seen their own value before the majesty of God, everything becomes simple and natural for them, no matter what happens.

This physical labor was in view of the spiritual work, which was most important and the one true work for which he had entered religious life, and Martin realized it perfectly. The religious life is ordained to the acquisition of perfection; to lead the soul to its full development of charity. St. Catherine compares the soul to a tree originating in love, which in order to nurture itself on love, in accordance with the needs of its nature, must plunge its roots into the soil of true and profound humility. Humility is the foster-mother of charity and of all the virtues which spring from the trunk of charity. "The first sweet Truth teaches us how to become great. How? Through the lowliness of true humility." The Saint of Siena wrote these words to the bishop of Florence, exhorting him to be virile in the practice of virtue, because "those who are not strong in virtue, are not constant." [1]

In itself, humility is a hidden virtue which escapes our perception. It exists in the depths of the soul, and no one can say with certainty if it is truly there or not, because no created eye can penetrate to those depths. But when humility exists in the soul, it has a companion which serves as an indication of its presence: patience, which holds the field for humility without avoiding assaults, but rejoices in the battle and "through suffering, wins." [2]

Martin therefore seized his broom and wielded it with good will in cleaning the passages, the cloisters, the corridors and the cells of the monastery of the Holy Rosary. He had a broom in his hands so often that it later became a distinguishing mark in the pictures and statues of Martin de Porres. Tiny brooms are still distributed to the faithful in Peru as a sign of devotion to him.

But the broom was not the only implement which Martin employed. The barber's shears, the lancet of the surgeon, and many, many other tools were soon to keep the broom company. And Martin, always active and always calm, knew how to alternate delicate and heavy labor throughout the course of the day, without allowing a previous physical task to render his surgeon's hand heavy, and without allowing the thought of an important duty awaiting him to cause him to neglect his broom. He threw himself completely into what he was doing, moment by moment. If he had not done so, he would have been incapable of performing all the tasks which, with the passage of time, were added to that first simple domestic responsibility, and which little by little became so numerous and so important that it seems impossible that one man could have sufficed for them.[3]

The duties brought along with them a throng of magnificent occasions for the exercise of patience. A very good one from this point of view was that of his work as a barber. Resuming his old profession in the monastery of the Holy Rosary, Martin found himself assured of three hundred clients, and not always the easiest to satisfy. Things went along well enough with the older religious, but Martin had to call upon his reserves of patience when the young ones came.

During the informative process for Martin's beatification, Father Francis Velasco Carabantes testified to an event which happened to himself during his early years in the Order, while he was yet a novice. He went to see Martin, but did not wish to have his head shaved; so he remained there, hesitating, unable to decide whether to go away or to have his head tonsured. His indecision was based on a definite reason: the miserable crown of hair prescribed by the rule did not please him at all, but he lacked the courage to ask the barber to spare his hair, for he knew that Martin was deaf when it was a question of relaxing the least point of the rule.

While he was plunged in his thoughts and hesitation, he suddenly found his head in Martin's hands, thoroughly wet, then covered with soap, then shaved, with the crown of hair down to the minimum prescribed by the rule. He leaped up furiously and began to inveigh against Martin, calling him a mulatto dog, a hypocrite, a cheat. Paying no attention to this deluge of insults, Martin dried Francis' head thoroughly and asked him to look at himself in the mirror, adding that Francis would see that the crown was not so badly cut as he had imagined.

Meanwhile, Father Alphonsus Gamarra, who had witnessed the scene, completed Martin's work with a stern rebuke, capping it by imposing on the novice a severe penance, as he had the right and duty to do as the disciplinarian of the monastery.

Partially because of Father Gamarra's intervention and partially because he saw in the mirror that he was less ugly than he had feared, Brother Francis grew calmer. Martin thereupon put his hand on the friar's head, saying: "If this head continues to flare up like this, it will have much difficulty in the Order."

But the matter did not end there. Anyone who insulted Martin thereby acquired the most secure title to his gratitude, and therefore Francis should not have to bear the penalty of the abusive language which he had heaped upon Martin. Consequently, Martin went to the master of novices and begged him to forgive Francis. The young novice was perfectly right in what he had said because he, Martin, was really a great sinner, and his mother was a poor Negress, and therefore the title of "mulatto dog" fitted him perfectly. Why punish someone who had spoken only the absolute truth? Francis did not deserve punishment, but a reward. And having secured the revocation of Francis' penance, Martin sent him a gift of fresh fruit the same day.

It is almost a natural law that souls thirsty for humiliation find other souls around them ready to satisfy this thirst. Every time Brother Francis wanted Martin to do something for him, he took care to sprinkle his conversation liberally with the same epithets which had succeeded so well the first time. Martin, always calm and unchanging, would laugh and give the young friar whatever he had come to seek, letting Francis believe that in order to please him he gave in to his caprices and his insults like a dolt.

Finally the inevitable happened. Francis' eyes were suddenly opened, and he saw things in quite a different light. He realized that Martin was wiser than he; he realized that, of the two, he himself was the fool. He changed completely and began to observe every action, to note every word of the Negro Brother, and to try to imitate his holy life. And having preserved fresh and intact even to his old age the memory of what he had experienced in his youth, Father Francis Velasco Carabantes was able to furnish one of the most vivid and valuable testimonies at the time of the informative process.[4]

In Martin's day the barber's trade extended to the field which today is reserved to doctors and surgeons. The superiors of the monastery of the Holy Rosary quickly saw how useful anyone skilled in this trade could be to the infirmary of the community. Martin therefore soon found himself entrusted with the care of the sick and he resumed the full exercise of his profession, exactly as he had carried it on before he entered the monastery.

He served the sick with love, taking care of all their needs, and especially the most repugnant, with utter devotion. Often he served them on his knees, "with the flaming heart of an angel," according to the testimony of one who had observed him.[5] That was the position he preferred, especially in the presence of the priests of the Order. He never sat down in their presence. His knees bent naturally, from an impulse of his humble heart, and his face was lowered to the earth to kiss the feet of the preachers of the Gospel of peace.[6]

Martin never lost his peace of mind, no matter how much others put it to the test. Often the patients repaid his care with insulting words, but Martin was not surprised. As a doctor he knew how suffering localized in one part of the human body can profoundly upset the normal balance of a man. He sympathized with his patients and was happy to serve as an escape valve for their bad moods.

One day the prior found him prostrate on the floor in a *venia* at the feet of a sick priest.[7] What could have happened?

"I was receiving the ashes, even though the first day of Lent is still far off," explained Martin, lifting his smiling face, as if he were amused by the oddness of the situation. "This Reverend Father reminded me of my humble birth and sprinkled the ashes of my defects on my head. In order to thank him, I am kissing, not his venerable hands which touch God every day and which I am not worthy to touch, but his feet, and I do it with great reverence because they are the feet of a minister of Christ." [8]

The truth is that Martin was sincerely convinced of his own worthlessness. We are all willing to say this of ourselves, but if we are happy to hear others say it of us, it is a sign that we really believe it. His "profound and consummate" humility, according to Father Joseph de Villarsbia, was "based on his knowledge of the greatness of God"; and in the light of that knowledge, it was not an exaggeration for Martin to think himself nothing, "the most imperfect, the most vile, and the greatest sinner in the world." Firmly rooted in this conviction, he found it completely natural that others should share the same conviction and tell him so plainly. He therefore felt that he should be grateful to those who did so. "I must take better care of him and love him more," he said of a patient who had treated him brusquely, "because he knows me better than the others." [9]

A virtue so manifest had to be tested by those who were responsible for Martin's spiritual life, and the superiors of the monastery of the Holy Rosary did not fail in their duty. Father Carabantes testified that it was not unusual for the superiors, in order to mortify him, to rebuke him severely, "as if he were gravely delinquent." Martin would thank them on his knees and his smiling face would manifest the joy he felt at being so mistreated. "I deserve much worse," he would say, "and God suffered much more for me!" [10]

Thus tempered, Martin's humility resisted all the pressure brought to bear upon it, bending under all the trials of his long life without ever breaking. His humility resisted praise as it resisted insults, and his reaction to the insults of those who were his superiors was the same as it was to the rudeness of those whom he helped in all sorts of ways and who could have been considered his inferiors.

It is true, of course, that in entering the Order as a coadjutor, Martin desired to avoid once and for all every distinction and every honor. But it is also true that his many skills and his genius for organization inevitably brought him duties to which were joined a certain authority. But humility had so firmly established him in the lowest rank—"I have chosen to be an abject"—that he could not imagine any position lower than his own.

And so, while he took care of his poor "with great meekness, docility and humility," he rejoiced, affirmed Father Christopher de Toro, "that everyone commanded him imperiously as if he were the personal slave of each one." But Father Toro furnished the motive when he said that in doing so, Martin saw these people as Jesus Christ.[11]

Many years were to pass before Martin would be able to

give the crowning proof of his humility and patience in his care of the poor. However, there is one event which is cited by the greater part of the biographers of Martin to indicate the full measure of his humility and abnegation. It happened in the early years of his religious life.

One day Martin learned that the prior had gone out to sell several valuable objects, not having enough money to pay certain debts of the monastery and to provide for the needs of the community. The news made him thoughtful. Certainly the prior must have been in great distress if he had decided to sell things belonging to the patrimony of the monastery. Could not some other solution be found?

Perhaps Martin recalled having heard how St. Dominic, in order to redeem a poor woman's brother from the slavery of the Saracens, had offered to go as a slave in his place. Martin may have said to himself that if his spiritual father had been able to think of sacrificing his precious life to console that poor woman, then it would not be at all strange that he, a mere nothing, should offer his life for the monastery to which he belonged.

So Martin ran through the streets of Lima after the prior, who was headed for the merchants' quarter. He overtook the prior and, still breathless, explained his idea, begging him not to sell the objects he had with him, but to sell him—Martin— since the monastery was wasting its funds keeping this poor idiot of a mulatto, while a slave merchant would pay well for him because he was strong and could work. And it would be a great blessing for him to find, at last, someone who would treat him as he deserved!

The prior was dumbfounded. At first he did not understand Martin. When he grasped Martin's plan, his eyes filled with tears. "Go back to the monastery, Brother. You are not for sale." [12]

➤ 5 ⤟

The voice of my beloved: behold, he cometh. . . .
Behold, he standeth behind our wall, looking through
the windows, looking through the lattices (Cant. 2:8–9).

HUMILITY is the nurse of the virtues, but prayer is their mother. The relation established between the soul and God by humility is at once a means of knowing and loving the good, and a channel by which every good thing comes to us from the Sovereign Good.

Religious life, which is a school of virtue, according to St. Thomas,[1] is inconceivable without an intense life of prayer. This is especially true of Dominican religious life, since the whole program of the Order of Preachers can be condensed into three words: *"contemplata aliis tradere,"* to give to others the fruits of contemplation. Contemplation is the necessary prerequisite of the apostolate; only those who have nourished themselves with the fruits of contemplation have a message for their brethren.

Martin had cultivated the art of prayer even before entering the monastery, and after his arrival he proceeded to intensify his prayer until it became almost continuous. Father Stephen Martínez attested that in every occupation Martin's soul found the means to lift itself almost spontaneously to the contemplation of the things of God. In all his duties, whether he was helping the sick, sweeping the floor, or aiding the poor, his thoughts were always fixed on God.[2] Such a state of prayer is generally not a gift, but the fruit of a constant and generous effort and much good will. "Perfect prayer," says St. Catherine, "is not acquired with many words, but with loving desire." [3]

Obliged to divide his time among so many occupations, Martin understood that he must use everything to nurture his life of prayer. For this, it sufficed only to look around. The very place in which he lived was a constant reminder of things of God and of the spirit. There were, for example, the holy images. In the corridors, on the landings of the staircases, on the walls of the infirmary, in the chapter room, in the cells, the Virgin smiled upon him, showing him the Infant Jesus; the crucified Christ opened His arms and His heart as if inviting him to a more intimate union with Him; the saints of the Dominican Order, in spite of the somewhat awkward stiffness of their images sculptured in wood or modeled in clay, ceaselessly encouraged him: "Courage, Martin, you are our brother; what we did, you also can do."

Martin loved all these images which sowed in his heart the seed of good thoughts, and when he passed them as he went about the monastery, he never failed to salute them by bowing his head or by dropping to his knees. He decorated them with flowers and candles, especially the image of a certain Madonna at the entrance to the dormitory. But above all, he tried to honor God, the Blessed Virgin and the saints with the offering of virtuous acts. His virtuous acts, joined to the devotion of his heart, exhaled "a better fragrance . . . than that of the nosegays and flowers that he put on the altars," testified the lay helper, Francis de Santa Fe. [4]

Then there was the church, with its tabernacle and its altars. The chapel Martin frequented most was that of the Queen of the Most Holy Rosary. He went there to tell her of the desire burning in his heart to love her Son, just as he took every difficulty to her, and there every night he begged her to watch over him and not permit him ever to fall into sin.

His love for Mary was spontaneous, the love of a son for his mother. Martin was always in the presence of Mary. His free moments, at night or during the silence of the afternoon, were passed in the chapel of the Virgin Mother. There was no danger that he would be absent from the rosary recited at night, or from the Little Office of the Blessed Virgin Mary, which preceded Matins of the Divine Office at night. Every morning before sunrise he was in the bell tower to send out over the city, with the strokes of the Angelus, the invitation to salute Mary, *"Aurora consurgens."* He never relinquished this duty, even when his advancing age and strength, diminished by ceaseless mortification, made it difficult for him.[5]

But these were only moments snatched out of the twenty-four hours of the day. Martin could not multiply indefinitely the visits to the chapel and to the images of Mary; he had too many other things to do. Fortunately, there was the rosary. Martin wore a large, fifteen-decade rosary around his neck, in accordance with the custom of his brethren of the Province of St. John the Baptist of Peru. He wore another one attached to his belt, or rather, he held it almost constantly in his hands, letting it hang from the belt only when his hands were occupied with work. But he took it up again as soon as his hands were free, and continued his praise of Mary, rejoicing with her joys, suffering with her sorrows, and exulting in her glory.[6]

Martin loved Mary. Even a child would have realized it, merely from hearing Martin pronounce her name.[7]

And Mary loved Martin. It pleased her to see him come to her as to a teacher, but since he was an attentive pupil, it sufficed to instruct him on a matter only once. Day after day, whether in the chapel of the Rosary or in the intervals between the Hail Marys of his rosary, Mary taught Martin many things. It was really she who told him he must gather up anything that could feed the ardent fire of his love, even the pieces of straw fallen along the way. It was she who explained to him that the thirst of the soul is slaked only in God, and that grace—which is God in the soul—is received in its fullest measure in the sacraments. It was she who made him understand that God is to be found in all His creatures, but especially in those in greatest need and in those who suffer most. She, who had kept in her heart every word of Jesus, love, sacrifice, obedience, purity, goodness—words which are but tinkling cymbals unless they become living realities. She made him understand what power these words had acquired after her Son, the Word of God, had spoken and exemplified them here on earth.

Mary taught Martin all this. And one night, when the lesson had been quite a long one, to let everyone see how pleased she was with her pupil and to prevent his stumbling in the dark as he ran to choir for Matins, she sent two angels in robes of purest white to escort him to choir with lighted candles.[8]

It is not surprising, therefore, that Martin succeeded in finding God in all things and in transforming his whole life into prayer. He was a most faithful and devoted pupil of Mary, Seat of Wisdom.

Another powerful attraction, a living and profound love, drew Martin insistently to the chapel of the Rosary. On the altar stood the tabernacle in which the Blessed Sacrament was reserved. Sometimes, instead of praying in the chapel, Martin climbed up under the roof of the church where he had discovered an ideal nook. There he could gaze at the tabernacle without being seen by those below. Francis de la Torre, an officer of the guard and his good friend, found him there one day after having searched fruitlessly for him in every corner of the monastery. Martin was on his knees, but raised some distance from the ground. Contemplation had been transformed into ecstasy. His unceasing fidelity had drawn this gift from heaven.[9]

Each time he passed along the upper cloister, in which there was a window that lighted the chapel of the Rosary, Martin dropped to his knees and adored the invisible Presence through the grating.

His great days were those of the Eucharistic celebrations: the feast and the octave of Corpus Christi, the third Sunday of every month, and all Thursdays. When the Blessed Sacrament was exposed for adoration, Martin passed hours before the monstrance, motionless. The faith and love of his humble soul shone forth in the very attitude of his body.

Each morning he assisted at several Masses, as he had done when he was at home with his mother. When the priests approached the altar to begin the first Masses, he was already in the chapel. There were many who celebrated Mass at that hour, and Martin was free of all duties. His devotion while he was serving at the altar was contagious. It was like a blazing fire which inflamed all those around him.[10]

In those days the lay brothers generally received Holy Communion on the great feasts of our Lord and our Lady, and every Sunday. Martin had obtained permission to add all Thursdays to these days. But his conscience would not leave him in peace and accused him of being too presumptuous. To quiet it a bit, and to reconcile his humility and his strong desire to be united to God, he imagined he was receiving Holy Communion on Thursdays as Viaticum. At the point of death, he thought, even anyone as unworthy as himself could ask for the Living Bread which our Lord left in memory of His death, to give us life.[11]

When he approached to receive Holy Communion, his face was lighted "like a burning coal."[12] He managed to be the last in the chapel, then disappeared into the chapter room, and no one could ever find him for some time after that. Did he hide in some dark corner, or did he become invisible in some spot visible to all? Perhaps both explanations are valid. It happened one way one time, and another way another time. The testimonies, in fact, speak of hours and hours of thanksgiving passed by Martin in the solitude of Limatambo, an estate at some distance from Lima belonging to the monastery, and tell of Martin's having been vainly sought everywhere in the monastery, and then presenting himself at the command of the superior without anyone's having seen him come. He was there suddenly, just as a moment before he had been absent.[13]

After a Eucharistic day passed at Limatambo, when Martin became visible again he returned in the evening and busied himself with the mules and cattle of the monastery farm. He put fresh hay in the mangers of the barn and changed the straw in the stalls. If someone remarked to him that it was not necessary to take this work upon himself since there were Negroes employed to do it, he replied that the Negroes had worked all day long while he had done nothing, and it was really a grace to be able to make reparation for such inactivity before night fell.[14] His humility made him take every precaution against pride, recalling the words of St. Paul: "Lest the greatness of the revelation should puff me up" (II Cor. 12:7).

Thus, the days on which he received the Holy Eucharist were days given entirely to uninterrupted prayer, to intimate and sweet conversation with his Lord. On those days, while he was immersed in the contemplation of the Gift *par excellence,* the flame of love was strengthened and refueled in him, to break forth later in such ardent words that he seemed an "Etna of fire" every time he spoke of the love which impelled the Word to become incarnate and to remain with us in the Sacrament of the altar.[15]

According to St. Catherine, all that we do, whether in word or in work, for the salvation of our neighbor, is true prayer, although we must consecrate some time to prayer in the strict sense.[16]

During the course of the day and in the midst of his various occupations, Martin heard the call to immerse himself in this oasis of the presence of God. "While he was performing his duties . . . he would hear the call of the Spirit, and the Servant of God would go to his cell, close the door, and fall on his knees in a corner, where he stayed as if the preceding labors were but a preparation for prayer." Such is the testimony of Brother Ferdinand de Aragonés, the head infirmarian, who had a duplicate key to the cell and twice surprised Martin absorbed in prayer. Two times, but not three, because the second time, seeing that it was useless to lock the cell door behind him and not wishing to be surprised in the intimacy of the divine colloquy, Martin fastened a bell to the door.[17]

Martin had certain periods completely free for prayer. Night was, naturally, the principal period of prayer. Martin's bed usually consisted of planks covered with a mat, with a piece of wood for a pillow. But he rarely slept at night. At best he napped a little during the day at odd moments while he waited for someone to call upon him. At night, if sleep overtook him in spite of his efforts, he slept anywhere at all, wherever he happened to be at the moment, sometimes in the most precarious positions.[18] But at night he had other things to do. Like the bride of the Canticle of Canticles, Martin went in search of his Beloved. After having begged Mary to show him the holy face of her Son, he went in search of Him, in the upper choir where he lingered after Matins. He searched for Him in the chapter room, where his fellow religious sometimes found him raised from the ground to the height of the great crucifix above the altar, his arms extended in the form of a cross, his hands on the nailed hands of the crucified Christ, as if he were embracing Him. He sought Him in the room under the bell tower, where he finished his night of prayer and penance while he awaited the moment to ring the Angelus.

Martin had very quickly learned an important thing that could not escape anyone who places himself under the tutelage of Mary. He realized that mortification is necessary for progress in prayer. St. Philip Neri, almost a contemporary of Martin and proverbially the most joyous among the saints, had said: "To wish to devote oneself to prayer without mortification is like a bird wishing to fly without first having grown feathers."

It may be said that Martin had learned this lesson too well. The saints, it is true, do not do things by halves, but he exaggerated, for he did things which surpassed the resistance of the human body. Nevertheless, he endured them. The only possible explanation is that because of his love of God, which led him to seek suffering so steadfastly, a gift of supernatural strength was given him to compensate for the weakness of human nature.

Father Gaspar de Saldaña once commanded him to say whether there was any truth in the rumors which were circulating concerning his mortifications. "It's really not worth talking about," answered Martin, overwhelmed with confusion. "In His own good time God will reveal anything that needs to be known about it." But since his superior was not satisfied with such a vague reply, Martin had to admit that every night he took the discipline three times, as his father, St. Dominic, had done. Then he begged Father Saldaña not to ask him any more about it.[19]

A certain youth named John Vázquez, who lived in the monastery and was a sort of voluntary assistant to Martin, had free access to all the parts of the monastery. He has left us some information about Martin's nocturnal mortifications.[20]

It was Martin's custom to take the discipline the first time in his cell, where he went immediately after the evening *De profundis*. There he prayed and flogged himself for three-quarters of an hour with a triple iron chain encrusted with points of iron. He offered his entire body, naked, to the blows because he wished to undergo what Jesus Christ had suffered when He was bound to a pillar, stripped and scourged. Martin's skin became swollen, broke open under the blows, and the blood flowed.[21]

Martin looked back over his life, at every action of his life as a religious, offered as a holocaust to the glory of God, and found it all so ignoble, so cold, so empty! He looked at himself in the dazzling light of the majesty of God; he belonged to that infinite perfection by a special choice, because of a free invitation freely accepted.

And what could he find that would be pleasing in the eyes of God, those eyes turned upon him? What had the most pure eyes of the Father found pleasing to Him upon earth through the course of all the centuries, if not His beloved Son and the painful offering of His love? But the passion of Jesus continues in His mystical body. Every member united to the Head and participating in His sufferings can hear words of ineffable sweetness coming from the Father: "You are also My beloved son, in whom I am well pleased."

Martin scourged himself with such force and rejoiced over the blood flowing from his wounds because he knew that the offering he was making to the Father of this blood in union with the blood of Jesus was pleasing to the Father. When he had finished, he called John Vázquez to help him treat his wounds. The remedy he used, strong vinegar, only increased the pain. John's flesh crept to see Martin in such a piteous state, and he begged him not to continue this kind of penance but to choose some other. Martin cut him short. "It's what I need for my health," he said gaily and laughing heartily. If he, a doctor, said that, what objection could John Vázquez make?

A quarter of an hour after midnight, Martin scourged himself the second time. The instrument was a knotted cord, the place the chapter room. This second scourging was for sinners, to make reparation for the offenses committed against God, to implore grace so that sinners far from God might return to Him.

Life at that time in Lima furnished ample motives for the vigor with which Martin wielded his instruments of penance. The city abounded in sin: the sins of the proud and unjust, of the avaricious who closed their hearts to the misery of their brothers, of the sensual who denied the spirit. Martin doubled the blows that rained upon his body. What a horrible swamp of mire the eye of Him "who seest the secrets of men's hearts" must have perceived beneath the wealth of the city, so beautiful with its newly built palaces, its churches, its streets stretching out toward the four points of the horizon! Every day, in the crowds of the poor coming to him, Martin had first-hand experience of the conditions prevailing in the city and he saw the disastrous consequences of the evil that was done and the good that was omitted.

But here, before the great crucifix of the chapter room, the thought of the love which held the God-Man fastened to the cross, where no created power could have held Him, a love which held Him there in order to make reparation for sin and to pardon sinners, overpowered every other thought. And from the painful humiliation of Martin's penitential exercises, our Lord drew him to Himself, lifted his body from the earth, opened up to him the inaccessible depths of divine love, the "secret of His heart." Several times John Vázquez came upon

Martin at prayer, raised from the ground to the height of the crucifix.

Having finished the second part of his nightly itinerary, Martin allowed himself a little rest. Without going up to his cell, he stretched himself out to sleep on the catafalque in the chapter room. The best way he knew to moderate the comfort of his rest was to join to it the discomfort of the catafalque and the thought of death.

Finally, near dawn, Martin began the third and most painful scourging. Even the place chosen for this penance had something horrible about it. It was a subterranean room, under the bell tower, dank and dark. Once more his shirt was torn from the wounds, still fresh from the preceding scourgings. But after the exhaustion of the first two scourgings, of the long, ardent and almost uninterrupted night of prayer, Martin no longer had any confidence in the strength of his own muscles. So he called on another to aid him. Sometimes it was young Vázquez, but more often someone he had helped, either Indian or Negro, whom he armed with a stout branch of a quince tree, begging him, if he had any gratitude at all, to strike him without mercy. These helpers were always strong men of simple hearts, ready to do a favor for a friend without questioning his tastes, and their muscles, strengthened by hard labor, were equal to this kind of early morning gymnastics.

In the darkness of the room, so like a prison, while the blows fell upon his pain-racked body and his wounds were re-opened, Martin united himself to those souls for whom the ineffable light of God is hidden by the prison bars of purgatory, those souls who cannot hasten the moment of their liberation but must hope to be aided by the charity of others. Possibly, in order to be more like them, Martin wanted to be scourged by his friends, feeling himself helpless, passive, without any other means of succor than his own voice. He did not employ his voice to cry out "enough" but only to plead and beg his friends to strike harder, without pity.

They stopped when the hour of the Angelus called Martin from the shadows of the underground room to the rosy light in which the bell tower was bathed. Perhaps at that very moment the souls for love of whom he had offered his prayers and sufferings—and who can say how many?—passed from the shadows to the vision of eternal light, and greeted the Queen of heaven in that dawning of their day without end.[22]

In this manner, inspired by charity, Martin joined contemplation to penitence during his nocturnal prayer. He looked at and loved his own soul and the souls of his neighbors in the light of the love of God. He looked at and searched after God and found Him by sharing in the sufferings of Christ. And if, when the night began, he took for his own the words of the Canticle of Canticles, "I will arise . . . I will seek him whom my soul loveth," as day broke, after having tasted the ineffable sweetness of divine union in suffering, certainly his soul repeated: "I held him, and I will not let him go." [23]

Once more he took up his day's work, resolved that he would not be separated from the object of his love. And he succeeded. Of him it could be said, according to Father Augustine de Valverde, what is said of St. Martin of Tours: *"Numquam spiritum ab oratione relaxabat,"* because he had learned to unite the activity of Martha with the contemplation of Mary.[24]

That is a beautiful ideal, easy to formulate but not easy to achieve. To many it seems altogether impossible. Martin found the key to the mystery in the Dominican spirituality, and by his personal and assiduous efforts he succeeded so well that he was a living example of the ideal of the mixed life which is characteristic of the Order of Friars Preachers.

He prolonged his pious exercises of the night throughout the day, prayer as well as mortification, wearing a hair shirt and an iron chain around his waist. And as he took the discipline at night in his cell, in the chapter room, or in the room under the bell tower, so he often went to scourge himself in the solitude of Limatambo during the day.[25]

In addition, he fasted continually, since to the times of fast prescribed by the laws of the Church and the Constitutions of the Order he added many more for his own personal reasons of devotion, with the result that he fasted practically the entire year. "For the said Servant of God, every day was a day of fast by precept," according to one of his colleagues, the lay helper, Francis de Santa Fe. To have some idea of the rigor of these fasts, it is sufficient to know what Martin's meals were on feast days. After passing all of Lent on bread and water, and after abstaining from all foods during the last three days of Holy Week, on Easter Sunday, "as a sign of rejoicing, he ate some root vegetables called *camotes* (sweet potatoes). And on Easter Monday he ate some bread stew and a little cabbage, but without eating any meat." [26]

To sum up, it could be said that Martin fasted on bread and water during his entire life, since the sweet potatoes took the place of bread in the diet of the Indians, and therefore should be considered only as bread.[27]

Martin was very generous with God, but God was not less generous with Martin. He flooded his soul with such sweetness that Martin was unable to restrain himself, and was almost forced to cry out: "How sweet is the Lord, and how worthy to be loved!" [28]

John Vázquez had been in the service of the monastery of the Holy Rosary only a short time when, one night around eleven o'clock, he was awakened by a violent earthquake. Thoroughly frightened, he leaped out of bed and called Martin, but was still more frightened when he saw the cell flooded with light and Martin lying face downward on the floor, his arms opened in the form of a cross and his Rosary in his hand. Almost beside himself, John leaned over him, clinging to Martin like a drowning man, calling him to get up, to beware lest the cell fall in ruins upon them.

The walls of the cell did a drunken dance and the beams creaked. Martin remained where he was, immobile, and John Vázquez felt he would go mad with fear. He gathered up his clothing, tucked it under his arm, and dashed into the cloister. There, while he was dressing, he saw another coadjutor, Michael de Santo Domingo, and related to him the great marvel of the night: the light enveloping Martin, who remained immobile in prayer while everything tottered.

"Oh yes, I believe it," replied Michael, "but if you stay on with Brother Martin, you'll see many things like that."

Nevertheless, to please him, Michael went back with him to the cell where Martin was still enveloped in the splendor of that light, though the walls had regained their normal stability and the whole building seemed more solid and compact than ever. Filled with pity for the frightened lad who had, as yet, seen little of such things, Michael led him to his own cell and prepared a bed for him there.

The next morning, when he returned to Martin's cell, John was told politely and firmly: "Take care not to talk about anything you might see in here. . . . It doesn't matter if you see something extraordinary, but don't go around chattering about it to everybody." [20] Martin wished to safeguard the "secret of the King."

*The light of the eyes rejoiceth the
soul* (Prov. 15:30).

ALTHOUGH PRAYER, mortification and a little sleep on the catafalque of the chapter room occupied the greater part of the
night, Martin had to set aside some time to visit the sick when
one of them was so gravely ill that he needed attention during
the night.

There was an old stairway in the monastery, dark and so
worn by use as to be almost impassable. To prevent anyone's
falling down the broken steps, the stairway had been closed
off. But Martin discovered that it was the most direct route
between his cell and the infirmary, and therefore used it when
he visited the sick at night.

One night he was following his usual way, his hands and
arms filled with supplies for the infirmary. When he reached
the stairway, he was confronted with an image that would
make one's blood freeze. A monstrous body barred his way,
and from the shapeless thing emerged a horrible caricature of
a human face, its livid eyes flashing with malice and hate. It
was not difficult for Martin to know who it was.

"What are you doing here, accursed one?" asked Martin.

The demons are said to be very intelligent but sometimes,
to judge by their actions, the contrary would seem to be true.

"I am here because it pleases me to be here," answered the
other impudently, "and because I expect to profit by being
here."

"Away with you to the cursed depths where you dwell!" cried Martin.

The other did not move, and Martin saw no point in losing time in fruitless discussion. He put down the brazier and the linen that he was carrying to the infirmary, took off the leather belt which held his tunic in place, and began to whip the monster with it.

The demon vanished immediately, certainly not because of the blows, which could not harm a spirit, but because he was convinced there was nothing to be gained by staying.

Martin then took a firebrand from the brazier, traced the sign of the cross on the wall, and knelt down to pray and to thank God who had granted him victory over the evil spirit. Some three hundred years previously, Martin's spiritual brother, St. Thomas Aquinas, had done exactly the same thing, after unmasking the enemy who, on that occasion, had chosen quite another disguise.[1]

It is quite natural that the progress in virtue made by a soul should annoy the enemy of good. That is why the saints, more often than not, have to undergo open or hidden struggles with him. On the other hand, it is much less natural that virtue should be displeasing to good souls. And yet sometimes it does happen, as can be seen in the lives of the saints of all times, as well as in our own ordinary lives. This envy, which may be aroused in good people by reason of the virtue of others, is one of the most vexatious and painful experiences on earth. It is like a snare which hinders action, or a needle which painfully penetrates into the very depths of the soul.

Martin does not seem to have experienced this type of suffering. It is true that many times he was badly treated. But if anyone called him a "mulatto dog," it was not through envy of his virtue. It was merely because some irritation had immediately aroused that complex of self defense which was rooted in the soul and temperament of the sixteenth-century Spaniard. Today we would call it racial prejudice. But it was done, if one can say so, in good faith, and Martin understood it that way, for he "knew" that whatever evil was said of him was true.

On the other hand, if reproofs, humiliations or harsh treatment came from a superior, they were administered much more calmly. Religious superiors have a duty to test their subjects and thus help them to walk along a more rugged path than the one our weak will so readily follows.

In Martin's case, his evident taste for humiliation had to be tested to see whether it was really genuine. It is relatively easy for us to put ourselves in the last place, but rather difficult to submit to being assigned the last place by others. The superiors of the monastery of the Holy Rosary had to find out how Martin would react when thrust down by another. They also had to test the authenticity of his many preternatural gifts as soon as reports began to circulate about the extraordinary graces this poor mulatto was receiving. It was not strange, therefore, that they scrupulously exercised their right and performed their duty.[2]

Nevertheless, from the beginning to the end there was a sense of fair play between Martin and his superiors, and between Martin and his brethren. He had to be put to the test to see how he would act under trials, and his superiors did so. But as soon as it was evident that he stood the tests admirably, they did not hesitate to recognize him as being of "good metal," without regard to his being black or white of skin.

To their honor it must be said that when Martin's sanctity became apparent, no prejudice of birth or color prevented the members of the monastery of the Holy Rosary from recognizing and admitting that sanctity. Members of the community, who by reason of their sacerdotal dignity were raised to a level superior to that of the coadjutor, took Martin as a model of life and even asked him to adopt them as spiritual sons.

This was all the more an honor for Martin, since those who thus esteemed him were not inexperienced men. Dominicans as a group are positive men, accustomed more to reason than to dream, not at all inclined to fantasy, exaggeration or unwarranted enthusiasms. This was especially true of the members of the monastery of the Holy Rosary, since it was a house of studies and the seat of the first university of the New World. They could therefore be considered as an aristocracy of the spiritual and cultural life. When these religious said, "Martin is a saint," it is certain they did not say it lightly. It remains to be seen how they came to this conclusion.

Father Francis Velasco Carabantes was of this opinion, as well as Father Andrew de Lisón, who was master of novices and therefore learned in spiritual matters. Father Andrew once declared to a group of novices and several professed: "This mulatto is a saint, and should be venerated as a saint. Last night he had a dreadful battle with the demon and conquered him." [3]

There truly had been a battle that night, not on the stairway to the infirmary, but in Martin's cell, and the master of novices had received an account of it from Martin in a long conversation. This time Martin was not alone with the adversary. Francis de la Torre, the officer of the guard who had found Martin in ecstasy under the roof of the church and had been sharing Martin's cell for several months, was present during the struggle and narrated the details later.

Francis occupied the back part of the room, separated from the front by an alcove. He was about to go to bed when he heard the door open and close, and Martin's voice, always so measured and even, was raised in an angry tone: "What have you come here for, you trouble maker? What are you looking for? This is not your room. Get out!"

This time the devil must have planned a grand attack and paid no attention to Martin's command, even though it was reinforced by a flow of invective. Perhaps the band gathered for the attack bore the name of Legion, like that which vented its anger on a herd of swine when the power of the Word forced them to depart from a human creature in whom they had taken up their abode.[4] Whatever the case may be, an infernal din followed Martin's words. The demons seized him and manhandled him furiously.

Francis de la Torre wanted to know what all the uproar was about and stuck his head out of his alcove. He saw Martin being rolled to and fro on the ground and hurled against the walls. He saw him flinch and then heard him moaning under the blows. But Francis saw not even the shadow of an assailant.

Suddenly the cell and everything within it burst into flames. Francis de la Torre was not timid. He ran to fight the fire, and he and Martin succeeded in putting out the flames. Then, as suddenly as it had begun, the great noise ended and everything was calm again.

Francis returned to his bed and Martin stretched out on his plank, placing near the stone he was using as a pillow, the skull which was his inspiration for pious thoughts. And both men fell asleep, tired but tranquil.

At three o'clock, when Martin arose to ring the dawn bell and left a lit candle for his companion, Francis leaped out of bed, curious to see what damage the fire had done. Marvel of marvels! Neither the walls, the furniture, nor the linen arranged on the shelves, all of which Francis had seen a few hours before enveloped in flames, showed the least trace of fire or smoke.[5] The "dreadful battle" had ended with the complete defeat of the evil spirits.

The judgment of the master of novices, Father Andrew de Lisón, was not solely upon this encounter, no matter how glorious. Extraordinary events cannot be the touchstone of sanctity. For a religious, the touchstone of sanctity is the common life. The hermit sanctifies himself in his hermitage, the layman in society, but religious have taken as their means of sanctification, the common life, which means fraternal charity and good example, but also firmness and resistance in the face of bad example, and tolerance and patience with differences of character. Martin's virtue proved to be pure gold in face of the frictions of community life.

Sometimes those who lead a very austere life become harsh in their ways and even, what is worse, a little acid. When this happens, it is a pity, because virtue, instead of being sweet and attractive, becomes repellent. Perhaps to prevent this, as well as to safeguard the freshness and purity of good works, the Gospel teaches that mortification, like prayer and almsgiving, should be offered to the Father in secret: "When you fast, do not look gloomy like the hypocrites, who disfigure their faces" (Matt. 6:16).

How well Martin understood this teaching of the Gospel! Everything he did was utterly simple, utterly appealing. The austerities by day and by night, the constant sufferings of his heroic constitution, were hidden, a secret confided to the jealous custody of the love which reserved the offering for the sight of his Beloved. But they were apparent, nevertheless, in the light of his smile, like joy springing from spiritual conquest.

If the portraits of Martin, or rather the various sketches left us by his brethren, are reliable—and how could they be otherwise?—he was the perfect type of the man who is complete master of himself. His whole attitude showed an inner control and a fidelity to the demands of the rule: the downcast eyes, the hands crossed on the breast or hidden in the ample sleeves of his habit. His was a "rare" silence, said Father Christopher de Toro, meaning that his silence was carried to a degree rarely found. Only when obedience or charity for his neighbor demanded it, did Martin interrupt that silence, and even then his words were "brief, few, holy, necessary," corresponding to the needs of his brothers. But when he opened his mouth, his speech was so filled with grace that his listeners would have been content to listen for hours on end. Father Anthony de Morales did not hesitate to use the word "style" when describing Martin's way of speaking, praising its efficacy, conciseness, eloquence, and emphasizing how amazing all these gifts were in the person of a humble lay helper.[6]

Martin had the power, perfected by his practice of silence, of saying "things" rather than "words." In his condensed, objective speech, every word counted; no word was idle. It was quite logical that this should be the case, when one thinks of the subjects of his conversation. "All his conversation, . . . when an occasion arose for speech, was of heavenly things, . . . expressing the hope that all should have of salvation through the merits of our Lord and Savior Jesus Christ and His most holy Mother."

St. Dominic always spoke either with God or of God. And Martin, little inclined to speech, followed the Saint's example in his own individual way, "speaking always more with God than of God."[7]

Nature had been generous with Martin. In his physique the best traits of the two races from which he sprang were in harmonious accord. The noble and regular lineaments of his Spanish father were blended with the slenderness and vigor of his Negro mother.

The moral gifts he had received were even more attractive:

a character naturally quiet, reflective, silent; a keen and active intelligence; a soul of integrity, loving truth, filled with goodness and compassion.

With the aid of divine grace, Martin had perfected all these gifts to the point where they were completely under the control of his will, until he was in full command of the city of his soul and never let a rash act or word escape him. Martin was like a "living sentinel."

But this does not suffice to explain why others, merely upon seeing him, felt an attraction toward the good, nor why the afflicted and suffering felt themselves consoled when they merely looked at him.[8]

The humiliating realization of our defects can create an abyss between ourselves and a man who has attained a high degree of perfection. Natural gifts, especially those we do not expect to find in someone whose social condition is inferior to our own, easily arouse envy and jealousy. Moreover, an inflexible fidelity to silence added to a certain exterior attitude —the eyes fixed upon the ground, the arms crossed and hands within the sleeves—can sometimes annoy rather than attract the beholder.

But in the case of Martin, all this was attractive. I believe it was because of his smile. This detail does not seem to have escaped any of the witnesses who sketched a profile of Martin in their deposition for his beatification. All of them had something to say about his smile.

It was not just an average smile. It was not a smile which came and went according to the agreeable or disagreeable events that occurred. Much less was it a smile provoked by a low tide in the affairs of others.

Martin's smile was veiled with sorrow by the sorrow of others, but when he himself was suffering it was more luminous than ever. It was a constant smile, but not a fixed one.

The purity and ardor of his soul were revealed by it, and in his contacts with others it had nuances of inexpressible delicacy, as light takes on indefinable tones and shades of colors from the objects on which it falls. His smile gave courage to the timid, comfort to sufferers, confidence to those who faltered, hope to the oppressed. Most important of all, it always aroused distaste for evil and love of good.

Virtue is true virtue when it arouses the desire of imitation. When anyone can continue to smile, as Martin did, in spite of all the annoyances involved in contacts with others, surmounting his own internal struggles, it is a sign that charity reigns in that soul. "O most sweet fire of love, filling the soul with all sweetness and delight!" exclaimed St. Catherine. "Neither grief nor bitterness can take possession of the soul which burns with this sweet and glorious fire." [9]

And what is sanctity, if not the reign of charity in the soul? Father Andrew de Lisón and the others were right in saying: "Martin is a saint."

Having formed this opinion, the Dominicans of Holy Rosary monastery drew a logical conclusion from it: since Martin is so holy, it is not right that he be denied any longer the grace of religious profession.

Father Anthony de Morales clearly states that the possibility of making his solemn profession was offered to Martin as a consequence of the reputation for sanctity he had gained among his brethren. Father Morales mentions the fact of his profession as a proof of Martin's reputation as a saint, "because, although the lay helpers, who in Peru are called *donados,* did not usually make solemn profession, the said Servant of God did so with full formality, as a real religious, and thus his profession was celebrated as exceptional, and the other religious esteemed the Servant of God as a truly professed religious." [10]

Martin had already spent nine years as a lay helper. When he had asked for admittance to the Order, his father had protested, demanding that his son be received at least among the lay brothers. But since his father's protests and demands were inspired only by wounded pride and vainglory, Martin firmly refused, as we have seen.

Then, during the nine years spent in the monastery of the Holy Rosary, Martin's understanding and knowledge of many aspects of religious life increased. It is not amazing. No mind, no matter how acute, can penetrate to the depths of things at first glance. No one seizes the full beauty of a landscape at first sight, or all the beauty of a literary work at the first reading. Similarly, the mere fact of having a vocation is not sufficient to allow one to grasp from the first moment all the profundity of religious life, which, in the grand symphony of the things of this world, is one of the most mysterious and puzzling melodies. One must plunge into that life and live it.

That is what Martin did. For those nine years, he had lived as a religious, with a fidelity that would have been praiseworthy in even a professed religious, in spite of the fact he was not bound by any tie other than that of his own constancy. But Martin realized that something was lacking—not to his ambition, not to his dignity, but to the demands of the impulse that had brought him to the monastery. He had offered himself, following that attraction; he had given himself by an act which, in his own heart, was definitive; and he had given proof of the validity of that act by the fact that, though free, he had remained faithful. Nevertheless, something was lacking to make his gift perfect.

In the chapter room, at the feet of the great crucifix that witnessed his prayers and penances, or before the tabernacle of the Eucharist and the picture of the Queen of the Holy Rosary, Martin could say: "Lord, in the simplicity of my heart

I have given Thee all with joy, and I have sworn to follow Thee whithersoever Thou goest." But he could not say: "Lord, Thou hast pledged Thyself to me, so that I may follow whatever path Thou showest me."

A religious vocation springs from love, it is carried out because of love, and love has its exigencies. It needs to give itself, but it also needs to know that its gift has been accepted. It is not by chance that religious profession is compared to marriage, in which each of the two who love gives himself to the other and accepts the gift of the other. In a religious profession, the Church accepts the gift in the name of Christ, her Spouse, and promises a divine exchange to the giver.

During his long novitiate, Martin must have felt the lack of this seal, of this solemn acceptance on the part of the Church, but he did not speak of it because, humble as he was, such a desire seemed presumptuous. But when his superiors invited him to take the step, he accepted with joy.

So one day, in the presence of the entire community gathered in the chapter room, after having implored the mercy of God and of the Order, Martin made his solemn profession, promising to obey God, the Blessed Virgin Mary, St. Dominic, and the superiors of the Order until death, in accordance with the Rule of St. Augustine and the Constitutions of the Sacred Order of Friars Preachers.

And Christ looked down with love from the great crucifix and, in the person of the superior who received his vows, gave him the kiss of peace.

⊱ 7 ⊰

*Put me as a seal upon thy heart, as
a seal upon thy arm* (Cant. 8:6).

EXTERIORLY, nothing was changed in Martin's life by his profession. The change was completely interior, in his spirit. Martin's soul received the seal of stability and was bathed in peace.
At the same time he discovered a new impulse to spiritual
progress by remaining faithful to the solemn obligation he had
assumed before God and his brethren. The joyous alacrity with
which he embraced all the duties of religious life recalls the
words of the psalm: "He hath rejoiced as a giant to run the
way."[1]

His life was "a living mirror of religious life, a model of
piety, a perfect ideal of regular observance."[2] Brother Lauren
de los Santos adds that Martin was so perfect in observance
of the three vows and of the constitutions of the Order that
he was never seen to fail on any of these points.[3]

The virtues which form the object of the three vows of religion had been Martin's daily bread even before he bound
himself to them by his profession. After making his vows, he
practiced those virtues with even greater effort, if such were
possible.

His way of dressing was such that it satisfied the requirements of poverty, humility and mortification. In addition to
having nothing as his own—which is an elementary obligation
for those who make a vow of poverty—Martin never used
anything new. All of his clothing was second-hand. But lest
his great love of poverty arouse praise, he concealed it under

the veil of a jest, saying that he preferred ugly and used things so that he would not have to take too much care of them or think much about them.

Any habit that aspired to the honor of being a part of his wardrobe had to be of the most wornout material possible. Having attained that honor, it was obliged to stay in service until the last moment that the warp and woof succeeded in holding together, and even when they began to part company. Patch was placed upon patch to prolong the life of the tattered garments. When the material was reduced to rags, it traitorously fell apart and revealed to the pious curiosity of the brethren the secrets it should have hidden: the undergarment of sackcloth and the shirt of horsehair.[4]

Martin's sister Joan once tried to give him a new habit so that he might wash the one he was wearing. "Why?" he asked. "When I wash my habit the undergarment suffices while the habit is drying, and when I wash the undergarment, I can very well get along with just the habit, as I always do. It would be altogether superfluous to have two habits."

And he refused Joan's gift. But he had a good reason for doing so. He had the example—as vital and efficacious for him as a command—of his father, St. Dominic, who wore "one patched habit always, using habits uglier than those of the other brothers."[5]

Martin had a hat, also very old, but since it seemed to him a form of self-indulgence to use it to protect his head against the rays of the equatorial sun, he usually let it fall back between his shoulders, suspended from his neck by a cord.

His shoes were chosen from among those discarded by his brethren. It seems that his principal source for this article of his wardrobe was Father John Fernández who, according to the Father Procurator of the monastery, was " a religious of exemplary life and good habits." That being the case, there is no doubt that he, too, practiced the virtue of poverty, and did not pension off his shoes until they had well merited their retirement.[6]

Martin had no cell of his own. The cell considered his was really the storage room or supply room of the infirmary, where he kept his famous bed of planks. The only ornament on the walls was a bare wooden cross and a rude picture of the Virgin and of St. Dominic.

As he had done before entering the monastery, he never touched a penny of whatever he was able to earn through his medical skill.[7] At a certain point in his life, the charitable works springing from his heart and his genius brought the alms of all Lima flowing into his hands, creating a kind of bank of charity. Then, more than ever, Martin remained poor. The money flowed in and out of his hands without ever leaving a trace on them.

Such intransigent love of poverty is all the more remarkable when it is considered in relation to the religious observance of the sixteenth century, which interpreted the vow of poverty in a rather wide sense. In fact, religious did not then live the common life with the fullness intended by the founders of the various orders, and to which Canon Law happily restored them in succeeding centuries.

The Rule of St. Augustine states that everything shall be held in common, and that anyone who tries to keep something for himself, even though it be a necessity, shall be punished as if he were a thief. How faithful the first followers of St. Dominic were in the observance of this concept of poverty is shown by an episode related by Gerard de Frachet in *Vitae Fratrum.* After having solemnly begged God to liberate the soul of a lay brother from the demon of avarice, Blessed Reginald punished him severely in the presence of the friars merely because he had accepted a piece of cloth as a gift and then hidden it for himself.

But in the sixteenth century, on the contrary, the individual religious were expected to provide for their own needs and therefore they were permitted to use, entirely or in part, whatever they succeeded in earning through their labors. Although this had the advantage of lightening the task of those charged with the material care of the community and of stimulating individual initiative, the custom nevertheless did not represent the perfect ideal of religious poverty. Moreover, it created disparities of life which were opposed to the spirit of fraternal charity, which is the soul of the common life.

Martin loved poverty in all its integrity, as St. Dominic had loved it and had urged his sons to love it, menacing with his curse anyone who might be guilty of infidelity in this respect. Insofar as its observance depended upon him personally, Martin practiced poverty as rigorously as if he were living in the thirteenth century instead of the sixteenth century, and tried to bring about a more strict observance of the holy virtue on the part of his brethren.

Neither the reason for its being nor its end are found in poverty itself. It proceeds from humility and from the desire of conforming oneself to the example of the poor Christ, and prepares the way for other virtues. St. Catherine thus explains the origin of poverty in humility: "The humble man has disdained riches, whence self-will would derive pride, and he desires true and holy poverty. For he sees that voluntary poverty in the world enriches the soul and frees it from bondage; poverty renders the soul mild and meek and liberates it from the vain hope of transitory things, and gives it lively faith and true hope; the soul hopes in its Creator, through Christ crucified. . . . Out of love of true riches, the soul despises vain riches and seeks poverty, espousing it for the love of Christ crucified, whose whole life was one of poverty." [8]

Poverty paves the way for the other virtues, closing the door to the vices which are the enemy of the soul: "By means of poverty, the soul flees from pride and worldly conversations and unworthy friendships. . . . Freed of vanity of heart and frivolity of mind, the soul delights in the calm of its cell . . . and arrives at perfect purity." [9]

The function of poverty is therefore to clear the ground of obstacles, so that the soul, now purified and serene, is opened to the action of grace. This being done, the soul naturally finds itself called to its center, to a pure, laborious and recollected life. But to return to the center of the soul is not to wrap oneself in egotism. It is, rather, like living in a cell, and not a prison cell, but a monastic cell. In this context St. Catherine stated: "His cell becomes a heaven because God is concealed in his soul."

In Martin's soul, poverty was the prelude and ornament of limpid purity. All those who knew him in life agreed that he preserved his virginity intact to the moment of his death. He had a profound love for the spiritual beauty of the soul, a jealous love which made him search for the proper means to preserve and increase it. He did so in conformity with the spirit of his Dominican vocation, not by isolating himself from all contact with his neighbor, but by using the means to protect the angelic virtue without impeding his apostolic action. The black mantle over the white habit was a symbol of his mortification through fidelity to the rule and voluntary penance, of his clearsighted humility, which was always on guard, did not suffer from illusions, and knew where to find help in weakness and a guide in doubtful paths.

Martin strove to increase and perfect this virtue in an ever more intimate union with the infinitely pure God, whose love renders the soul chaste, whose contact purifies it, and who, in giving Himself to the soul, consecrates it a virgin, as the liturgy sings on the feast of St. Agnes. To protect and intensify the virtue of purity, Martin made good use of the sacrament of penance. We are sometimes amazed to see how assiduously the saints used this sacrament. But we forget a very simple fact: in the ascent towards sanctity, the eye of the soul is purified and sharpened so that it sees more clearly the beauty of the end to be attained, the false steps to be avoided, and the least deviations from the straight line leading to it. We also forget that confession has a positive value because this sacrament immerses the soul in the blood of Christ as in a bath which not only purifies it, but renews all its forces by a new infusion of grace.

The saints neither forget nor ignore these simple things, and that is why they become saints. This was true in Martin's case. The sacrament of penance refined his soul and increased its brilliant whiteness, so that when absolute purity had become his habitual state and the indispensable air breathed by his soul, it also became his most efficacious instrument in the apostolate.

In the corridors of his monastery and in the sunny streets of Lima, at the bedside of the sick and among the poor who came to ask for food at the door of the monastery, Martin concealed his treasure under his patched clothing and simplicity of manner, but the perfume of his virtue spread abroad and, almost without his knowing it, awoke in others a taste for the things of God. "Every gesture, action and word manifested the purity of his heart" and his countenance radiated such grace that it "aroused others to devotion. Merely by looking at him, the afflicted were consoled." [10]

Poverty and chastity went hand in hand, and together they

led Martin far along the path of sanctity. But surely the third and most important virtue of religious life was not neglected. St. Catherine calls obedience "the third column which preserves the city of the soul," and it is really obedience which is the firm foundation of the whole edifice.[11]

Martin realized this perfectly. On the day of his religious profession, he had pronounced only this vow, the only one which can contain and imply the other two. If he was thereafter bound to the observance of poverty and chastity, it was by reason of the vow of obedience in accordance with the constitutions of the Dominican Order.

This summing up of all the obligations of religious life in the one vow of obedience, peculiar to the Dominican tradition, is the most effective means of emphasizing the fact that the very essence of religious life consists in the giving of one's whole being to God in a perpetual holocaust, consumed day by day with the full consent of one's free will, which is man's noblest possession. It is the means by which the religious is conformed to his Divine Master, whose whole life St. Paul summarized in the concise statement: "He humbled Himself, becoming obedient unto death." [12]

Martin's fidelity to the subordinate virtues of poverty and chastity, if one may thus term them, was sufficient to show us how faithful he was to the principal virtue of obedience. Besides, we have ample direct testimony concerning his obedience. In Martin this virtue was based on such a deep sense of respect for authority that it amounted to veneration. This applied to all authority, whether ecclesiastical or civil, because he saw in each a participation in the authority of God. Father Anthony de Morales testified that he knew by experience that Martin "obeyed and revered both religious and diocesan prelates, and all persons invested with either ecclesiastical or secular dignity, as if venerating God in them, His authority and

His delegated power." [13] He therefore obeyed promptly and induced others to obey.

Father Andrew Martínez affirmed that Martin never evaded any command, but did everything he was told. Indeed, he even sought out the wishes of his superiors. [14]

"He fulfilled the vow of obedience with a prompt, joyful and virile will," stated a lay brother, James de Acuña, and it would be difficult to express more complete praise in so few words. [15]

True obedience is the virtue of strong souls. If among all the moral virtues, whose function is to free the soul of the tyranny of created things so that it can be united with the Creator in charity, that virtue has the greatest excellence which exercises its dominion on the free will, which is the greatest of all created goods, then obedience, more than any other virtue, must possess the quality of *"virtus"* or manliness.

St. Catherine saw it clothed with the beauty of regal dignity: "O obedience, always united in the peace and obedience of the Word, thou art a queen crowned with strength!" And she numbers fortitude among the virtues which accompany it: "This virtue is never alone in the soul, for it is accompanied by the light of faith, based upon humility . . . with fortitude and perseverance and the precious gem of patience." [16]

Elsewhere the Saint of Siena draws a picture of the truly obedient man which seems, by anticipation, to be a portrait of Martin: "The truly obedient man does not obey only in one way, in one place or one time, but in every way, everywhere, always. . . . With all care he keeps his rule, respects the customs and ceremonies, fulfills the will of his superior with joyfulness, desiring neither to judge nor question the superior's intentions. He does not ask: 'Why is a heavier burden laid upon me than upon another?' He merely obeys peacefully, calmly, and with a tranquil mind." [17]

[55]

Father Francis Velasco Carabantes said of Martin: "He exercised this virtue to the fullest, with such joy of spirit, prudence, constancy, profound humility, and so religiously, that all knew . . . that the said Servant of God sought his own will in nothing, but only that of those who commanded him, and with such virility of soul, with such solid constancy, that nothing, however slight, could ever be found in him in opposition to this virtue." [18]

This insistence of Martin's brethren upon the quality of joy and strength in his obedience is admirable. It is likewise useful, because seeing it as an actuality in the life of a saint, we can form a more exact idea of this virtue. Obedience is not a "passive virtue," as many seem to think who look at it in the grayish perspective of such expressions as "blind obedience," "obedient as a corpse" and the like. These expressions are often used and abused in contemporary spiritual literature.[19]

Obedience is certainly the renunciation of one's own will, but a renunciation effected by a free act of the will which, in view of the object to be attained, goes contrary to the tendencies of what St. Catherine calls the "sensitive will," that is to say, the love of one's own satisfaction and indulgence. It is therefore a virtue in the fullest sense of the word (*virtus*); a virtue which, more than any other, makes demands upon the free will of man. According to St. Thomas, the more obedience compels the will to overcome natural repugnances, the more it is genuine and pleasing to God.[20]

In view of this doctrine, it is easy to understand how Father Velasco could praise Martin's obedience by saying: "He obeyed . . . with joy of spirit and *of his own will,*" which is to say that he obeyed with all the force of his will, in an intelligent manner, as is worthy of a being endowed with free will and intelligence. And Father Velasco could add, without any shadow of contradiction, that Martin was "obedient to the very end of his life, without seeking his own will in anything whatsoever." [21]

In an almost paradoxical manner, St. Catherine of Siena explains how activity and detachment can be reconciled in the practice of obedience, when she invites her disciples to "run as dead men" in the footsteps of Christ crucified. She praises the victory of obedience in the following words: "O sweet obedience, which never causes pain! Thou killest self-will and thus makest men live and run even though they are dead; and the more they are dead, the more swiftly they run, because the mind and soul that are dead to the love of a perverse sensitive will, run the race more easily and are united by love to the eternal Spouse." [22]

Another attractive aspect of Martin's obedience appears in the testimony of those who knew him: its simple constancy and sobriety. One would look in vain among the details of his life—so rich in other respects with remarkable facts—for "miracles of obedience." In his garden there are no cabbages planted with their roots in the air, no water poured on rows of dry sticks.

I do not say this to criticize the masters of the spiritual life who thought it wise to test the virtue of their novices with such expedients. If one is to believe the legends, the Lord showed that He was pleased by these examples of ingenuous faith because sometimes He put His power at their service and worked miracles.

Rather, I say it only because I am happy that, in Martin's case, no miracles were needed. God never works a miracle without a serious purpose, and the purpose in the case of the "miracles of obedience" is to induce someone to practice this virtue. But Martin never had any doubts about the value of obedience and he never had to be convinced that it must be practiced. From the very first day, he understood and practiced obedience in all the occasions offered to him by life in the monastery of the Holy Rosary. This simple, "unvarying constancy" and "long perseverance" is much more impressive than any miracle. A virtue that lasts through a whole life, in the obscure succession of ordinary events with which every day is filled—day by day, year by year—in addition to being heroic virtue, can also serve as a model for others.

Martin's will was resolutely submitted to that of his superiors. He constantly followed every indication of their will, not only in the easy paths—as when he was ordered to sweep the cloisters and to do humble and tiring work—and not only in intricate paths—as in the accumulation of duties which he fulfilled, without being overwhelmed by them—but also in the steep and thorny paths, when obedience imposed upon him something repugnant to his humility. Thus, Father de Saldaña imposed the formal precept of obedience (without which he could not have overcome the resistance of Martin's humility) to make Martin talk about his nocturnal mortifications.

It may sometimes happen that the virtues, which normally get along well together and help each other, contend with one another, so to speak, and one strives to prevail over another. Something like this once happened when Martin was ill. Martin was often ill and usually paid no attention to the fact. In winter he suffered from quartan fever but went on working. He took to his bed only when he could no longer stand on his feet, but even then, his bed of planks did not offer him much relief.

During one of these malarial attacks the prior ordered him to make up a bed for himself like the others, with mattress, sheets and blankets. Naturally, Martin obeyed, but without deliberately willing to do so, he looked beyond the intention of the prior and slipped under the sheets wearing his habit, undergarment, hair shirt and also, I believe, the shoes of Father John Fernández. He fell asleep, happy to have reconciled obedience and the spirit of mortification, which at first seemed about to break off relations.

Someone reported the facts to the prior, who judged them in the worst possible light. He called Martin, gave him a good lecture, and accused him of disobedience.

Martin defended himself brilliantly. "But Father, how could I have believed you intended to give to a poor mulatto slave like myself, here in a monastery, a luxurious bed such as I could never have had in my own home? It was too comfortable for me, even in the way I used it."

When the same thing happened again, the prior, who was then Father John Surate, smilingly replied to the one who had come to inform him of Martin's new "disobedience": "Let him alone; Brother Martin is a good master of mystical theology and understands the laws of obedience very well." One need only add that the master of novices and the master of students held Martin up to their charges as a model of obedience and the "renunciation of one's own will." [23]

Martin found himself engaged in a duel to the death between humility and obedience when Felician de Vega, the archbishop-elect of Mexico, fell ill in Lima while he was traveling to his residential see. When all the remedies prescribed by the best doctors proved useless, Father Cyprian de Medina, the archbishop's nephew, said to him, "Why haven't you called our Brother Martin? He certainly could cure you."

It seemed a good idea to the archbishop, and he at once charged Father Cyprian to ask the Dominican provincial to send Martin to him.

When Father Cyprian arrived at the monastery, Martin could not be found, for he was invisible in one of his Eucharistic ecstasies. But at the command of the superior, he appeared instantly, wearing his black mantle, his hands crossed in his sleeves, his eyes cast downward—his usual appearance, composed and tranquil.

"Are you already prepared to go out? Very well. You are to go at once to see the archbishop of Mexico and to do anything he asks of you. And you are not to return to the monastery until the archbishop is healed."

Martin was still somewhat absorbed in ecstasy. He did not completely grasp what he was to do and therefore did not take along any medicine.

Martin had worked many marvelous cures during his long medical career, previous to this particular occasion. Whenever he found he must heal some incurable malady, he took clever precautions to divert all suspicion from himself, letting the credit go to the very innocent remedies he used—a few leaves of herbs or a glass of sugared water. But it is also possible that on this particular occasion the Father Provincial did not give him time to go up to his pharmacy to collect his supplies. Martin went on his way, consoling himself by reflecting that, after all, a glass of water and a lump of sugar could surely be found in the palace where the archbishop was staying.

But as often happens, when he arrived there, things did not go at all as he had anticipated. He was led immediately into the presence of the archbishop, who began to upbraid him because he had not come earlier. Martin fell on his knees near the bed to take his scolding. The archbishop told him to get up, and Martin rose to his feet and stood waiting. Then the archbishop commanded Martin to give him his hand.

Martin began to scent the danger and tried to defend himself. "But what would a prelate like Your Excellency want with the hand of a poor mulatto?"

The archbishop knew that his was a case of life or death,

and he calmly replied, with the secure dignity of those accustomed to command: "Didn't the Father Provincial tell you to do whatever I said?"

"Yes, my Lord," was all that Martin could reply, seeing all way of escape shut off.

"Then put your hand here," ordered the archbishop.

He was suffering from an acute and unremitting pain on the side of his chest, a pain which hampered his breathing and left him no rest by night or day. Hardly had Martin's hand touched the spot, when the pain vanished.

Martin was aware of the marvel he had been forced to perform and, blushing to the tips of his ears and perspiring as if he had swept the entire monastery, he tried to withdraw his hand.

"Isn't that enough, my Lord?" he asked gently.

The archbishop inexorably held Martin's hand with both of his own. "Leave it where it is."

He was right in insisting, because after a little more of the treatment, not only was the pain gone, but the fever and all discomfort as well.[24]

Only then was Martin allowed to return to his monastery without further delay, and the humility which had been forced to give way to obedience at once sought revenge. Martin remembered that certain toilets needed cleaning. One of the Fathers, finding him absorbed in that unpleasant work and knowing that the archbishop had called for his help, said, "Brother Martin, wouldn't you be better off in the palace of the archbishop of Mexico?" He doubtless thought that Martin's time could have been better employed in talking with the archbishop, who so greatly esteemed him, than in doing work that anyone at all could have done.

Martin gave him the famous reply with the words of the Psalmist: "I have chosen to be an abject in the house of my

God," and added, almost paraphrasing unconsciously another verse of the same psalm: "Father John, I think one moment spent in doing what I am doing right now is more important than many days spent in the house of the Lord Archbishop." [25]

Martin was no longer young when he said that. In fact, he was in the last year of his life. The reply he gave to Father John de Ochoda, preacher general, was a proof that he had faithfully carried out, year by year throughout his whole life, the program he had selected in his youth: the practice of humility in the house of obedience, out of love for the humble and obedient Lord Jesus.

It was also a profession of faith and love of an ideal preserved intact: "I have chosen to be an abject in the house of my God . . . for better is one day in Thy court above thousands" (Ps. 83:11 and 10).

CHAPTER

⊱ 8 ⊰

Say to wisdom: thou art my sister (Prov. 7:4).

WHEN Martin decided to embrace the religious state of life, we do not know why he chose the Order of Friars Preachers and not one of the many others which in his day had monasteries in Lima. Perhaps it was because of his love for the Queen of the Most Holy Rosary, whom the Dominicans venerate as their special patroness. Perhaps it was because the Most Holy Virgin had given to St. Dominic the mission of preaching and propagating the devotion of the Rosary as a remedy for the many evils of his time and of all times. Perhaps it was because of his love of the crucified Christ, a love which is so strong in Dominican hearts from Henry Suso to Catherine of Siena. Perhaps it was because of his love of the Holy Eucharist, whose poet is St. Thomas Aquinas. The possibilities could be discussed indefinitely.

Someone has hazarded the hypothesis, which is humanly possible, that because of his great love of animals, Martin's attention was drawn to the figure of St. Dominic on account of the dog with the flaming torch in his mouth, invariably represented at the feet of the Holy Patriarch.[1]

From a natural point of view, it is possible that any one of these reasons could have exerted some influence, because it is true that many factors play a part in the choice of every vocation. But over and above the natural attractions and repulsions, there is the supernatural element: that mysterious, quiet, interior voice which speaks to the soul and makes it ardently desire a kind of life still unknown, without the soul's being able to define its reasons. The reasons are known to Him whose voice is heard in the soul, who with infinite wisdom chooses for each soul the path by which it can attain perfection.

As soon as he had entered the monastery of the Most Holy Rosary, Martin realized what a perfect choice Eternal Wisdom had made for him, and he loved the Order of St. Dominic with a strong, unfailing love to the end of his life. "The lines are fallen unto me in goodly places," he could have repeated with the Psalmist, "for my inheritance is goodly to me."[2]

His love was compounded of esteem for everything in the Order, of fidelity to all the requirements of the rule, of untiring labor, of zeal for his own perfection and that of his brethren. His love was expressed by a constant effort to instill in his own soul the spirit of his father, St. Dominic, by the imitation of his example and the acquisition of the virtues which characterize Dominican life in its double aspect—the virtues of the interior life which flower in the virtues of the apostolic life—and in this way to give to others something from the abundant treasure in his heart. The crowning proof of Martin's love of the Order is the fact that his was a lifelong effort to actuate the Dominican ideal in his own life and in the lives of others.

But here a difficulty arises. If Pope Honorius III, in approving the Order of Friars Preachers, called the followers of St. Dominic *"pugiles fidei et vera mundi lumina"* (defenders of the faith and true lights of the world), it seems evident that the perfection of this ideal cannot be attained without a profound knowledge of the science of divine things. "And if you look at the bark of your father Dominic, My dearly beloved son," we read in the *Dialogue* of St. Catherine, "you will see how perfectly he constructed it, wishing that his sons seek only My honor and the salvation of souls by the light of science." [3]

This light should be the guide of all Dominican activity if it is to conform to the ideal of the founder. But how can the perfection of the Dominican ideal be realized in a simple lay helper, absorbed all day long in a thousand material occupations, without ever having an opportunity to study? This is one of the most surprising aspects of Martin's life. Because he understood the indispensable need of study (a thing rather rare in those who do not study) and its importance in the formation of a Dominican, Martin helped the students as much as he could, trying to eliminate at least some of their difficulties. He was always ready to furnish them with paper, pens, ink, and even the books needed for the various courses of study. He took special care of the clothing of the students and the professors, and since they had no time to take care of their own needs, because of the many hours they spent in teaching, Martin freed them of all preoccupation on that score and took the tasks on his own shoulders.

Of course, that is the duty of the brothers in a Dominican monastery. They share in the merits of the apostolic life by taking over the material preoccupations so that the priests may be free to devote their time exclusively to study, preaching and the priestly ministry.

The religious state is a living exemplification of the dogma of the communion of saints. No Christian—and, for that matter, no man—can ever consider himself an isolated individual, independent of all. But he who is a member of a religious community, by the very fact of his membership, is constantly reminded of the relations existing between him and the other members, bound together in one corporate body for the attainment of a common end to be reached through an effort which is at once individual and collective. It is the effort of the individual in the collectivity from which he receives and to which he gives his contribution.

Martin's collaboration in the effort to provide the best possible conditions of study for the young members of the community was so intelligent and so solicitous that one could say that he was what he was supposed to be in the Order: a note in perfect harmony with the whole. But Martin did not stop there. With almost a paternal love he looked after the younger members of the community who were the hope of the future of the Order. He wanted them to be perfect in all respects. If he felt that love of study was lacking a little in one or the other, he recalled the delinquents to their duty either individually or in groups. "Boys," he would say, "study attentively because the credit and glory of the Province will one day depend upon you." And abandoning his reserve and habitual silence, he employed words filled with fire to enkindle anew their enthusiasm for the ideal of their Order.

He went even further than that. One day when classes were over, two students began discussing a difficult theological question about the perfection of essence and existence in God. They had been engaged in the discussion for some time, without making any progress, when Martin happened to pass by. It may seem strange to us, but to them it seemed very simple and natural to ask him what he thought about the point under discussion. They turned to him, moved by the same impulse and using the same words: "Brother, Brother Martin! What do you think of this? What is your answer?"

It certainly was odd to question pointblank a lay brother who was going about his own affairs, slipping the beads of his huge rosary between his fingers; a lay brother who perhaps a moment before had put his broom in a corner and a few moments later would be pouring out soup in the refectory. Why put a problem to him that would have more easily been clarified by the professor who had just finished the lecture they had attended? Surely they were trying to make a fool of the mulatto brother!

No, the two students were not joking. And the question did not seem at all strange to Martin. He replied very simply, with his usual gentle smile: "Does not St. Thomas say that existence is more perfect than essence, but that in God essence and existence are one?" And he went tranquilly on his way.[4]

The two students were speechless. Thy went to see the master of studies and repeated Martin's reply. He confirmed its exactness and explained to the young friars that Martin was capable of replying so correctly and with such assurance because he was far advanced in the "science of the saints."[5]

On another occasion, a large group of students had launched into a discussion that threatened to degenerate into a dispute. The discussion began calmly enough but gradually grew heated, and each one began to raise his voice in order to be heard above the others.

At the height of the argument, Martin arrived and asked

the reason for all the noise. Brother Bernard de Valilla replied that they were discussing a certain question proposed by the Angelic Doctor. "But why get so excited about it," asked Martin, "when St. Thomas himself resolved the difficulty?" And at once he gave Brother Bernard the exact place in St. Thomas with the number of the question and of the article.[6]

What explanation can be offered for such a direct and precise knowledge of the *Summa Theologica?* Did Martin consult the monastery library during his free time? But what free time did he have? It was already a miracle that he managed to carry on all his ordinary duties in the course of a single day. The question remains enigmatic, as do many other things in the life of St. Martin. What is certain is that events like this were not sporadic if, in a Dominican house of studies, as was the monastery of the Holy Rosary, Martin was "esteemed, considered and reputed to be a learned man." [7]

His was the "science of the saints," which is not acquired simply by the exercise of the intellectual faculties, but is a gift which God grants to His chosen ones. It is the gift by which the Psalmist says he has been enriched because he was faithful to the Law; the gift which the Gospel promises to the pure of heart.[8] St. Dominic acknowledged that he had learned this science from the book of charity, and St. Thomas stated that he had learned much more in the contemplation of the crucifix than in books.

But admitting that the gift was divine does not diminish the fact that Martin was endowed with a keen intelligence. A proof of it is the rapidity with which he completed his studies of medicine and the short time in which he mastered all the secrets of his profession, and to such an extent that he equalled his teacher. Sometimes, in hopeless cases, his use of medicine was only a screen for his supernatural gifts of healing, but that was true only of hopeless cases. For all the others, Martin acted like a doctor, conscientiously and intelligently applying the remedies of his profession. I remember once speaking with a doctor of the treatment Martin had used for a patient. The doctor told me, "Martin did exactly what was proper and necessary."

Grace perfects nature, and natural abilities are gifts of God no less than the gifts of grace. God Himself created the earth and the seed, and if He wills that the seed bear abundant fruit, He makes the earth more fecund. Or, if He wishes, He can make the desert burst into bloom.

From the naturally rich soil of Martin's spirit, the supernatural gifts of knowledge and wisdom flowered splendidly in the furrow prepared by his love of the faith. And in this respect also, Martin imitated his father, St. Dominic.

Out of love of the faith, St. Dominic pursued the sacred sciences. The doctrine of which he made himself a master was not cold and arid, but a burning knowledge of divine things, drawn from the fountain of charity. Following St. Dominic's example, Martin dedicated to the faith his purest and liveliest affections, nourished by charity.

Love of the faith, which had impelled St. Dominic to acquire a solid theological doctrine, also inspired him to work for the faith with a vehemence comparable to that of "a torrent that a high vein forces." [9] Martin's love of the faith was likewise a principle of action. Good works are a sign of the vitality of faith, but faith, in its turn, is the soul of good works.

Good must necessarily diffuse itself. "As it is better to enlighten than merely to shine, so it is better to give to others the fruits of one's contemplation than merely to contemplate." [10]

These three words, *"contemplata aliis tradere,"* contain the essence of the whole Dominican program of life and action:

to give to one's neighbor the fruit of one's own contemplation.

This most perfect form of charity springs from the love of God, whom one wants to make known so that He may be loved as He deserves, and from the love of neighbor, who will be elevated and ennobled by knowing and loving God. A Dominican should be concerned with this form of charity more than any other. It is the *"caritas veritatis,"* the gift, given out of love, of "that truth which lifts us so high." [11]

St. Dominic was keenly aware of the ravages produced in Christianity by error and he realized that heresy had taken root because the land was overgrown with the weeds of ignorance and neglect. Preaching and teaching the truths of the faith were obviously the sole means of restoring Christian society to health and freeing it from the basic causes of the evil.

St. Dominic yearned not only to restore Christianity to its pristine beauty, but also to extend it by preaching the Gospel to nations still numbered among the infidels, and he hoped to seal his apostolate with the testimony of his blood. Even though the express will of the reigning pontiff constrained the Saint to remain on the battlefield, waging war against the Albigensian heresy, some of the earliest of his followers were missionaries and martyrs.

From its inception, the apostolate of the Dominican Order was directed to these two ends: the restoration and consolidation of the faith in the heart of Christendom, and the propagation of the faith among the infidels. The aims were the same in the time of St. Martin, the only difference being that the contemporaries of St. Dominic found mission lands near at hand in eastern and southern Europe, while in the sixteenth century the missions of the Friars Preachers extended around the earth.

In his desire to spread the truth, Martin was a true son of

St. Dominic. His love of the faith, nurtured by contemplation, was the activating principle of his whole life, and his life became a magnet which drew souls to the faith.

Martin loved souls by the light of the faith, he loved them in the light of their glorious destiny. He saw them as precious stones destined to be used for the construction of the celestial Jerusalem after they had been purified and refined by the trials of life.

Martin loved the City of God and souls with a jealous love. He desired them to be, even upon earth, free of all stain. Had he been able to do so, he would have wished to see the light which shines on the Church triumphant shining as well on the face of the Church militant.[12]

His love found expression in good works: his labor, his prayer, his penance, his efforts to persuade others by word and example to seek the good. It is true that Martin could not preach in a pulpit or teach in a classroom, but when the heart overflows with love, the tongue cannot be silent. Poverty and illness brought him so many pitiable creatures seeking material aid. He tried to help all of them materially, but to that he added spiritual assistance as well.

Every day, after he had served dinner to the sick and the servants of the monastery and had distributed food to the poor who waited at the door, he gathered together in the infirmary a group of young boys and other laymen who worked in the monastery of the Holy Rosary. Then, as he gave first aid to the sick, he taught them Christian doctrine and prayers, and explained what must be done in order to live a life in accordance with the faith.[13]

When he went to Limatambo to spend the day, he did the same thing there for the servants and Negroes of the farm and those of neighboring estates.[14]

His talks were not complicated. In his limpid and simple

style he explained the principal points of dogma, but when he spoke of the means whereby one might live a life worthy of the name of Christian, his words acquired an extraordinary sweetness. He seemed to supplicate rather than to admonish.

His words had great efficacy. Martin knew what he was saying, for his own was a life conformed to the faith. For that reason the servants and the poor listened to him eagerly, and what was more important, they tried to put his teachings into practice.

Love of souls is proved by good works, but does not end there. Good works are necessarily limited, and love tolerates no limits. When action has exhausted all its resources, there is still an infinite field open to desire. To love souls efficaciously means taking upon oneself "corporal labor, with much anxious desire, as the Son of God did, who endured bodily torments and the pain of desire." [15]

Martin, too, suffered the "pain of desire," longing to carry out to the fullest the Dominican ideal of an apostolate among the faithful and the infidels. Peru was a recent conquest of the Church. The missionaries who had evangelized the nation belonged to the generation of Martin's grandparents. It could still have been considered missionary territory because there were vast areas as yet unexplored. But the preaching of the Gospel in Peru could no longer be considered a perilous undertaking, since the conquistadors supported and protected it.

Far from Peru there were regions into which missionaries ventured at their risk and peril, sustained only by their trust in God and their own resourcefulness, with nine chances out of ten of crowning their apostolic work by martyrdom. China and Japan, impenetrable until the middle of the sixteenth century, began to open up to missionary efforts between the last decades of the 1500's and the first decades of the 1600's.

While Martin was still alive, Blessed Alphonsus Navarrete

and more than one hundred Dominican missionaries, among whom was the Italian, Angelo Orsucci, heroically shed their blood for the faith in Japan. Nine years after Martin's death, in addition to giving China its first mssionary and first bishop, the Dominican Order was also to give that country its first martyr in the person of Blessed Francis de Capillas.

Martin's eyes turned to China and Japan. He longed to work for the spread of the faith, and to give the supreme proof of his love of the faith by martyrdom.[16] But God exacted from Martin, as He did from St. Dominic, the sacrifice of his own desires.

At the same time, however, He showed Martin how pleasing that desire was to Him, fulfilling it partially by means of a miracle through His omnipotent power. Witnesses have stated that Martin was seen several times in China and Japan. The novelty of the surroundings did not disturb his habitual calm, and with the same naturalness and simplicity with which he taught catechism in his infirmary, he gathered the native children around him and taught Christian doctrine to them.

One can easily imagine the scene: Martin's tall, slender figure towering over the little crowd of street urchins, whose black pigtails hung down their backs straight as a plumbline, their intelligent, almond-shaped eyes becoming thoughtful and serious as they listened to him speak of God and of the love which impelled Him to live among us and to die for us. Then those almond eyes would suddenly shine with childish delight at the end of the lesson, when the catechist unclasped his hands, hidden under his scapular, and brought out of the measureless depths of his sleeves all those trifles so pleasing to a child: candy, little holy pictures, exotic fruit of a new and strange taste.[17]

Were these merely dreams, rooted in his ardent desires?

Sometimes desire carried Martin to comfort Christians who were prisoners of the Turks and were in grave danger of losing the faith. The Turks deliberately maltreated them as a means of making them renounce the faith.

One day a Spaniard came to the monastery of the Holy Rosary. He had reached Lima a short time before, from Algeria, where he had been a prisoner of the Turks. Seeing Martin pass by, he greeted him enthusiastically as his father and his liberator.

"Welcome," replied Martin, "but now I am busy. We'll see each other later." And he disappeared.

The traveler was not disconcerted by his rather cool reception and told the friars his story. He had been a slave of the Turks for many years when Martin began to visit him and his companions in slavery and to give them what help he could. Martin brought bread, money and other needs, took care of the sick and healed them, and exhorted all the prisoners to remain firm in the faith. Martin's visits were the sole moral support he had during the long years of imprisonment, and he had been able to pay his ransom only because Martin had brought him the money little by little.[18]

Charity of truth, in this case too. And charity knows no limits.

≻ 9 ≺

*She hath sought wool and flax, and hath wrought
by the counsel of her hands* (Prov. 31:13).

BROTHER Martin and Brother Christopher were walking one
morning along the roads which divided the sections of land
on the estate of Limatambo. John Vázquez, Martin's faithful
helper, was with them.

It was the sowing season. In the fields the farm workers
were going to and fro, scattering the seed the length of the
parallel furrows opened by the plow in the brown earth.

The two brothers and the young lad stopped on the road.
They watched the steady, measured coming and going of
the workers and the incessant repetition of the cycle of move-
ments. Each man's hand plunged into the sack he held, drawing out a handful of seed sufficient for the area he would
cover in the next step; then, with a sweep of his arm, he
scattered it in front of him, then to his left.

They watched, fascinated by the rhythm of the movement
and the fine rain of grain disappearing between the clods of
earth. Perhaps they were thinking of the mystery of life and
death which would be renewed in the germination of the
seed: "Unless the grain of wheat falls into the ground and
dies. . . ." [1]

Suddenly Brother Christopher said, "Do you see that un-
cultivated piece of land, up there beyond the plowed fields?
It would be ideal for an olive grove. I've thought about it for
a long time, and it should be planted this year. But we will
have to wait until the sowing is finished, for all the men are
too busy just now."

Martin's eyes followed the wave of Brother Christopher's hand. Beyond the plowed fields the land rose sharply, almost as if flaunting its unsuitability for cultivation.

"Is this the right moment to plant it?" asked Martin.

"Yes, but it is impossible now. We haven't the workers."

"Have you the young olive trees?"

"Yes, but what good are they under the circumstances?"

Martin went in search of a small hoe. With John Vázquez carrying the young trees, he went to the spot chosen by Brother Christopher for the olive grove and began digging holes in the hard earth. He spent the whole day there, digging, putting the young trees in the holes, filling the holes with earth and tamping the earth firmly around each tiny trunk. By evening the work was finished.

Martin lifted the hoe to his shoulder and carried it to the tool shed. "Thank you," said Brother Christopher. "Will you come back tomorrow to go on with the work?"

"No," replied Martin, "because we planted all the trees."

"All?"

If it had not been dark, Brother Christopher would have gone at once to see this marvel with his own eyes. But night had fallen and he had to wait.

When he went to see the new olive grove the next day, how astounded he was when, even before reaching the spot, he saw silver gray leaves trembling on the young trees! And on top of each shoot, outlined against the background of the rugged terrain, the breeze stirred the new leaves under the bright rays of the sun.[2]

It was always like that. Martin gave of himself without measure every time there was something to be done to help others. And God gave to Martin without measure. He bestowed a benediction which rendered his efforts efficacious beyond human possibilities. *"Non recuso laborem,"* Martin could have said with his great namesake and patron, the Bishop of Tours. He could have added even more, because in addition to not shunning work, he continually went in search of it; not for the mere pleasure of being busy, but out of sincere love of his community and each of its members.

"Express your love by your good works," said our Lord to Sister Mary of the Trinity. And He added, "When you love more, you will do things more swiftly; work will flow from your hands." [3]

Work flowed from Martin's hands. It flowed so naturally that he never seemed to be busy. No matter how many duties piled up on him, he was not perturbed. He acted with calm and orderly precision, without confusion. Like a river running rapidly but smoothly between its banks, work flowed out of his hands.

His ability to carry out so many different duties, each one of which would normally have required the full time of one person, was a proof to his brethren of the presence of God in Martin and a motive for praising the liberality of God. "He gave himself totally to the service and consolation of his neighbor, without keeping an hour for himself either by night or by day," said Brother Christopher. And the latter said he had "seen with his own eyes and touched with his own hands the power of the grace of God which can turn a man made of flesh and blood into a seraph aflame with the fire of charity." [4]

Among Martin's many occupations, his care of the sick was the best demonstration of the degree to which he loved his brothers in Christ. He served them with a paternal affection and an unflagging solicitude. When Martin approached a sickbed, his serenity and his smiling face comforted the patient instantly. It seemed that Martin had nothing else in the world to do but to give all his attention to that one patient. He never said, "Wait a moment," or "I'll be there right away." He was there when he was needed, silent and seemingly the complete master of his time.[5]

One year there was an epidemic of measles in Lima. Naturally, it penetrated the monastery of the Holy Rosary. More than sixty religious were stricken with the disease, some seriously, and several of them died. The illness was characterized by an extremely high fever which no medicine could lower and it produced a delirium akin to madness.

Martin nursed the sick without repose. He watched over them as a guardian would protect a treasure against the cupidity of thieves. He pitted his own strength against the attack of the malady, sustaining the forces of those stricken, trying to render the torment of the fever and burning thirst more bearable with refreshing beverages. He searched for remedies that might ease the patients' sufferings—unctions, medicinal extracts, herbs.[6]

He was with the sick day and night. He came and went from one to the other, without delay and without agitation. He passed from the community infirmary to that of the novitiate, sovereignly indifferent to locked and bolted doors.

Among those sick was a novice, Brother Matthias de Barrasa. His youth and delicate constitution gave him little chance of surviving. Feeling himself growing worse one evening, he began to ask for Brother Martin. At that hour of the night the door of the novitiate was locked and the master of novices had the key. The porter of the novitiate, Brother Francis Guerrero, ran to the master of novices and asked and obtained permission to bring Martin in. Keys in hand, Brother Francis was on his way to unlock the door. As he passed the cell of Brother Matthias, he decided to tell him the good news at once, but when he looked into the cell, he saw Martin already beside the bed, calmly talking with the sick novice. Martin's words must have been consoling and beautiful, for a radiant smile illumined the face of the dying novice.[7]

Every morning Brother Ferdinand de Aragonés, the head infirmarian, made the rounds of the sick and found that during the night Martin had visited them all, bringing each one precisely what he needed: a refreshing drink for those burning with fever, clean sheets and a clean tunic for those bathed in perspiration, and for all of them, encouraging words and a kindly smile.[8]

Sixty patients is a large number in a religious house which, after all, is not a hospital. With that many to take care of, the infirmarians could have considered themselves justified in doing things superficially. But Martin did not know the meaning of doing things by halves when it was a question of safeguarding the good of the community. And what was more important to the community than the lives of its members? At the height of the epidemic, overwhelmed with work by the increase in the number of the sick, he continued to treat each one as if he were the only patient in the house. He divined their wishes even before they were expressed. Without seeming to do so, he often remedied the harm done by the ignorance or the incorrect diagnoses of the doctors.

One of the stricken religious felt an unconquerable repugnance for any kind of food. The only thing for which he had any appetite at all was a certain kind of fruit. Martin appeared, the longed-for fruit in his hands. The sick man ate it with relish, and only after he had recovered did he realize that he had asked for a fruit which was out of season and could not be found in the market in Lima at that time of the year.[9]

Sick people normally welcome refreshing drinks, but during the epidemic there was one patient who never wanted to drink anything. Martin knew he must take a large quantity of liquids in order to recover. Every night he carried a mixture of sugar and water to the bedside, and did not leave until the sick man had drunk all of it.[10]

In Martin's eyes, a man stricken with illness was much more than a "clinical case," interesting only from a purely scientific point of view. He was a man engaged in a struggle that could absorb all his physical and spiritual forces, a man undergoing a trial that might be decisive and final. And his condition, humiliating from many points of view, demanded the greatest respect for his person.

An elderly priest, stricken with paralysis, had lost the use of all his members. He could not walk; his arms hung inert. His greatest affliction was his inability to make himself understood. In spite of their good will, the infirmarians could not gather what he wanted to say from the disconnected sounds issuing from his mouth. The priest's mind had remained lucid and he suffered greatly because he could not communicate with others. It was such an anguish to him that often he became impatient, and finally the situation became so painful that no one wanted to wait on the poor old man. All of Martin's sympathies were aroused. "Ask God to give him back the use of his tongue and his hands," he said to Brother Ferdinand, "even if he can't use his legs!"

God heard the prayer—the prayer of Brother Ferdinand, according to Brother Martin; the prayer of Brother Martin, according to Brother Ferdinand—and the sick man was able to speak and use his hands for many little things, including feeding himself. From then on his impatience was changed to patience, "he was as gentle as a lamb," and to such a degree that he became an admirable example to others during the long years of infirmities and ailments that still remained to him.[11]

During the epidemic two sick novices were in the same room. One had grown much worse, and in his delirium he rambled on endlessly in senseless phrases. The other, whose fever was not high and who retained full control of his faculties, amused himself by listening to the incoherencies of his companion and laughing as he recounted them to anyone who happened to pass by.

Martin did not laugh when Brother Francis Martínez tried to repeat some of these pleasantries to him. He could not endure anyone's mocking a sick man hovering between life and death. He said, "Brother Francis, you should thank God that this religious is now out of danger and think about yourself, for I do not know if you will come out of this as well as he." Several days later, at the end of the second week of his illness, Brother Francis died.[12]

Martin had the gift of knowing how an illness would end, independently of the indications given by its course. At first the doctors would cling to their own opinions, but after they knew Martin better, they unquestioningly accepted whatever he said.

This gift allowed him to bestow his attentions in accordance with the need. For Martin, there were two privileged categories of the sick: those whose disease was most repulsive to nature, and those nearest death. "Don't worry," he said to patients who complained that he had neglected them, "when I am rarely at a bedside, it means that the illness is not dangerous." There was even a saying among the friars of Holy Rosary: "That brother will soon die, because Martin goes to see him often." Not even those dearest to him were any exception to this law.[13]

Father Cyprian de Medina had fallen ill. He was so gravely ill that five doctors had withdrawn from the case, saying that the only thing left was to administer the last sacraments. Since death was all he could expect, Father Cyprian awaited it with resignation. Only one thought left him no peace: Martin had abandoned him and had not come to see him for several days.

Night had fallen and several religious watched around his bed, thinking he would not live until morning. Father Cyprian was overwhelmed by a desire to see Martin, linked to a feeling of revolt against his absence at the moment of greatest need. At his request, those who were with him went to look for Martin all over the monastery. He was not to be found.

It was between three and four in the morning. The night had already lasted so long that it seemed it would never end. A first ray of light began to shine through the window. At that moment, when everyone had given up all hope of finding him, Martin entered the room.

A thrill of joy went through the heart of Father Cyprian. At once he began to detail his woes and to complain that Martin had abandoned him. Did he not remember how he—Cyprian—when he entered the order as a boy, had begged Martin to adopt him as a son and had always venerated him as a father? And the paternal care Martin had always given him during all the years of his religious life? Why, at the very hour the doctors despaired of saving his life, should he have to resign himself to dying without seeing "his" Martin again?

Martin let the words pour out. A little outburst was perhaps good for the sick man. He listened in silence, the smile in his eyes veiled by the half-closed lids, his head inclined.

When he judged the moment had arrived to raise his head, he looked directly into Father Cyprian's eyes, talking to him in his humble and soothing tone of voice which, this time, had a touch of reproof in it.

"Father, you should have realized that you were not in

danger. Everyone knows that when I make frequent visits to the cells of the sick, it is a bad sign. Do not be upset if you have grown worse. This crisis will only serve to end your illness more swiftly. But you will not die now. God wills that you should live and give Him glory by continuing to serve him in religion."

Events a few days later confirmed Martin's words. Father Cyprian improved visibly. Shortly he was able to resume his teaching and preaching and he continued his labors for the glory of God for many years.[14]

When death was really at the door, Martin would return with increasing frequency to the bed of the friar who was about to embark on that mysterious journey. Without neglecting the physical attentions, he sought to strengthen the soul. He spoke of the infinite goodness of God with the assurance of one who had experienced it. He spoke of the mercy of God, seen in the outspread arms of Christ crucified, ready to embrace anyone who turned to Him. He spoke of Divine Wisdom offering Himself as a remedy for our weakness and ignorance, of the blood of the Lamb and of His immaculate body transmitting to us a source of life capable of surmounting even the barriers of death.

When he feared he could not say enough, he called to the bedside of the dying man the religious he considered better qualified to utter words of comfort and confidence, while he withdrew to pray and discipline himself so that the words would be efficacious and grace would innundate the soul of the dying man. He knew God would never refuse his petitions.

When the battle was over, Martin would not allow anyone else to perform the last and most painful service. He washed the corpse, reclothed it, and with the aid of the other religious carried it to the place of burial. And he urged them to pray.

But sometimes he said nothing, and a celestial joy shone from his face. Then everyone understood that the soul of the departed brother was already in the arms of the Father.[15]

The post of infirmarian carried with it more than the care of the sick. When Martin began to work in the infirmary, he found even the most indispensable equipment lacking, such as beds, blankets, linens. Funds to buy them were lacking, too. The monastery was poor. Anyone else would have said to himself, "If I am not given the necessary money, how will I buy supplies?" Martin's reaction was, "The sick should have everything they need, and even a little more, so the money must be found."

And he initiated a campaign to find it.

He was aided by the fame of his sanctity, which had begun to spread abroad. When he set out to knock at the doors of the rich and the powerful, Martin was not unknown. His life of humility and prayers, the extraordinary things told of him —his ecstasies, miraculous cures—were already being talked about in Lima.

As a matter of fact, Martin had never been unknown in Lima. His father held one of the highest posts in the government. When Martin had lived in poverty as a child with his mother and little sister; when he had become the apprentice of Rivero after the interlude of Guayaquil; and when he had renounced the advantages of a position gained through his own work and had put on a religious habit, Martin had never been lost among the unknown faces of the anonymous crowds in Lima.

But his life had become even more luminous after he had hidden it behind the walls of the monastery, because the irresistible power of sanctity shone out from him. The monastery was not an ivory tower, withdrawn from the world. All classes of people came and went.

There was Francis de la Torre. When he was not on duty, he went to Holy Rosary and was free to go all over the monastery and to sleep at night in the supply room of the infirmary near Martin. When he was on duty, he went back to the city to command the guard and recount the things he had seen, to the edification of those who listened to him.

There was Marcel de Rivero, Martin's teacher, who often came to the monastery to visit the sick and saw Martin in ecstasy, raised from the floor to the height of the crucifix in the chapter room.

There was John Vázqez, as well as many others who, after they had witnessed something extraordinary, could not deny themselves the pleasure of telling their acquaintances about it.

Martin himself often had occasion to mingle with the crowds of the city, and his worn habit and unassuming manner revealed more than all the tales of his admirers.

Martin certainly did not think about all this when he went in search of help for his sick. He thought only of the needs of the religious. For love of them, he was ready to risk harsh words or refusals. He was pleasantly surprised each time people listened to him and then responded generously, and he praised God who had put into their hearts such sentiments of compassion and generosity.

There was immense wealth in Lima. It was almost a relief for the conquerors to do some good with it, since they had appropriated it, often by illicit means. Do not the Scriptures say that almsgiving covers a multitude of sins?

No matter how indifferent they were to the misery surrounding them, the conquerors were moved by the appeals of this man who was charity incarnate, and they gave generously of the plentiful wealth they had found in the New World, wealth so abundant that it would have seemed a fable or a dream in the Old World.

Little by little, Martin built up a group of benefactors to whom he could always have recourse. The viceroy was at the head of the list. And then, going down the line, riches flowed to him from all sides, from all the ranks of the government, of the aristocracy, of commerce. It was a flood of imposing proportions.

Martin was not swept away by it. He had discovered a way to tap the hidden vein and he knew how to employ what he received by sagely directing it where it was most needed. To do so, he brought into play those gifts of his character which are among the most appealing from a human point of view; in other words, his genius for organization.

First he took care of the most urgent needs. Then, as the flow of alms became greater and steadier, he planned and carried out a division of the offerings which permitted him to enlarge the field of his charity far beyond the walls of his monastery.

As was entirely natural, he began with the needs which had prompted him to ask for alms: the necessary supplies for the infirmary, and the garments needed for the infirmary and the community.

In reorganizing all this, the source of Martin's zeal was doubtless his compassion for the sick who lacked all of the most indispensable equipment. It must have been like a knife in his heart not to find a pair of sheets or a tunic to give to a patient who needed them urgently.

But at the same time he was spurred on by a motive of a higher order. Custom had legitimized a wide interpretation of the observance of the vow of poverty, but it had gone too far and fatally led to the disregard of certain prescriptions of the rule. Being obliged to find a way of furnishing their own clothing, it was inevitable that the friars used almost anything they could get and wore articles they had received as gifts, but were not entirely in conformity with the rule. As a result, many of them wore cotton or linen habits instead of woolen ones.

These infractions of the rule distressed Martin. Even though they are of secondary importance, such details do have a role in a state of life which should be a testimony of faith and of love. To bring his brethren back to a more perfect observance of poverty, Martin assumed the task of making it possible for them.

Consequently, he went in search of wool with which to make the needed habits. He had gathered a little money and he found the merchants willing to sell him the needed cloth at greatly reduced prices. As a result, he was able to provide more than eighty new woolen habits. Then there was the problem of making the substitution in such a way that no one would be irritated by it. Martin worked out a plan which included the organization of the wardrobe of the community and the supplies of the infirmary, as well as the regular care and distribution of all the clothing. He not only planned it, but put it into practice, taking upon himself, as usual, the burden of the work.

This is what he did. Each time a linen habit arrived in the laundry, he substituted a woolen one of the same size for it. The original habit, washed and ironed, went into the reserve supplies of the infirmary to be used for the greater comfort of the sick. Every new piece of clothing he gave out was marked with a number, and each member of the community had his own number. In the wardrobe room he had numbered a series of shelves divided into sections, and each one's clean linen was arranged in his own section.

Every Saturday Martin went from cell to cell with his big basket filled with clean clothing and distributed it to the religious. On Monday he made the rounds again to gather up the clothing to be washed.[16] In this way Martin furnished not only habits, but all other articles of clothing to those religious who had no way of securing them, either because their families were poor or because they were too occupied by their duties in the monastery to be able to earn money through other activities. The less fortunate ones who might have been ashamed of their indigence discovered that they were really the most fortunate because, thanks to Martin's solicitude, they were provided with everything in accordance with the most strict observance of religious poverty.

Martin was not yet satisfied. It was good to have the garments and linens of the community in order, but it was not enough. In addition to begging for money to supply these needs, Martin asked for Mass stipends. Again the response was generous and regular. The governor himself became Martin's almoner, and every Monday he brought Martin the Mass stipends he had collected. Martin prepared a complete list of all the priests of the monastery, from the provincial down to the last newly ordained priest. Each received Mass intentions in turn, going all the way down the list until the offerings had all been uesd.[17]

It was a satisfaction to know that the infirmary was now supplied with a fair number of cotton or linen tunics, even if they were more or less worn, for which woolen tunics had been substituted. But there were still so many other things needed! The beds were few and in a deplorable condition; blankets and sheets were almost non-existent. And every once in a while a sheet had to be torn up to make bandages even before it was completely worn out, for there were no bandages at all.

Gradually Martin managed to secure all that was needed. Father Alphonsus de Arenas estimated the value of the various articles secured by Martin at "more than six thousand gold pieces," and rejoiced over the contrast between the personal poverty of the custodian of the supply room and the wealth his industry had brought to the community. "Being, as he was, so perfectly poor himself, he had control over all the donations of the laity." [18]

Martin was naturally a jealous custodian of all he had acquired by his industry and efforts. One day a man came to be bled, and in the course of the operation, he fainted. Just at that moment Martin was called out of the room for a few moments and left his patient seated on a chair which he kept there for that purpose. He knew it was nothing serious, a reaction to the sight of blood, as happens to many.

In a few moments his patient regained consciousness. Finding himself alone, he decided to take advantage of the situation. He took two soiled sheets from a basket of linen and slipped them into his trousers. At that period very wide trousers were in style, with plenty of room for voluminous objects. Very sure of his ability to maintain an innocent air, he greeted Martin indifferently when he returned and then prepared to leave. But he heard himself recalled. "Come back, brother. Come back into the room and replace in the basket the sheets you are carrying off in your trousers."

Martin's tone of voice was very firm, but without the slightest trace of harshness. He could have called him "thief," but instead he called him "brother." He added, almost as if to excuse himself for not allowing his visitor to carry away the sheets, "The sick have so little linen that they cannot even get along without this pair of sheets." And the would-be thief, overcome with shame, returned and replaced the sheets. [19]

Once a mattress disappeared. Martin had put it out to air and then forgot it. Even the saints can forget something now and then! Late in the evening Martin remembered that the mattress was still waiting to be brought in and went to get it. But he discovered that the mattress had not waited for him. Without wasting time asking questions of one person or another, Martin called Brother Ferdinand and went with him to a dark storeroom in the cellar where the mattress had been hidden temporarily.

Another time an entire bed disappeared, the bed of a Negro who worked in the infirmary. "I can't find my bed," the Negro told Martin. Martin answered, "Wait for me here." He went straight to the spot where the bed was hidden, and to the religious whose servant had taken it, saying to him frankly, "Father, if that servant has no bed, please see to it that he gets one, but he should not take the bed of the Negro who works in the infirmary."

When it was a question of others, Martin knew very well that anyone who had worked all day long had a right to a sound night's sleep on a good bed. And the Negro got his bed back.[20]

Another enemy, more to be dreaded than any occasional petty thief, threatened all that had been accomplished with so much effort. An inexorable enemy, an invincible enemy: mice.

When the mice found their way into the wardrobe room, it was a great worry for Martin. Day after day the clean shirts and sheets put on the shelves with such care came out with holes showing the marks of nibbling teeth, and instead of the pleasant odor of clean linen, an unpleasant odor arose from the sheets.

Several days went by. The mice seemed to delight in gnawing the best and newest things, leaving intact those almost worn out.

The head infirmarian was weary of this underground warfare. He knew a remedy and felt any defense would be legitimate against this pest. "Shall we spread some poison around?" he proposed. Martin would not hear of it.

"The poor little beasts," he said; "they have to do something to live. They don't find their meals ready for them in the refectory as we do every day."

Martin finally caught one of the vandals. Would he inflict the sentence of justice upon him, in order to give an example to the other malefactors? Not at all.

Martin held the mouse in his hands. The heart of the little animal beat rapidly against his fingers, the bright eyes glanced about desperately in every direction.

Martin smiled. Then he spoke to the mouse. He delivered a discourse similar to that given to the thief who had taken the sheets, but this time it was a little more difficult because it was a question not only of persuading the mouse that he must respect the possessions of the sick, but of winning him over as an ally to persuade the others. Martin said to him, "Little brother, why are you and your companions doing so much harm to the things belonging to the sick? Look; I shall not kill you, but you are to assemble all your friends and lead them to the far end of the garden. Every day I'll bring you food if you leave the wardrobe alone."

The mouse grew calm as Martin talked, and at the end of the discourse his little eyes looked straight at the Brother, as if he were saying, "Agreed; I accept the offer."

Martin opened his hands, and the mouse jumped to the ground and disappeared.

At once a great rustling began, and other pairs of bright eyes shone everywhere. From under the wardrobes, on top of the wardrobes, from the joists of the ceilings, and from the cracks in the floor, mice sprang out. Who would have thought that one room could hide so many of them? Now that the army was out in full array, there was reason for rejoicing that these brave soldiers had been content with so little. If they had gone about it seriously, not a thread would have been left!

When the whole company was assembled, the procession started towards the garden. Helter-skelter they went on their way, the swifter and more agile leaping over the slower and heavier ones. Martin's long stride accompanied the tiny, hurried steps of the little creatures. They went to the far corner of the garden where there was a fine hedge and bushes and enough open ground for an entire city of mice to dig holes, and the mice gleefully took possession of it all.

Every day, after he had served dinner to the sick, to the servants and to the poor, Martin went out to bring the mice their meal. It was a service he rendered directly to the little animals, but it was also a service rendered indirectly to the community. He knew that if he kept his word, the mice would respect the pact. From that time on, no mouse ever put a foot into the wardrobe room nor, what was more important, a tooth into the linen of the monastery.[21]

Martin guarded the goods of the community jealously, but he used them freely for the sick. Once he had brought into the infirmary a man found in the street after a brawl, bleeding and covered with mud. Several days of nursing restored him sufficiently so that he was able to walk and return to his own home. But when he got out of bed, the color of the sheets was beyond description. A lay brother showed them to Martin and in a moment of ill-humor muttered, "And now to try to get them white again!"

Even the saints have at least one weak point, and if they are attacked on this weak point they react as the rest of us do. Only we have dozens of weak points, and they are not always the most praiseworthy.

Martin gave him a look as piercing as a blade and cut short his grumbling. "Brother, with the application of a little elbow grease, water and soap, the sheets will be white again, but the soul needs other things! Only tears and penance can cleanse it from the lack of charity." [22]

That was Martin's weak point: charity. He would not tolerate joking on that point. A lack of fraternal charity was a thorn in his heart, and his speech took on an impetuosity and an unsuspected authority. While he was ready to accept any and every insult directed at himself, he could not bear the thought that he should ever be accused of a lack of fraternal charity. If he multiplied his attentions for those who insulted him, it was "so that they would know that they had not lost their place in his heart because they had offended him." [23]

It was both his weak and his strong point.

Charity was the source of his prodigious activity, it was the strength that lifted him out of weariness, that kept him ready for work at all times.

It was also the source of his patience in putting up with difficult people, and with the demands of the sick. It was the source of his habit of always giving and never asking, of being constantly, untiringly at the disposition of all.

"Charity, of which it is said that it does not seek its own, must be understood to mean," admonishes the Rule of St. Augustine, "that things held in common shall always be placed before one's own, and not one's own before those held in common."

That is precisely how Martin understood it. Out of love for his brethren, he went begging, he took upon himself all kinds of work, he sacrificed his own rest, day after day, with unflagging heroism. And out of love for the true good of the brethren, because he had become enamoured of spiritual beauty, he was constantly in the presence of our heavenly Father, asking for the daily manna of grace.

"A fraternal charity in Christ Jesus," as St. Catherine of

Siena had said, "is drawn from the abyss of His charity." [24]
To draw love from the abyss of the charity of Christ means
to find in the love of the Word made flesh the motive and
example of our love for our brothers in Christ. Contemplating
this love in the work of our redemption, which is its most
striking manifestation, St. Catherine exclaimed, "O madness
of love! You were not content to become incarnate; You willed
also to die for us." [25] Anyone who seeks to penetrate the depths
of this abyss in contemplating the passion of our Lord, will
finally share in the "madness" of Eternal Wisdom, in some
degree or other.

Martin was no exception. The indubitable proof was his
proposing to the prior to sell him as a slave instead of giving
up some valuable object when the monastery had no means to
meet the demands of its creditors. That happened, without a
doubt, during the early years, when Martin was simply a lay
coadjutor. There is very little probability that a similar sug-
gestion would have been agreed to after his profession, and so
it would have been useless to make it.

But the same "madness" governed all Martin's actions all
through his life: the days filled with work after sleepless
nights, the unceasing alternation of prayer and penance and
work, the service of others with no thought of himself.

To the moment he died, Martin obeyed the "law of love"
of the Master: "Christ did not please Himself" (Rom. 15:3).

CHAPTER

⊱ 10 ⊰

Words from the mouth of a man are as deep water;
and the fountain of wisdom as an overflowing stream (Prov. 18:4).

NOTHING SHOWS MORE CLEARLY how much Martin loved his
Order than his relations with the novices.

In any form of society the young represent the hope of the
future and attract the love and attention of those who live to
the full the life of that society. In a family the problem of the
training of the young is relatively simple because of the restricted number involved and the close affinity between the
members of the family. But the problem is very complex in
a religious community, where subjects who must be raised to
a higher plane of life are accepted with wide differences in
origin, habits and characters. Perhaps because the problem
of training is such a difficult one, and because so much in our
life depends upon the training we receive, we love the young
in a particular way. We most readily bestow the affections of
our heart upon those who have cost us the most time and
thought.

Martin could not ignore the presence of the novices in the
monastery of the Holy Rosary. He loved the Order, and he
could not fail to love the novices of the Order. And since to
love means to desire the good of the person loved, Martin
could do no less than to try to promote the best interests of
the novices.

Martin was always as attentive to the needs of all as if he
held the place of father for each one. Every time a brother
needed something—whether it was a shirt or a notebook or a
book—he "went immediately to help whoever was in need,

[94]

and was such a great consolation to the needy that they were encouraged and cheered simply by hearing his name." He outdid himself for the students and novices, "in order that they should not be downcast by the lack of anything in religious life." [1]

Needless to say, Martin never dreamed of usurping the authority of the master of novices. For the novices he was simply an additional guardian angel. If one of them were ill, Martin had no scruples about breaking the strict seclusion of the novitiate, as happened when Brother Matthias de Barrasa so ardently desired to see him before dying.

Martin often passed through locked doors, carrying voluminous objects with him, such as sheets and other linens, or his famous brazier filled with burning coals. He would suddenly appear to a sick member of the community in the middle of the night. Placing the brazier on the floor, he would throw a branch of rosemary on the coals, and at once the cheerful crackling and delightful perfume of the rosemary dispelled the heaviness of the vitiated air in the cell. The patient would open his eyes. There, beside his bed, was Martin, offering him the restorative of which he had dreamed during his restless slumber: a fresh tunic in exchange for the one saturated with perspiration, a drink of cool water, a juicy piece of fruit for his lips burning with fever.

Even in serious cases, Martin's visits were always followed by a marked improvement, and sometimes by a complete cure. One of these was the case of Brother Francis Velasco Carabantes, who was attacked by a serious form of dropsy while he was in the novitiate. It should be added that Martin's cooperation in the healing of Brother Francis was not their first encounter. Martin had been involved in the circumstances surrounding the beginning of his illness.

This is how it came about. When Francis had been in the

novitiate of Holy Rosary about a month, his father, who was the secretary of the treasury, came to visit him. He came with a definite end in view: to take Francis home. As secretary of the treasury, he had received notice that the King had granted him the authorization to leave his coveted post in the government to his son as an inheritance. This was a marked and extraordinary honor granted to the treasurer in return for the many services he had rendered to the crown. It was to be the consolation of his declining years, and his heart was filled with justifiable pride to think that the King was so satisfied with his services that His Majesty wished to ensure their continuing, beyond the limits of the life of the father, in the person of a son judged to be capable of carrying on the work he had begun.

This recompense aroused the most delicate sentiments of a fatherly heart and seemed to the old treasurer like a flower unexpectedly blooming in the aridity of a life passed among registers and figures. While he walked to the monastery of the Holy Rosary, a new joy filled his heart and brightened the memory of the long years spent in tedious toil.

Perhaps Brother Francis offered some resistance to the proposal of his father, but he ended by giving in. Not being certain he could keep his resolution if he had to inform the master of novices of it, he agreed to flee that night through a break in the wall near the church of the monastery. And the father and son agreed upon midnight for the escape.

Night fell and the bell called the religious to the refectory. As the youngest of the novices, Brother Francis headed one of the long double lines going processionally to the refectory. Suddenly a figure hurried up to him out of the chapter room and drew him aside. "Are you going to take off the habit of holy religion and leave the house of God for the office of the secretary of the treasury? This will never do! You will not do that. It is better to serve God and assure your salvation than to live in your father's house. Believe me, what you were unwilling to do out of love of God, you will do out of fear of God."

We do not know what Brother Francis said to the Negro Brother who, without any preamble, showed that he knew what Francis was trying to hide under his unconcerned behavior. Perhaps he pretended not to understand Martin's words and quickly escaped from the embarrassing conversation.

What we do know with certainty is that when he rejoined the religious in the refectory and sat down at table, he began to shiver and to develop such a high fever that he was forced to rise before the meal ended and ask the master of novices for permission to go to bed.

And there, curled up under the covers with his teeth chattering, he certainly recalled Martin's words, words to which he had closed his ears a few moments before: "What you were unwilling to do out of love of God, you will do out of fear of God." The project vanished into thin air, at least for that night.

Brother Francis did not admit defeat. A month later, when he was cured of the fever, he once more began to make plans for his flight. But at the moment of putting the plan into execution, the fever struck him again and for the second time he lay helpless in bed. The headstrong young novice was hardly on his feet again when he renewed his plans for escape a third time. And for the third time, the fever stopped him.

The third warning accomplished what the first and second warnings had failed to do. Francis surrendered. He finally understood that God wished at all costs to save the vocation he had been ready to barter for a mess of pottage. A profound gratitude to God arose in his heart, joined to a deep admiration for Martin, whom he venerated as a holy man.[2]

Francis' third attack of fever was so severe that he was at the point of death. The doctor declared that there was no hope, and the superiors of the house prepared him for death and administered the last sacraments. But the crisis passed, and they sent him into the country to recuperate. But the change of air did him little good, and he returned to the novitiate with a persistent fever and all the symptoms of dropsy. Every possible care was given him, and even the personal physician of the viceroy was called in. But Dr. Cisneto shook his head. He could do nothing for this case.

Day by day Brother Francis grew worse. His breathing became labored, for he almost suffocated from the fluid in his pleural cavities. His superiors would not give up hope of seeing him cured, but, fearing that some overly sympathetic companion would give him water or other harmful liquids, they put him in a cell of the novitiate and locked the door.

At that point, Martin intervened. It was about one o'clock in the morning or a little later. Francis lay on his bed, oppressed by his suffering and by the solitude and tedium of insomnia. The door was locked. He suddenly became aware of the presence of someone in the room. Martin was smiling at him out of the shadows. In his hands was an old brass brazier filled with live coals, under his arm was a clean tunic, and a branch of rosemary peeped from one of his sleeves.

Was it a hallucination induced by the fever?

Martin put the brass brazier on the floor, approached the bed, asked the sick novice to rise, helped him sit down on a stool near the brazier, and wrapped him in a blanket. Then he took the rosemary out of his sleeve and dropped it on the lit coals. A thin, gray-blue thread of smoke rose and spread into a light, perfumed cloud.

Not a word was spoken through all this.

Francis finally overcame his amazement and broke the silence to ask Martin how he had entered the room at that hour when both the doors of the novitiate and of his own cell were locked.

The reply was no encouragement to carry on a long conversation. "My boy, who told you to meddle in such things?"

Then giving him a playfully light blow, as if to soften the harshness of the words, Martin added in a gentler tone, "You are not a great Bachelor or Doctor of Arts; you are fortunate to be alive!"

He turned the mattress and remade the bed with fresh sheets; sponged Francis' body and put a fresh tunic on him, warmed and perfumed by the rosemary; helped him back into bed; and then covered him up well.

Francis hazarded one more question. Would he die of this illness?

Martin replied with another question. "Do you really want to die?"

"No," said Francis.

"Then you will not die," concluded Martin, and disappeared as he had appeared.

A great peace and sense of well-being filled Francis' soul, such as he had not experienced for a long time. He fell asleep and, for the first time in two months, he slept soundly until morning.

When he awoke, every sign of his illness had disappeared. The difficulty in breathing, the discomfort, the fever, the swelling—all were gone. Three or four days later he was on his feet again, as well and bright-eyed as any lad of his age, and Dr. Cisneto stared with amazement and proclaimed it was a miracle.[3]

This was the same Francis Velasco who was once extremely

rude to Martin and then, seeing that the Negro Brother seemed to delight in being insulted, acquired the habit of giving Martin generous measures of such treatment. He must have been, as we would say, a "difficult character." And it is probable that Martin's constancy in putting up with his outbursts of ill-humor, and his firm belief that Francis could become a good religious, helped Francis overcome this stumbling block.

Even the best of us can experience moments of dismay when we realize the length of the path before us, or moments of incertitude when the road seems difficult. A helping hand held out at those moments can change the course of one's entire life.

One evening the master of novices sought out Martin and confided a great grief to him. Two novices had disappeared and could not be found anywhere. They must have fled.

Martin promised the master of novices he would do his best to help find them, and began to pray. When he had finished, he went to ask the prior's permission to go out. Knowing what had happened, the prior granted the permission, even though it was already night.

Martin walked several miles and then stopped before the door of a house. The door was closed, but that made no difference to him. He entered and found the two fugitives tranquilly asleep on two cots.

Martin awoke them without one word of reproof. Instead, he began to speak in his pacifying and convincing tone of the beauty of the religious state, of the dignity of a life intimately united to the life of God, of the boundless field opened to love when man closes his heart to the attractions of his lower nature and disposes himself to receive the light from on high.

His whole discourse seemed so logical to the young men that they found it hard to believe they were really guilty of having fled from the monastery the day before. They heartily wished they had never done such a foolish thing. All they could think of now was how to get back into the monastery. That problem was simple for Martin. As long as the two culprits were sincerely repentant, everything else would take care of itself.

Just as he had entered the house alone through locked doors, he re-entered the monastery through its barred doors with the two novices. Thus, no one knew of their flight except the prior and the master of novices, and no shadow was cast on their honor as religious. They became good religious and remained members of the Order until their deaths.[4]

Even the sight of Martin was sometimes sufficient to decide a vocation.

"I've said it and I've repeated it millions of times," Father Ignatius of St. Dominic used to say, "that I decided to become a Dominican because I saw Brother Martin de Porres in prayer, lifted high above the earth, almost embracing the crucified Christ in the chapter room."

No matter how many million times Father Ignatius had repeated it during his lifetime, once his eyes were closed in death he could no longer reiterate his assertion. And it was just that point that grieved Father Christopher of St. John, who had never had the joy of seeing Martin in ecstasy, when it was his turn to give testimony during the process of Martin's beatification. "Oh, if Father Ignatius were only here," said Father Christopher one day to Marcel de Rivero, the surgeon.

"And isn't my testimony enough?" replied de Rivero a little testily. "I also saw him, just as Father Ignatius did, high above the ground, in the chapter room, and my word is just as good as his!"[5]

Cyprian de Medina was another novice whom Martin helped

overcome his initial difficulties. Cyprian entered the monastery of the Holy Rosary when he was only about fourteen years old. In spite of his youth, he realized at once that Martin was holy, and in addition to entrusting himself to Martin's paternal care, he observed him constantly and strove to imitate him.

Cyprian was clumsily built, short and fat, and ugly as well. Because of his physical defects, his companions often made him the butt of their jests and stinging remarks. One day the students were awaiting their turns in the room where Martin cut hair and shaved beards. As usual, Cyprian and his ridiculous stature served as a subject of amusement to pass the time, and he was miserable about it. A religious should be above such petty annoyances, but at fourteen a boy has a legitimate ambition to grow tall, at least as tall as his own father, and if he is undersize he feels humiliated.

One of the students said to Martin, "Brother, shave Brother Cyprian, the 'wild man' of our monastery."

Brother Cyprian had so much hair on his face that he looked like a bear.

Brother Martin answered calmly, "You call him 'the wild man' and laugh at him because he is so little. But wait a while. He will grow so much that he will tower over all of you; and he will be an outstanding religious who will bring honor to the Order."

No one answered and no one dared to continue teasing Brother Cyprian. Behind Martin's simple words there must have been something mysterious, perhaps a real prophecy. Events very shortly showed how truly Martin had spoken. Brother Cyprian was stricken with a fever which confined him to his bed for four or five months. When he recovered, he had grown so much that his garments no longer fit him. A whole new set of clothing had to be made for him. But he outdistanced his companions even more in his intellectual and moral development. The others did not distinguish themselves in any special manner, but Cyprian was appointed to important posts and he was consecrated a bishop while he was still young.[6]

Sometimes the master sent his novices to Martin during recreation. One afternoon several students turned up in the room that served as Martin's general headquarters, asking for an afternoon lunch. They did so every day, following the lecture on theology.

"Wait for me," said Martin, "I'll be right back."

The students entered and began to rummage about. There was a little fruit in a drawer, so without ceremony they began their lunch. There was also a small silver coin, and since students are usually full of high spirits and in need of relaxation after their classes, one of them took the coin and slipped it into his shoe.

Martin returned with some fried fish, bread, apples and other bits of food, and while he served the food with his habitual graciousness and invited the young men to enjoy the good things provided by God, he remarked that they were entirely right in having taken the fruit out of the drawer, for it was there for them.

Suddenly he became serious. The lunch was finished and the students were about to leave. The brother who had taken the silver piece feigned innocence. Did he perhaps wish to see if Martin really knew hidden things, as everyone said?

He heard his name called. "Brother, put the money back where you found it; it is not ours; it belongs to someone else."

The young brother tried to carry it off with an air of innocence. "What money? Who has taken any money?"

Martin smiled confidently. "Take it out of your shoe. It is wicked to take what belongs to Jesus Christ's poor."

One can easily imagine the astonished face of the culprit and of all the others.[7]

Another time, thirty novices went for a walk in the country with Martin. In entrusting them to Martin, the master of novices instructed them to return home before nightfall, and Martin promised to be punctual.

They set out on their way at a good pace, happy to have the long hours of study interrupted by an afternoon of freedom and a pleasant walk.

They arrived at the hill called *"de los Amanches"* and admired the view. Then Martin brought out the picnic provisions and the young novices, seated on the grass, needed no urgent invitation to consume everything. When the lunch was consumed, Martin perhaps began to speak of spiritual things, as he knew how to do so well, and the young men and he, completely absorbed in the conversation, forgot everything else.

In the meantime, the day was drawing to its end and no one thought of their return to the monastery. When they suddenly realized how late it was, the novices were frightened. Their master of novices tolerated no nonsense! When Martin realized what time it was, even he was disturbed by the thought of the penance which would be imposed on the young novices (he certainly did not think of his own punishment) and above all by the fact that their tardiness would constitute an infraction of the rules and of the orders he had received.

But he did not became agitated. He recollected himself for a moment of prayer, then had their knapsacks gathered up, telling the novices to trust in God. Finally he said, "On our way now, let us form ranks and start for home."

They descended from the hill and in closely drawn groups set off for Lima in silence, concentrating all their energies on walking. They were half a league from the monastery when the *Ave Maria* bell sounded. Then, without knowing how, they found themselves at the door of the monastery in about the length of time required to recite the *Credo* four times.[8]

The bell was ringing for Compline and the religious were on their way to the choir. The novices joined them. They were in their places by the time the bell stopped ringing.

Everything had happened so rapidly, so naturally, that they hardly had time to realize the prodigious speed of their return. As they knelt in choir, Martin's invitation to have confidence in God came back to their minds, bringing with it a new and deeper understanding of the many expressions of confidence in God's goodness with which this hour of the Divine Office abounds. "Thou, O Lord, art among us . . . ; forsake us not, O Lord, our God. . . . Keep us, O Lord, as the apple of Thy eye. Protect us under the shadow of Thy wings. . . . Into Thy hands, O Lord, I commend my spirit."

They left the stalls of the choir and ranged themselves in double lines to salute Mary with the chant of the *Salve Regina* procession. Having invoked her as "our life, our sweetness and our hope," they knelt down, imploring her to "turn her eyes of mercy towards us." Perhaps then they remembered the words of the Blessed Virgin to St. Dominic, after she had given him a sign of her maternal protection for the Order: "I am she whom you invoke every night, and when you sing *'eja ergo,'* I too prostrate myself before my Son to pray for the preservation of this Order."

If they remembered her words, they saw behind the events of the afternoon the hand of Mary, who had admirably protected her sons of predilection, and they understood what it meant to be under the protection of her mantle.

Perhaps it was precisely what Martin had hoped to accomplish: to make them grasp this truth and see it clearly in the simple but solemn ceremony of the *Salve Regina,* which is one of the ceremonies dearest to the heart of every son of St. Dominic.

Martin knew and appreciated the power of the *Salve Regina.* He used it once to bring to the "holy flock" a lamb who persisted in wandering outside the fold. This recalcitrant lamb was called Anthony de Mancilla. Martin knew him well, for he lived near the monastery and had attended the school of the Dominicans of Holy Rosary until he was eighteen. Anthony then went on to study rhetoric at the Jesuit College of St. Paul in Lima.

Every time he met him, Martin would say: "Listen to me; God wishes you to be a Dominican." Martin had a discerning eye and if he said that a boy had a vocation, one could be certain it was true.

But in spite of having a religious vocation, Anthony had not the slightest desire to follow it, and he always answered clearly and frankly that the only aspect of a monastery that pleased him was the outside, and that rather than become a religious. . . .

"Very well," Martin said to him one day, "but remember that before I die, you will enter my holy Order."

These were Martin's last words to Anthony de Mancilla when the young man came to bid him good-bye before leaving for the upper provinces of Peru. He set out in search of whatever kind of work he could find, provided it was different from what the friars did.

Almost four years passed. Anthony was established, or nearly so, near the city of Cuzco. One Saturday afternoon he felt an irresistible desire to hear the *Salve Regina* chanted. Just as the religious were finishing Compline, Anthony reached the monastery of St. Dominic in Cuzco. He entered the church, torn between his long resistance to the divine call and this imperious desire which led him there almost against his will.

But there, in the church of St. Dominic, Mary was waiting for him. At the first notes of the *Salve Regina,* an intense, sweet emotion invaded Anthony's soul, and he knew that from that moment on, there was nothing to do but admit that he was conquered. When the last notes of the chant died away, Anthony had reached the decision he had tried to avoid for so many years: to go to confession and ask for immediate admission to the Order.

As the friars marched back to their choir stalls in procession, they sang their customary evening prayer to St. Dominic: "O light of the Church, doctor of truth, rose of patience, precious ivory of chastity. . . . O preacher of grace, unite us to the blessed."

At that moment the company of the blessed, for Anthony, was that double rank of men clad in white, following their father securely along the luminous and straight path of truth, even if the road ran between the roses and thorns of patience.

Anthony approached one of the friars who was coming out of the choir—according to legend it was Father Anthony de Valverde, professor of theology—and asked to go to confession. He then begged the Father to ask the prior to accept him as a postulant without delay, because he had decided not to leave the church until he had received the habit of St. Dominic.

Such haste, after so much temporizing!

Fortunately, some of the friars at the Dominican monastery in Cuzco had known Anthony when he used to go to the monastery in Lima as a boy, and the prior quickly gathered the necessary information about him. Anthony de Mancilla received the habit of the Friars Preachers on August 23, 1639;

just in time to fulfill the prediction made by Martin four years previously.

"Before I die," Martin had said. And on August 23, 1639, Martin had less than three months left to live.[9] The Virgin most faithful had collaborated with Martin so that his words might not be in vain.

These incidents show how Martin watched over the young members of the Order, not only to ward off danger of spiritual or physical evil, but also to increase in their hearts that joy which is the companion of the love of the good: "Love of true good, full of joy." [10]

CHAPTER

⤝ 11 ⤜

I have called you friends, because all things that I have heard from My Father, I have made known to you (John 15:15).

WALKS WITH THE NOVICES were not a daily occurrence for Martin, not only because he did not have enough leisure to go out every day, but also because he did not devote all of his free time to the novices.

In spite of the accumulation of duties imposed upon him by obedience and in spite of the supplementary occupations he voluntarily assumed out of charity, he did have some leisure hours from time to time. He could dispose of these periods as he wished, and he consecrated them to friendship.

It would have been impossible for Martin not to feel the occasional need of the company of a soul living on his own level. He felt that need as all those do who, day by day, consume their spiritual energies in the constant vigilance required by contact with persons who constantly ask for help. In his everyday relations with the sick and the poor, with the novices and students, and even with the priests of his monastery, Martin was constantly giving.

It is strange, when one realizes that as far as dignity was concerned, that he occupied the lowest rung of the ladder and he desired to remain there out of humility, but his charity, which made him "the father of all," as his own brethren said, had given him a much higher rank. He was obliged to look down a little every time he had anything to do with his companions, like the father of a family in the circle of his little ones.

Martin was always surrounded by faces looking up at him. And he was forced to look down. He did so with extreme simplicity and humility, realizing that there was no danger in dominating the groups surrounding him as long as he kept his feet on the ground. But it was quite natural that he felt the need, at least now and then, of gazing into eyes on his own level.

Divine goodness, which clothes the lilies of the field and feeds the birds of the air, provided the spiritual companion Martin needed, a friend capable of reciprocating Martin's friendship on the plane of the highest spiritual perfection. Providence chose that friend carefully, disregarding a distance of thousands of miles and leading him in a strange concatenation of events from a little village of old Spain to Lima.

When John Massias arrived in Lima, he was still very young but had already had a rich variety of experiences.[1] He was the son of a noble family, but had known only poverty and sorrow since his infancy. His family had lost its entire fortune and John grew up as an orphan, cared for by his uncle. He earned his living by tending sheep.

His humble social position seemed to be a mockery of his

ancient and noble blood, but John had acquired illustrious friends. Often, as he watched his flock, St. John came to keep him company. St. John the Evangelist was his patron, and it was quite fitting that he should be interested in young John.

It was marvelous to sit with a companion like that, engaged in familiar talk. Above all, it was marvelous to listen to the heavenly visitor as he spoke of the Lamb of God, of the Good Shepherd.

In such company the hours passed swiftly. When the sun grew huge and red as it sank towards the horizon, it seemed to John that the day had finished almost before it began. He gathered together his sheep, counted them one by one, and led them to the fold. Not one was ever missing; not one was ever hurt or lamed.

The Beloved Disciple initiated the boy into the secrets of divine love, instilling into his simple soul a love for the spotless Lamb and for the Mother of the Lamb of God. Mary came down from heaven, bringing to the orphan the maternal tenderness of which he had been deprived early in life. The valley in which he passed his days with his flock, and everything in it, seemed beautiful and transfigured by Mary's presence.

John's love for Mary dated from the moment he attained the use of reason, which was very early. When he was only five years old he could be trusted to carry out perfectly any duty entrusted to him. At about that age, he had begun to recite the entire rosary every day and had resolved to do so all during his life. Five decades were for himself; five decades were for sinners; and five decades were for the souls in purgatory. To the end of his life he kept the resolution he had taken as a mere child, and Mary rewarded him with the gift of purity and the consolation of her visits.

Mary's visits bore fruit. Like one athirst, John drank in Mary's words and teaching, and his love for her grew so great that for her he would have gone to the ends of the earth.

One day, after having shown him in a vision something of the heavenly land, the Virgin Mary told him she would like him to leave his fatherland, cross the ocean and begin a new life in the New World, out of love for her.

John entrusted the sheep to his uncle and embarked.

On the other side of the Atlantic he did various kinds of work, moving from place to place several times, until finally, after crossing the entire continent, he arrived on the shores of the Pacific and reached Lima.

His long journey was ended, but he had not yet attained its true goal. He was employed by a rich landowner as a herdsman, his old trade. The colloquies with St. John began again among the sheep. John was confident that St. John would reveal God's will to him, and two and a half years later he knew with certainty what it was.

He asked his employer for the wages due him and gave the money to the poor. He then went to the monastery of St. Mary Magdalen in Lima, where with tears he begged to be admitted as a lay brother. He received the Dominican habit and began to lead a life which, in its love of prayer and mortification, its inexhaustible charity, its preternatural gifts of miracles, ecstasies and prophecy, was the duplicate of the life led by Martin de Porres in the monastery of the Holy Rosary.[2]

Martin was delighted to spend his free hours with John Massias. Whether he went to St. Mary Magdalen, whether Brother John came to Holy Rosary, or whether they went together to Limatambo, the program of their recreation periods was always the same. They spoke of God, sharing the experiences, gifts and graces the divine goodness had bestowed upon them in such abundance, and encouraged each other to run along the path to God like athletes who seek at all costs to win the prize.

They spoke above all of their mutual great Friend, in whose name they were united in the bond of a holy friendship; of Him who, at the moment of giving the supreme proof of His love to His own, had called them "friends," because His death freed them from the slavery of sin. Together they meditated upon the infinite love which impelled Him to undergo His bitter passion so that men might be His friends and sons instead of servants. For them the words of St. Catherine to the prior of the Benedictines of Cervaia were verified: "When the eye of the intellect is enlightened and sees the infinite goodness and love of God, suffering seems sweet and delightful, and it seems impossible to delight in anything else; and the soul seeks suffering out of hatred for its own vileness." St. Catherine also wrote to Blessed Clara Gambacorti: "When your heart and mind are one with Christ crucified, you will love suffering as a means of being conformed to Christ crucified." [3]

"Out of love of hatred," that is, hatred springing from the soul's awareness of its own misery and the vivid memory of its offenses against God, which demand reparation; but most of all, because of a need to repay love with love: "for love of love." For these two motives rooted in love, John and Martin ended their holy conversations by disciplining themselves to the point of blood.

On feast days their penance took on an altogether different character. On ordinary days the predominant idea of expiation and reparation lent an austere and sorrowful tone to their penances, but the penance of feast days had a joyful and exultant tone for Martin and his holy friend. It was the fuel thrown on the fire of love so that it might burn more brightly.

On solemn feast days, Martin put on a hair shirt that reached to his knees, and drew his iron chains so tightly about his body that he could barely walk upright. With overflowing joy he offered this gift of a friend to his Friend.[4]

In addition to John Massias, Martin had another intimate friend, a Franciscan religious whose name is unknown. Martin shared hours of holy conversation and penance with him also, under a crucifix attached to the trunk of a tree in the cloister of the Franciscans.[5]

Charity consists in receiving as well as in giving. This is especially true in the spiritual sense. St. Catherine stated this with great clarity in a letter to the Abbot of Sant'Antimo: "To manifest the magnificence of God, and out of respect for right order in the exercise of charity, it is necessary that the servants of God use and share with each other the lights, graces and gifts they receive from God, so that the light and magnificence of sweet Truth are shown to be infinite . . . and we humble ourselves by acknowledging the light and grace of God in the servants of God. He has placed them on earth like springs; one sort of water comes from one, another sort from another. They are upon earth to acquire life for themselves and to console and refresh the other servants of God who thirst for this water, which is the numerous gifts and graces which God bestows upon His servants." [6]

This is what occurred during the recreation periods of Martin and his friends. In a mutual sharing of the gifts of God, they adored and praised the Giver and deepened their own humility.

According to St. Catherine, this is one of the most important objects of fraternal charity: "that we should humble ourselves by acknowledging the light and grace of God in the servants of God." The higher a soul mounts, the more charity must fulfill its imperative duty. It is admirable to scale the heights of perfection, but to feel that one is isolated, almost cut off from the rest of men, can induce dizziness and the temptation to look down on the great mass of humanity which is incapable of advancing along the steep and difficult path of sanctity.

This peril of isolation is greatly diminished in a religious community. All are there for one purpose—to attain perfection—and there is no way of knowing who has attained the highest degree of perfection and who is still at the lowest level because, for the most part, spiritual progress is hidden from human eyes. But a religious community is a little like a family with numerous children, each one of whom has varying capacities. Because of their diversity, the individuals complement each other and form a harmonious whole. The stronger members are happy to help the weaker, and the weaker members are happy that someone is there to help them, without anyone thinking himself a "superman." And when no one considers himself a superman, humility is safeguarded, and with it, charity.

Martin had climbed very high on the path of perfection. Divine Providence gave him the companionship of several souls like himself in order to protect him from the vertigo of the heights.

Martin was not yet thirty years old when Archbishop Turibius died, and the archbishop was to be numbered among the saints.

Martin was a little more than thirty when another saint closed his eyes in Lima: Francis Solano, son of St. Francis of Assisi and marvelous apostle of the New World.

Martin was not yet forty when the Dominican, Rose of Santa María, ended her brief and angelic existence. He had undoubtedly met the holy tertiary, for she frequently attended the Dominican church of the Holy Rosary and her spiritual director was Father John de Lorenzana, who, as provincial, had received Martin into the Order. Moreover, Martin certainly witnessed the triumphant tribute paid to the Saint at the moment of her death. We are told that the entire population of Lima rushed to the house in which the soul of the pure virgin had answered the call of her Spouse, and an enormous crowd accompanied her body to the church of the Friars Preachers. Martin was probably present two years later at the exhumation and translation of the body of Rose, and smelled the perfume of that incorrupt body, of that fragile vase which had served the virgin of Lima in her virile practice of mortification and charity towards her neighbor under the impulse of her burning love of God.

Martin was then a mature man, at the height of his powers. It is probable that he felt himself a weakling when he considered the indomitable courage of little Rose. In like manner, the thought of the young virgin martyrs during the first centuries of Christianity had inspired St. Gregory to the following sentiments of humility: "What shall we bearded and weak men say, seeing young girls pass through iron to the kingdom of heaven?" [7]

Martin was in good company, surrounded by so many privileged souls who aspired to the heights of perfection.

There was another soul intimately united to his, though without his own aspirations to the heights of sanctity. His sister Joan was always ready to grant even his half-expressed wishes and to help him carry out his plans. Joan de Porres was married and lived in the suburbs of Lima, almost in the country. When the readiness with which Martin gave his own bed to the sick or wounded he found on the roads was finally judged to be excessive by his superiors, they forbade him to bring strangers into the monastery. At that point Martin asked his sister to take in his protégés.

It was a strange thing to ask a young wife to do. She risked seeing her house transformed into a hospital for serious and urgent cases. Perhaps prudence should have counseled her to refuse. But Joan agreed. She proved worthy to be Martin's sister. In a certain sense she was even more heroic than Martin, because she ran the risk of irritating her husband by bringing germs into a home where there were children. Urged on by her saintly brother, she closed her eyes to the danger and trusted in the providence of God.

Events proved her trust was well-founded. In spite of the fact that she turned her home into a branch of Martin's first aid clinic, no harm ever came to her or to her family.[8]

Naturally, Martin was vigilant. Even without seeming to do so, he always watched over his own.

One day the serenity of the little family was menaced by an unfortunate discussion between the wife and husband which seemed to be leading to a serious misunderstanding. The discussion began during a family reunion in the home of Joan and her husband. Seeing that the argument was growing heated, the other members of the family decided that the best thing to do was to leave their hosts alone, and they began to saddle their mules for the return to Lima.

Martin, on the contrary, thought it best to talk to Joan and her husband and convince them of the futility of their dissension. So he suddenly appeared, a walking stick in his hand and on his arm a large basket overflowing with good things—a fine cake, fruit and wine.

"May the peace of God be with you!" he cried cheerfully as if he had not even noticed the tension casting a pall over the spirits of the group. "It's a long walk here! But I've brought a few little things to eat. Shall we lunch together?"

The mules were unsaddled and sent back to the fields to graze. Young and old formed a circle around the brother and his basket. But the cloud of discord was not yet dissipated. Their faces were still dark.

"I know why you have such long faces," said Martin, and he detailed the points of the argument concisely and exactly.

His relatives looked at him, stupefied. Martin knew every detail of the situation, but how could he have followed their argument while he was walking along the dusty road leading to their home?

Upon reflection, however, they realized that was not the strangest thing. What they really could not understand was why the subject of their disagreement seemed to lose all its importance when it was put before them so clearly and exactly. It was deflated by the mere fact of being enunciated, as a sail on a mast hangs limp when the wind dies away.

Peace was restored, the little group fell upon the provisions which Martin took out of his famous basket, and a long, joyous conversation ensued in an atmosphere of serene intimacy.

When evening fell, Martin assured his sister that she need not worry about him, for he had a place to sleep. Early the next morning, before starting out again for Lima, he came to bid her good-bye and to assure himself that the peace had lasted.[9]

Shortly thereafter, Joan had occasion to go into Lima. She met one of the brothers who worked with Martin in the infirmary and felt impelled to tell him what her brother had done to restore peace in her home.

"But I don't understand," the brother interrupted her. "Martin did not leave the infirmary the afternoon and night you are talking about. We had several patients in need of constant attention, and we took care of them in turn, Brother Martin and I, as we always do!"

Once more divine power had provided Martin's presence so that he might bring the aid of his charity where there was need of it.[10]

Martin found ways of helping his neighbor materially with

a generosity that was truly prodigious. No less amazing was the effusion of his charity in friendship, in that form of friendship which consists of aiding others to advance in sanctity, and is an anticipation of the joyous communion of the blessed in each other's merits.

"For by so many more there are who says 'ours,' so much the more of good doth each possess, and the more of love burneth in that cloister." [11]

CHAPTER

➤ 12 ➤

As I have loved you, that you also love one another (John 13:34).

AT THE DINNER HOUR, Martin usually grew restless. His proverbial calm seemed to abandon him. A strange agitation, almost an impatience, became apparent in him.

At that hour of the day the poor began to gather at the door of the monastery, and Martin seemed to hear them coming. He had no peace until he was in their midst.

Armed with a cup and a kettle, Martin made the rounds of the refectory to gather everything he could possibly find. His own portion went into the kettle first. Bread and water were enough for him. But others must be served.

When the pot was filled, or when at least he had gathered all that was to be had from the meal of the community, Martin went to the kitchen of the infirmary, where his clients were waiting for him. It was a varied and many-colored clientele: Spaniards and Negroes, Indians and mulattoes, sick and well—even dogs and cats! And, as if that were not enough, there was a long line of bowls belonging to the poor of the neighborhood who could not walk. Some kind souls had brought their bowls to the monastery.[1]

A truckload of food would have been needed to feed the crowd; not a mere kettle and a cup! But Martin was not dismayed.

One Wednesday, a day of abstinence for the monastery, Martin went to collect food for his poor in the small refectory reserved for those who were indisposed, though not bedridden. They were, of course, dispensed from the abstinence. But on that particular day the religious dining in this refectory were far more numerous than Brother Sebastian, the assistant infirmarian, had anticipated in providing for their dinner. Martin arrived at the worst possible moment, while Brother Sebastian was absorbed in the difficult problem of dividing a small quantity of food into many portions, but portions which would not appear too skimpy on the plates.

"Really, you can't take anything for the poor," protested Brother Sebastian, "for I haven't even enough for the refectory!" And he went on dividing and subdividing the servings as if he were confronted with a desperate task.

"Don't worry, Brother," answered Martin, moved by pity and a little amused as well by Brother Sebastian's difficulty. "You should not be discouraged or downcast by such a minor problem. God surely can provide, since He sustains the world." Martin took the ladle out of Sebastian's hand and went on preparing the plates himself. There was enough for everyone, and the portions were generous. There was also a great deal left over for the poor.[2]

Martin was never dismayed by the large number of the poor when he came before them with his faithful cup and kettle. The mere fact of being with his poor brothers filled his heart with joy. All shadow of restlessness vanished. Martin became himself again. He glanced over the little crowd and smiled. He greeted them with his habitual salutation: "Salvation, above all else. Let us save our souls through the merits of the blood of Jesus Christ!"

Before he distributed the food, he blessed it, saying simply: "May God increase it through His infinite mercy!" and then began to fill the cups, the bowls, the little pans. Francis de Santa Fe, who often helped him, carefully watched the quantity of soup in Martin's kettle. There was not enough for more than four people, or six at the maximum. But the poor continued to come and Martin continued to pour out soup until he had filled the last bowl of the last of his poor. At the end, all had had sufficient, "and all were satisfied, even the dogs and the cats," noted Brother Ferdinand de Aragonés.[3] And how could it have been otherwise? Martin had given up his own meal, and then called the infinite riches of divine mercy to his aid.

It would be difficult to determine how many poor were habitually fed by Martin at the monastery of the Holy Rosary. Blessed John Massias fed about two hundred persons every day at the monastery of St. Mary Magdalen.

When the hunger of the poor was satisfied, Martin regained his calm. But his charity did not end there. He went on revolving great plans in his mind. From the doorstep of the monastery, Martin looked into the distance. The needs of his brothers called him forth, and he went.

In Callao, the port of Lima, there was a detachment of soldiers for whom no one provided and they were near starvation. Martin thought it unjust to let them die of hunger. Every day he made the trip from Lima to Callao—five miles going and five miles returning—weighed down by provisions, in the heat of the sun and the dust of the road. He did so as long as it was necessary, which was for several months.[4]

Today it seems strange that a handful of soldiers could have run the risk of starving if it had not been for the charity of a lay brother. But in Peru in the sixteenth and seventeenth centuries it was not strange. Much remained to be done at that period. The social structure of the New World was like a stream of lava still flowing down the slopes of a mountain, a shapeless mass still requiring the passage of time before it acquired a stable form. The provisional arrangements following the conquest left much to be desired. Life in the overseas possessions was full of unknown factors, and those who left the homeland to undertake its risks were, for the most part, men without scruples. There was no organized movement of immigration. The stronger or more tyrannical seized the sources of riches, while the weaker and more timid, even though they had survived the perils of the journey from the Old World, lived in misery because they had not succeeded in finding a means of livelihood in the new land.

Martin aided many of these immigrants who had not found a way to solve their own difficulties. He housed them temporarily in the infirmary, went looking for work for them, and allowed them to leave the monastery only when he had made satisfactory arrangements for them.[5]

The case of John Vázquez was typical. It illustrates the intelligent charity exercised by Martin. He was not satisfied with giving only the indispensable help at the moment of urgent need, but sought a way of assuring the needy person's future through his own work.

One day in 1635 Martin discovered John Vázquez in the church yard of the monastery of the Holy Rosary. He noticed him particularly among the other immigrants because he was very young and very poor. John was fourteen and had not even a shirt on his back.

"Where were you born?" asked Martin.

"In the city of Jerez de los Caballeros, in the province of Estremadura, the kingdom of Spain," replied John listlessly. He wondered how many times he had repeated that tedious tale since the day he left Spain. But what had ever come of it?

"Have you a trade?"

"No."

"Then come with me."

John's eyes widened. Could it be possible that this brother really intended to help him?

Martin led him to his own cell, gave him a clean shirt to put on, and fed him, "grieving greatly," John said, to see one so young in such misery. When John felt a little better, Martin told him he could come back there every day to eat and sleep, but that he must think about choosing a trade so that he could earn his living in the city.

John gratefully accepted the offer of food and lodging, for he had no place to go in Lima. But the question of a trade left him perplexed. One was as good as another because he did not know where to turn to learn one.

"I see," said Martin. "I'll have to take care of that for you."

Martin was a "master barber." Since he had to launch John into some kind of trade, it was natural that he should teach him his own. He gave him several theoretical lessons and then, to give him practice, he permitted John to give him a shave and haircut.[6]

John did not leave Martin when he had mastered his trade. He was won over by the goodness of the Negro brother and begged to be allowed to stay with him as an assistant.

Martin was delighted. By this time his works of charity had multiplied and widened, and the help of a clever, serious lad like John would be very useful. John justified Martin's confidence, and Martin entrusted to him one of the most delicate sectors of his charitable work, that of aiding families who had known better days.

Martin had a long list of these poor. They had once been so well known that now they could not bring themselves to ask for alms. And the memory of a life of ease made their misery all the more painful.

For the most part they were widows or orphans of Spanish grandees who had held important posts in the army or the government. The pride of the conquistadors and rulers was too strong in their hearts to permit them to descend to begging in public. Rather than draw attention to their present condition, they preferred to get along as best they could in obscurity, in spite of the fact that help might have come to them if their needs were known. To these poor, who asked nothing, it was imperative to give in secret, in silence.

If Martin had been less holy, and therefore less humble, he might have found pleasure in making those he helped see that the normal positions were reversed: that he, a member of the despised Negro race, was furnishing the livelihood of the proud whites.

If Martin had been less holy, he could have displayed the worst possible taste in a spirit of class struggle.

But Martin had nothing to struggle for. He saw in the diversities of fortune a manifestation of the providence of God, and he loved all souls without restriction, for the love of God. So, with a delicacy inspired by charity, he hid behind John Vázquez, and his help for the families who had formerly been powerful and wealthy passed through the white hands of the young Spaniard.

The aid was given in money as well as food, clothing and candles. Every Thursday, for two and a half years, John Vázquez made the rounds of the families supported by Martin.[7]

Another category of the needy who aroused the Negro brother's compassion were those in prison. In that period of history, anyone who fell into the hands of the law, no matter what his crime had been, was truly to be pitied.

Martin visited the prisons periodically. He brought food and clothing, but above all he endeavored to help those souls ensnared by evil and its consequences to find the path of true liberty, of freedom from sin.

Once, almost at the end of one of his visits, he realized he had run out of provisions and that two prisoners had received nothing.

"I'll be right back," he said to the prisoners.

He left the prison and pawned his old hat, faded by the sun and misshapen by the rain, to the first old clothes dealer he met on the street. What could the dealer possibly have paid for such an antique? A few pennies, hardly enough to buy a a little bread. But that was all Martin needed at the moment. He bought the bread and returned to the prison to console his friends.[8]

One of them, a Spaniard named John González, asked Martin one day to pray for him because he had been condemned to death and the thought of facing the judgment of God frightened him. When he reached the monastery, Martin began to pray, and a little later he sent word to John not to worry; he would not be executed. But the next day the guards led John from the prison to the place of execution. While he was going to the gallows amid the insults of the mob, poor John asked himself how Martin could have deceived both of them in that manner. Just as the hangman was preparing to slip the noose over his neck, a figure waving a white handkerchief appeared on the balcony of the viceroy's palace. It was the Countess of Chinchón, wife of the viceroy. She had availed herself of her privilege and granted his pardon.

John González was liberated, but his future seemed very uncertain. He had no money and his prison record could not be offered as a recommendation in the search for work. Martin took care of everything. He found a way for John to earn his living, and gave him what he needed to start out, plus thirty *reales* for his initial expenses.[9]

To be saved from execution when all hope seems lost is assuredly a cause for rejoicing, but it is better still not to fall into the hands of justice. That is what two men thought when they sought asylum in Martin's cell. The court officer and guards who were pursuing them appeared at the door of Martin's cell to conduct a search. The two knaves, whether guilty or innocent, trembled in a corner of the cell. If the police entered, there would be no escape. If only Martin would not open the door!

Martin began to pray and had the two fugitives pray. Then he opened the door and allowed the guards to enter. "Would you like to see what is in this room? Please look around. There is nothing here but these baskets of laundry." The guards did not wait for a second invitation. They had seen the malefactors running at top speed towards the monastery, and who but Martin could have given them asylum? So they turned everything topsy-turvy. They went to the baskets and lifted the laundry to see if anyone was hidden under it. The fugitives concealed in the baskets, actually felt the guards' hands touching them and thought all was lost, but the guards could see and feel nothing but the laundry. They then left, begging Martin's pardon for having disturbed him.[10]

In addition to criminals wanted by the police, Martin frequently took into his cell the abandoned sick poor or, even more frequently, men he had found lying wounded in the street after a brawl, quarrel or assault. Two or three of such sick or wounded were almost always to be found in his room, which was the supply room of the infirmary. To be sure, they were not lying on his bed of planks, but on comfortable beds complete with mattresses, pillows and sheets. He fed them good, substantial food to help them regain their strength and even tried to take into consideration their tastes, wishes or caprices.[11]

Someone in the community, however, did not look favorably upon this kind of first aid treatment within the walls of the monastery. Perhaps it was the brother who complained because he had too much work washing the sheets. Granted, it was a bit irregular to bring all kinds of people into a monastery, but for a while the superiors let Martin do it. Then a little storm began to gather, and one day the lightning struck: the sick must be cleared out of the supply room.

It was then that Martin thought of asking his sister's help. Joan agreed, and Martin transferred his little hospital to her house. The house was about a mile and a half from the monastery. Martin did not consider that a serious inconvenience, since the bother of going to and fro would be his. In Joan's house the sick had the advantage of quiet and of the pure country air which would hasten their convalescence. Martin went there every day to visit them and take care of them. If an occasion arose when he was not able to do so, he sent his old teacher, Marcel de Rivero, who gladly took his place.

One evening, a few steps from the door of the monastery, Martin found an Indian who had been stabbed and had almost bled to death. It was too late to take him to Joan's house; the patient would have died before reaching it, for his life hung by a thread. Marcel de Rivero was not to be found.

Taking everything into consideration, Martin felt that the gravity of the danger justified at least one exception to the general rule and he carried the Indian into his room, as he had done before the prohibition was issued, with the intention of transferring him to Joan's house the following day.

But one of the usual zealous souls went straight to the prior to tell him that Martin was disobeying the orders he had received and was once more taking the sick into his cell. In a few moments a categorical order came from the prior, demanding that Martin transfer the wounded man elsewhere at once.

Happily, Martin had time to cleanse, medicate and bandage the wound. Aware of the sentence of expulsion hanging over his patient, he begged God to heal him immediately since he must put him out of the monastery.

The next day, Marcel de Rivero went to visit the Indian, and found him as well and strong as if he had never lost a drop of blood. He removed the bandages and discovered that only a fine, pink scar remained. Martin, meanwhile, was given a penance and he performed it in complete peace.

A few days later, the prior had occasion to call Martin to see him. Martin seized the opportunity to beg his superior's pardon for having displeased him. But how was it possible, the prior asked, that Martin could have disobeyed such a definite order?

Martin explained what had happened, saying that the urgency and gravity of the case had led him to presume the prior's permission. In other words, he had judged that the precept of charity took precedence over the precept of obedience. He begged the prior to tell him whether or not he was mistaken in his judgment so that he would know how to act another time.

The prior was silent. The affair had not been presented to him in that light by the brother who had come to complain about it. He was sorry he had listened to the tale; he was sorry he had acted under the impression made by the brother's words; he regretted having forced Martin to remove the wounded man and having given Martin an unmerited penance.

"You judged correctly, Brother," he finally said. "Do the same thing the next time." [12]

The sufferings of his brothers and sisters in Christ called Martin out of the monastery and little by little drew him into the stream of life in the city. As a preparation for a wider battlefield, he had forged his first arms behind the walls of the cloister by helping his brethren. After God bestowed upon Martin the gift of His presence in the secret of his cell, He came to the doorstep and invited him to go out. He now presented Himself to Martin in the person of the poor.

Even the appearance of those who came to the door of the monastery proclaimed the endless misery of the new, rich city. Then there were the sick who were untended and abandoned in their huts; the victims of violence lying along the roadside; the penniless nobility, living in hidden privation beyond the reach of help because of their pride; the prisoners in the filthy jails.

But a particular group stirred Martin's charity in a special way: the abandoned children and orphans. In his earlier years Martin had known what it meant to be a child without a family, to be forced to depend on the help of strangers, to be treated without affection, to feel oneself hardly tolerated.

There were many children without families in the streets of Lima, and they got along as best they could. The authorities should have taken care of them, if for no other reason than the fact that these neglected children would be a source of trouble when they grew up; but they did nothing.

At that period of history, social problems were not discussed as they are today. Nor had Martin ever studied social questions. But Martin saw, as clearly as he knew that two and two make four, that if these abandoned children were left to their own devices, they would never know the happiness of loving God, of living in His friendship. Sooner or later they would become delinquents. From the point of view of society, at least of the society of his time, a delinquent was only an individual who annoyed others and therefore would eventually be justly deprived of his liberty. From the Christian point of view, a delinquent is a man who has missed the whole point of his life because he has not attained that perfection of his being which renders him worthy in the eyes of God of receiving gifts superior to those of the other creatures on the earth. That is as sad as a violated promise, as an arrow fallen short of its mark.

This tragedy weighed unsupportably upon the soul of Martin. He could not bear the thought that men like himself, capable of living, as he did, in a world rendered luminous and joyous by the grace of God, should remain far from God, so far away that they did not even suspect the existence of God. He could not endure the thought of the souls who remained outside the wedding feast in exterior darkness, and in the cold night of sin.

He knew very well that if divine providence had not led him by the hand from his very first years, he too could have been one of their number. He likewise knew that providence used men to carry out its hidden plans. He realized that he was an instrument chosen by providence to show the little abandoned ones of Lima the path to the house of their heavenly Father.

As soon as he had realized all this, the only thing he could do was to go to work. It was an undertaking completely different from anything Martin had done up to that moment. It would not be a small undertaking; not like helping the poor who came and went, or visiting them in their homes, or bringing two or three sick into his cell for a short time. It was a question of gathering together a large number of babies and children from the streets and educating them. They would need constant help over a long period of time so that their future could be assured. In short, it meant establishing an orphanage.

Today that seems to us the most natural thing in the world. But then it must not have seemed so simple, since neither the civil nor ecclesiastical authorities had been willing to undertake the task. Martin appealed to both, and received no encouragement. In their opinion the idea was sheer madness. As to the authorities of his own Order, there was no hope of their financing the orphanage because of the restricted means at their disposal. All they could do was to give Martin permission to seek the necessary funds, but with the debts which weighed upon the community, he could not hope to get any financial hlep from them. All in all, the outlook was far from encouraging.

If it had been only a passing fancy or some vague philanthropic idea which inspired Martin, he would have been overcome by the first obstacles. But his love of souls sprang from his love of God. His respect for souls was based upon his veneration for the blood of Christ, shed for our redemption. His greeting, "Let us save our souls through the merits of the blood of Jesus Christ," was not mere words. It expressed his living, unfailing desire that the price of our redemption should not be wasted for even one soul. Those who look at themselves in the mirror of the fountain from which all things spring, find in God the source of the dignity of His creatures, and in creatures the goodness of God, and "feel they must love their neighbor as themselves, because they see that God loves them with an infinite love." [13]

Our self-love is the most deeply rooted of all our affections. We never renounce, we never can renounce, the desire of our own good. We overcome obstacles which, in the path of our neighbor, would seem ten or twenty times beyond our powers.

That is why the Gospel demands that we love our neighbor as we love ourselves.

It can truly be said that Martin loved his neighbor as he loved himself, because he never went to greater pains for himself than he did for his neighbor. And at least for his own physical well-being, Martin did not consume even a small fraction of the energy he used to serve his neighbor. All he did for his neighbor was done under the impulse of the most genuine charity.

An authentic proof of this fact was the success of his efforts for the orphaned children. He began to work alone, without financial support and in an atmosphere of hesitancy sufficient to weaken the strongest spirit. Nevertheless, the orphanage of the Holy Cross rose from nothing and prospered. It was built on such solid foundations that the *Colegio de Santa Cruz* still exists and shelters the children of Lima today.

In addition to his charity, in this undertaking Martin exercised the full measure of his farsightedness and his genius for organization, which turned the school into a small masterpiece. It would not have been worthwhile to overcome so many difficulties just to give the children a refuge. They had to be educated. Obviously, Martin could not be responsible for the work of education, neither alone nor with the help of others, since obedience placed him elsewhere. Nor did he wish to administer the school. He asked his friend, Matthew Pastor, the greatest benefactor of the project, to do that. All Martin did for the orphanage was to conceive the idea, to seek and find the means of carrying out his idea with a trust that overcame all obstacles and, lastly, to organize the school.

To educate the little guests of Holy Cross and turn them into men and women who would lead solid Christian lives, it was necessary to have a staff completely dedicated to this work. Martin chose his teachers and assistants with care, and to secure the best, he did not haggle over salaries. He wanted the best, at all costs.

It was not Martin's habit to do things by halves. Once he had taken up the cause of the abandoned children, he carried the work to completion. He realized that a good education would enable a boy to face life with a fair chance of solving his problems, but that was not sufficient for a girl. A girl needed a dowry. And Martin arranged for the girls to receive an adequate dowry when they left the orphanage of the Holy Cross.[14]

How did he secure the financial means to carry out such a grandiose plan? His system was simplicity itself. He gave all he had to give and waited for providence to give the rest.

Giving all he had to give meant giving his own food to the poor who waited at the door, depriving himself of rest to give his time to others, going about begging for help, and before going out to beg, living a life which inspired trust and confidence. Rich people, noblemen, and even the viceroy gave to him willingly and with great generosity because they knew "how well and faithfully" he distributed what he received. Everything that went through Martin's hands reached the poor, down to the last penny. Sometimes even money not intended for the poor went to them, as when Martin "invested" in clothing for his beloved ragged protégés a large sum of money which his niece Catherine had deposited with a merchant. When Catherine learned that the money intended for her trousseau had been used in that fashion, she wept. Her uncle smilingly assured her that she had lost nothing. As a matter of fact, the next day one of Martin's rich friends heard of the affair and gave Catherine the amount of money that had been spent.[15]

Giving all he had almost meant that Martin planned the

distribution of the riches which flowed his way in order to make good use of everything. The alms which rained upon him from all directions were varied in kind and in source. The Count of Chinchón, viceroy of the King, sent him one hundred thousand pesos every month. Every year Frances Vélez furnished the repast of the novices and students on Holy Thursday, and on Good Friday she "sent sufficient bread for the whole community for the fast of bread and water kept on that day, likewise sending cinnamon to be taken with the water so that it would not be harmful." Elizabeth Mexías gave Martin the revenue from one of her houses for the needs of the students. The governor, John de Figueroa, brought him generous Mass offerings every Monday and, now and then, special alms for the lay brothers, "asking that they remember him in their prayers and rosaries." [16]

And then there were the offerings that arrived little by little, every day, from all kinds of voluntary contributors. Martin felt he should divide all this by assigning it to various categories of his poor according to the different days of the week. The alms received on Monday and Saturday were transformed into suffrages for the souls in purgatory, whose merits at the moment of death had not been sufficient to balance their spiritual debts. The alms received on Thursday and Friday were for those who had embraced voluntary poverty: novices, students or priests. The offerings of the other three days of the week were at the disposition of the unending stream of his beloved poor, with the exception of the Sunday offerings, which were reserved for Negroes and Indians, who were the poorest of the poor.[17]

At the end of a week these various offerings amount to an amazing total. But Martin always gave more than he received. The Dominicans of Holy Rosary realized this and they considered as a continuous miracle the inexhaustible source of help given by the lay brother who went about clad in the most worn, patched and faded habit anyone had ever seen. "It was something that made us marvel and was considered a constant miracle by the religious," said Father Gutiérrez, "to see that a poor lay religious, dressed in rough clothing, humble and ragged, had the means of helping as many poor as came to him, so that it seemed that alms rained down on him. Although wealthy people in the capital and outside of it, who knew him, aided and assisted him with their alms for this purpose, it did not seem that these alms alone could be enough, but that God in His mercy worked with him by increasing the sums he received so that the ardent desires and affections of His servant might be fulfilled." [18]

The added contribution of divine providence was needed, since Martin could not be satisfied with giving only a little help but had at all costs to give all that was needed. He felt it was a small thing to help ninety-nine poor, if the hundredth had to be sent away emptyhanded. To be unable to help a poor man would have been a great grief for him, a sorrow he could not endure. "He grieved so deeply," said Brother Lauren de los Santos, "when a poor person came asking for alms and he had nothing to give, that he begged our Lord to give him something to help the poor man in his necessity.[19]

Martin made his request, not as one who wishes only to be able to say to his own conscience, "I have done all I could," but as one who wishes to obtain what he asks at all costs. He made his request with his irresistible prayer, composed of flaming desire and limitless trust and reinforced by his heroic exercise of penance. When Martin had nothing to give, he prayed and flagellated himself until divine mercy opened the treasury of its infinite riches to him. This was another of his ways of paying, in his own person, the price of the exercise of charity towards his neighbor. It was one more of the characteristic and original aspects of his charity.

Another originality of Martin was that he was not satisfied to use only the wealth of others to aid the poor, but he also worked to produce wealth. Just as one day, in order to help his brethren of Limatambo, he had planted a whole olive grove with the help of John Vázquez, so whenever Martin went along the roads branching off from Lima into the countryside, he planted rows of a variety of fruit trees along the way. As the trees grew and produced their fruit, the poor found food along the roads, food that belonged to everyone because it grew on public land, and they were saved from the temptation to climb over the hedges and steal from the orchards. In this instance, too, the charity of Martin was aimed at the good of souls even while he was providing for their bodily needs.

In addition to the trees planted along the roads, he established a plantation at Limatambo to provide the sick poor with medicine. It was a plantation of all the herbs employed by the medical science of his day for their therapeutical properties. It enabled his clinic to function without augmenting the expenses of the monastery.[20]

Martin established no monopoly in his exercise of charity. Quite the contrary. It made no difference whatsoever to him if the aid he gave did not always come from his hands. He was happy to develop in those who offered their alms the habit of helping the needy directly. "Many illustrious and wealthy authorities of the republic . . . gave generously to the poor, as much by the hand of the Servant of God as by his counsel." [21]

Among these alms given directly were the dowries for twenty-seven young women, one after the other. Martin, who had himself experienced the truth of the words of the Lord, "it is more blessed to give than to receive," encouraged his pupils in the school of charity by obtaining an augmentation of their wealth for those who were so generous in giving to the poor. When they opened their purses to the poor, God increased their capital.

Martin's contemporaries called him father of the poor, father of charity, father of all, and he was truly paternal in his beneficence.

He was paternal in the way he received everyone, without distinction and without preference, unless his preference could be said to have been for the weakest and neediest. He was paternal in his compassion for the sufferings of others, in his desire to alleviate them at all costs. But above all, Martin was paternal in the spirit which inspired his charity, in his desire to generate the life of Christ in souls.

In his commentary on the words of Jesus, "Whoever does the will of My Father in heaven, he is My brother and sister and mother" (Matt. 12:50), St. Gregory says, "Whoever believes can be considered the brother and sister of Christ, but he becomes His mother if he is a means of generating the love of God in the heart of his neighbor." [22]

Martin's whole apostolate of charity had only one purpose: to awaken the love of God in souls; in all souls, without exception, in the souls of the rich as well as those of the poor. Some people do not know how to love the poor without hating the rich. They really love only themselves, and are the hypocrites who sound the trumpets when they give alms so that they may be honored by men.

Martin loved all, rich and poor, because from "the ardent love with which he loved the Divine Majesty . . . was born the love he had for his neighbor, loving him in God and for God." [23]

In Martin's eyes the rich and the poor were not two irreconcilable opposites, two extremes of opposition. They were simply two different ways of life in the infinite variety of the universe, two states willed by uncreated Goodness so that men might exercise the divine work of charity among themselves. "The things necessary for the life of man," the Eternal Father said to St. Catherine of Siena, "I have given in many ways, and I have not given them all in one way way so that you may necessarily have the means of exercising charity towards each other. I could easily have created men endowed with all they need for both soul and body; but it is My will that they should have need of each other, and that they should be My ministers to administer the graces and gifts they have received from Me. Whether a man will it or not, he cannot help acting as charity requires." [24]

That is precisely how Martin understood it, and his desire to transmit to all the souls the divine life of charity was the source of his profound compassion and love for the poor, of his effort to kindle compassion and love for the poor in the hearts of the rich, and of his effort to free the souls of the poor from hate and revolt against misery and human injustice by showing them how the providence of God watched over them.

And if a glass of water given out of love will not go without reward in the kingdom of God, we can believe that the reign of supernatural charity was established in the hearts of those who responded so generously to Martin's pleas. Therefore his contemporaries called him not only "father of the poor" but "father of charity" as well. And they were right.

*Even the dogs under the table eat
of the children's crumbs* (Mark 7:28).

MARTIN WAS TEARING an old sheet into strips, preparing dressings, when Brother Francis Guerrero entered the room. It was one of those tranquil afternoon hours when the morning's work was done and the afternoon's work had not yet begun.

"Is someone in the house hurt?" asked the lay brother.

Martin glanced up from his work, an amused smile glinting in his eyes. "At the moment, no, but shortly someone will need these dressings."

Before Brother Francis had time for conjecture, a pathetic patient entered the room. It was a very big dog. He had a large wound in the belly, from which his intestines protruded.

The dog came up to Martin, greeted him like an old friend, and seemed to beg for his help.

"Now you see how the dressings will be used for this poor beast, which is also a creature of God," said Martin, while he replaced the entrails in the dog's body and sewed up the wound. He then prepared a bed of sheepskins on which he stretched a piece of coarse cloth and ordered the wounded dog to lie down on it.

The dog docilely obeyed all the commands, as if he understood them.

Martin kept him for several days, feeding him and dressing the wound. When he was healed, Martin said to him, "Now go and work for your master!" Just as he had obeyed the doctor during the period of treatment, the animal obeyed the benefactor who was dismissing him, and went back to his master.[1]

All the witnesses who testified concerning Martin's life are unanimous in considering his love for animals as a manifestation of his charity. Marcel de Rivero had known Martin before he entered the monastery, and altogether had the good fortune of being associated with him for about half a century. When speaking about the charity of his ex-pupil, Marcel said he did not have "sufficient words to explain it." To give at least some notion of the breadth of Martin's charity, Marcel affirmed that he "exercised it even towards the animals," to such a point that while his brethren were having recreation during the community visits to Limatambo, Brother Martin would go off to take care of the cattle and other animals of the farm.[2]

Martin devoted himself passionately to taking care of others. It mattered little to him whether or not his patients were gifted with reason. If men came to him, he took care of men; if animals came to him, he gave them no less attention. How could he have had too high an opinion of his medical skill to employ it for animals, when the Gospel speaks of our heavenly Father's solicitude for the birds of the air and the lilies of the field?

Martin felt that it was entirely natural to take care of animals. He loved them spontaneously, with that pure love of charity which makes us love God in all His creatures, and all creatures for the love of God. "To the soul who loves God, all times and all places are His." [3] Martin would have added: and all creatures are His creatures. Everything in the world is filled with God. For those who have ears to hear, everything in the world speaks so clearly of the power that gives and conserves life, of the wisdom that orders each being to its proper end and creates harmony amidst the variety of beings, of the goodness which lovingly provides for the needs of all creatures! How can a man refuse to love created things which speak so eloquently of the First Love?

The Canticle of Brother Sun rose from Martin's heart: "Be praised, my Lord, in all Your creatures," because praise goes up from all creatures without exception, and the soul which loves God and sees in the perfection of creatures the reflection of the infinite perfections of God, is filled with praise.

But praise is more perfect when love is freed of self-seeking and freely forgives offenses: "Be praised, my Lord, for those who forgive for love of You." Martin gave proof of this heroism of love which pardons when he did not condemn the mice for their destruction of the linens. Each time an occasion arose, he gave proof of heroic love, always ready to serve others, and the occasions arose frequently.

Martin did not go in search of the animals, at least not in the majority of cases. The animals came to him, drawn by the infallible attraction of instinct. Animals always seem to know who will caress them and who will kick them. But even the meanest animals went to Martin with confidence. There are wide diversities, even among animals, and only those who love them can understand them.

The dog that came into the supply room while Martin was tearing up the sheet must have been a good dog, one of those dogs who would let himself be killed in defense of his master and his possessions, but one day a patient of another kind came to Martin's first-aid room. This dog was one of those mean animals that delight in picking a quarrel on any occasion. He had been stabbed twice. The weapon had penetrated from one side of his body to the other, and blood was flowing from four gaping wounds. This big bully did not wait to see if Martin would have compassion on him, looking at him with pleading eyes and wagging his tail. He pushed his way through the sick waiting in line and drew Martin's attention with two insolent yelps.

His antics amused everyone and even aroused the curiosity of Father Cyprian de Medina. Notwithstanding his dignity as a master in sacred theology, the priest stopped to admire the scene from the upper gallery of the cloister, and then came down to see how it would end.

Martin turned to the dog and spoke to him in a fatherly way. "Brother dog, where did you learn to be such a bully? See what your insolence has brought you!"

This little admonition was enough to subdue the dog. Instead of yelping, he began to rub his muzzle on Martin's habit. Martin took him by the ear and led him off to his own room, where he washed the wounds with wine in which rosemary had been heated—one of his infallible remedies—and then began to sew them up.

Naturally the dog growled and turned his head towards the surgeon's hands, pulling back his lips and baring his teeth. Not at all disturbed, Martin went on sewing, and to calm the dog, he said: "You had better be quiet and learn to be good, because bullies end badly."

When he had finished, he arranged two or three sheepskins on the floor and said to the dog, "Lie down here!" The dog stretched out on the skins but then began to roll about, his feet in the air, rubbing the wounds against the sheepskins because the sewn skin pulled and itched.

"Lie down and be quiet!" ordered Martin. With a deep sigh, the dog stretched out in a more dignified position, and with his muzzle on his forefeet, watched the brother with pensive eyes.

Martin fed him but gave him no other treatment, and at

the end of a few days the dog was better. He expressed his gratitude by following Martin everywhere and not wanting to leave him out of his sight.

In spite of Martin's good advice, the dog's character had not changed. Even in his manifestations of affection, he was still the brigand he had always been, with no concern for good behavior. A good dog stays near a benefactor and defends him in case of peril, but how could this bully claim the right to forbid anyone to approach Martin or have anything to do with him?

And yet that was the case. He growled and showed his teeth at anyone who came near Martin. One day when a lay brother was asking Martin for some information, the dog almost bit him. Martin held him back and with his usual patience made another attempt to train him. "Brother," he said, "when are you going to learn to be good? Look out, or the next time you will be chased out of the house with a stick!"

The dog had been warned, but he refused to mend his ways. A few days later he attacked another religious, so that three or four of the friars armed themselves with sticks and thrashed the dog thoroughly, then they pushed him out of the door and closed it, leaving the stunned dog in the middle of the road. But before doing what they did, they must have made sure that Martin was out of the way, for he would never have permitted them to do this, even though he predicted it was liable to happen.[4]

These two were not the only dogs Martin healed. Father Velasco Carabantes said that many times he had seen Martin treat "some for wounds, some for the mange." One dog who had been too seriously hurt to lick his own wounds came to seek the help of the "father of charity"; another, wounded in the belly, was invited by Martin to come to the monastery when he found him on the road. He ordered all his canine patients to be quiet and not to leave his room, and as soon as they were healed, he sent them on their way.[5]

Dogs were not the only animals who benefited from his care. Cats came to his clinic, too. One day, while he was passing through a courtyard with Brother Ferdinand, Martin noticed a cat mewing desperately on the doorstep of a cellar. Someone had thrown a stone at her and half crushed her head. "Come along with me and I'll take care of you," Martin said to the cat. "Do you know that you are in bad shape?"

The cat must have realized it, because she seemed to understand his words and followed along behind the two brothers. When they reached the infirmary, she was as good as could be while Martin treated her wound and sewed it up. When he had finished the treatment, he made a little cap for her out of a piece of cloth, fitting it to her head and sewing it on. Then he said, "Now go away, but come back tomorrow morning and I'll take care of you again."

The next morning Brother Ferdinand was curious to see if the cat would come back. He went to Martin's room very early and found the cat sitting in front of the door. It was a well-bred cat, for it preferred to wait rather than to arrive late for an appointment! [6]

With equal punctuality, and as long as it needed care, a wounded turkey came to Martin to be treated every day.[7]

With such a mixed clientele, unpleasant incidents might have arisen. Even a well-mannered dog would growl if he found a cat near him at mealtime. But Martin did not permit that. If they came there to benefit from his charity, they were not to treat each other as enemies. "Now, little brothers," he said to the dogs and cats, "don't fight, and eat together like good brothers. Otherwise I must send you away!" [8]

Those who watched always marvelled to see Martin persuade the dogs and cats to eat in peace, side by side.

Once a cat and a dog chose the cellar under the infirmary to give birth to their young. Martin feared the two little beasts would suffer from hunger, since they would not leave their brood even to eat. Every day he carried a good bowl of soup to the cellar, one bowl for both of them. Putting it on the ground, he said, "Come and eat, but be quiet and don't fight." Then he delightedly watched the two heads plunge into the soup, which vanished in a twinkling.

One day a mouse appeared, attracted by the odor of the food. He came out of his hiding place and stood watching at a distance. He would have been happy to share in the banquet, but what would the other two guests think, sworn enemies of his kind?

Since he did not dare approach the soup bowl, perhaps the mouse thought of feasting on one of the little ones while the two mothers were intent on their dinner.

Martin saw the eyes gleaming in the darkness of the cellar and understood "Brother Mouse's" temptation. He called to him in his calm and persuasive voice, "Brother, don't disturb the little ones! If you are hungry, come and eat without getting so excited, and then go your way in peace."

The mouse drew near the bowl and put his muzzle into it, while the other two continued to lap up the soul without even appearing to be aware of the newcomer's presence. They went on eating in peace so long that Martin had time to go and call Brother Ferdinand, and they both came back to enjoy the spectacle.

It was really worth seeing! Animals can be tamed with much time and patience, but not everyone can make animals obey instantly, speaking to them as one would to a Christian. Brother Ferdinand was so struck by this sight that twenty years after Martin's death he could relate it in all its details as if he had seen it the day before.

What was most striking, said Brother Ferdinand, was that whenever Martin appeared, the animals went to meet him and welcomed him warmly. "When he went to the chicken yard of the infirmary, the chickens welcomed him, let him handle them, circled around him, seemed to greet him with joy, as if grateful for his charity. It was the same if he entered the stalls of the mules and the other animals. They demonstrated a singular joy and affection. The same thing was true of the dogs, cats and other household animals, who seemed eager to be petted whenever they saw him, showing as best they could their delight in seeing him by touching him, licking his clothes." [9]

And not only the household animals.

One time three young bulls and one full grown bull were brought to the monastery during a holiday celebration. They were left there for the diversion of the young professed, who were to take care of them. But as often happens when a duty it assigned collectively, at the end of four days the bulls were still unfed. Martin found out about it and towards evening was seen carrying water containers and bundles of fodder to the enclosure of the novitiate. It was around midnight when he finished bringing all he needed for the animals. At that hour the door was locked, but locked doors were never an impediment to Martin's charity. The doors either opened or let him pass while they stayed closed. This time the door opened and Martin carried in his provisions of water and feed for the animals.

The four animals, locked up in a small enclosure, were maddened by hunger and thirst. As soon as Martin appeared in their midst they became as gentle and meek as lambs and licked his habit, almost kissing it. From a window above,

Father James de la Fuente heard Martin talking to the big bull: "Brother, don't be so domineering just because you are the biggest. Let the little ones eat!"

Martin went as he had come, but he left behind the empty jugs so that the animals would have something with which to amuse themselves. The next morning the pieces of the broken containers testified to Martin's nocturnal visit.[10]

On another occasion the novices were given two young calves for their amusement during recreation. But the novices did not enjoy the calves. They were so gentle they seemed to be made of wood. If they could get a young bull!

Martin found them a young bull. For two days all went well, but the novices teased the bull so much that "the third day he became *bravo*," that is, enraged, and the terrified novices ran and locked themselves in their cells. When the bell rang, calling the friars to choir, the novices were still so frightened of the angry bull that they did not dare leave their cells. Martin was near the door of the choir and saw all the older religious coming in, but not one novice appeared. What could have happened? He then learned that the novices were locked in their cells for fear of the bull raging in their cloister.

Martin armed himself with a fresh reed with a cluster of thorny leaves at the end and went to the novitiate. The bull was in a corner, head lowered and ready to charge. Martin prodded him with the leaves of the reed saying, "I didn't bring you here to frighten the religious and prevent them from fulfilling their duties. Now go away!" And the bull, meek as a little lamb, trotted through the courtyards of the monastery and returned to the farm from which he had come.[11]

Martin dealt with all kinds of animals on a basis of familiarity, and made them understand and obey without difficulty. "Martin loved God with his whole heart," writes E. Doherty. "He loved every human being and every animal God had put on this earth; and every animal, every man, woman and child, and God Himself, loved Martin." [12]

But among the chickens that fluttered around him, and the cattle and horses and mules that greeted him from their mangers, among the dogs and cats and mice, Martin reserved a place of honor for the dogs. The other animals could come and go, but the dogs had the privilege of staying in the supply room until they were completely healed. Joan's house sheltered the dogs evacuated from the infirmary of Holy Rosary, just as it did the sick. When a little dog lay down on the tomb of its master who had been buried in the church of the Holy Rosary, and for two weeks no way could be found to make it leave, Martin brought it something to eat every day, filled with compassion for the grief of the little animal.[13]

And finally, Martin's charity obtained a miracle from the omnipotence of God, just for a dog. The dog in question was eighteen years old and belonged to Brother John de Vicuña, the "prior of the kitchen," the procurator or steward of the monastery. Eighteen years is an advanced age for a dog, and one can easily imagine the condition of Brother John's pet when one knows that mange had been added to the infirmities of age. Those who knew the situation well, asserted that the dog had a disgusting odor.

Taking everything into consideration, the procurator thought he could no longer ask the community to endure the presence of the poor beast, and he ordered a Negro to kill it. The Negro went in search of the dog and found it in the garden, unsuspectingly stretched out, asleep in the sun. It seemed a good opportunity, so the Negro picked up a large stone and threw it at the dog's head. The stone must have been quite large, for the dog was killed almost instantly.

The Negro was happy to have solved the problem so neatly and was on his way to throw the dog's body into the river when Martin stopped him. He reproved him very severely, took the dog from him, revolting as it was, and carried it in his arms into his cell and laid it on the floor. No sooner had the dog touched the pavement than it pulled itself to a sitting position, lifted its muzzle towards Martin and began to move its poor wounded head slowly to the right and left. Martin took the dog's head between his hands and cleaned it of the mixture of earth and blood which covered it. "I'll go and get a little wine!" said Brother Lauren, who had witnessed the whole scene.

In the length of time it took the brother to go to the refectory and return, Martin had sewed up all the wounds in the dog's head. When the wine arrived, it served as a good external disinfectant for the rejoined parts. Piece by piece, Martin had removed all the dirt he found in the wound.

The dog was stretched out on a pallet in a corner. Between the dizziness induced by the wine and the blow he had received, he fell asleep immediately without eating.

"How's the dog?" asked Brother Lauren as soon as he saw Martin the next morning.

"I don't know; I haven't seen him yet."

Together they went to Martin's cell, taking along a large piece of meat. The dog was sleeping soundly, but when Martin patted him, he sighed.

"Get up, you're not going to die from such a little thing!" said Martin.

The dog stirred a little and yawned. Finally, smelling the odor of the meat, he opened his eyes, got up on his feet, and wagged his tail. And when Martin gave him the beefsteak, he devoured it.

The dog stayed there for three days. Brother Lauren was interested in the case because he had seen the dog return to life. On the fourth day, he met Martin and asked him, "How is the dog getting along?"

"Why, this morning," replied Martin, "when I left to ring the morning bell, the dog slipped out between my feet. That means he is cured."

The dog was completely cured, not only of the head wound but also of the mange, and could appear in public without running the risk of further disagreeable adventures. Since he had spent eighteen years with Brother John de Vicuña, he went back to him, and Brother John was happy to have his old dog back, healed and rejuvenated. After all, it was only out of consideration for his brethren in the monastery that he had reluctantly decided to have the Negro kill the dog. But his grief over the decision was augmented by Martin's reproaches. As soon as Martin had sewed up the dog's head, he sought out Brother John and told him, even though he used "mild, humble words, full of forebearance," that "he had not done well in ordering a companion of so many years to be killed."

In addition to Brother Lauren, Father Joseph de Villarsbia and Father Ferdinand de Aragonés were witnesses of the episode of the dog, and all three attested that the dog was killed by the Negro and recalled to life by St. Martin.[14]

In these little stories of the animals, furnished by the witnesses during the Process, the abundance of details is remarkable. It indicates the great importance they attached to these episodes, for they considered them necessary to complete the portrait of their holy Brother and to point out the lengths to which his disinterested charity went. And his charity towards animals most certainly was disinterested.

But of all the animals Martin loved and cared for, the mice —those tiny animals so little loved by humans—seem to have had the privilege of showing their gratitude to the "father of charity." He saved them from the death by poison which their deeds had merited, and then day after day patiently fed them, lovingly carrying food for them to the garden. Even after his death, they continued to obey him.

Even today, it is said, when mice threaten to become a plague, it is sufficient to invoke St. Martin to be freed of them.

And Martin, the humblest of the humble, wished or permitted the tiniest and most modest of those he aided to be associated with him in iconography. A picture of St. Martin is rarely found which does not show at least one little mouse at his feet.

But perhaps even in this the Saint of charity obeyed the dominant impulse of his whole life. By giving them a place in his own images, he has ensured a glance of friendship and gratitude from his devotees for the despised little animals. Love must necessarily inspire love.

CHAPTER

≻ 14 ≺

I am the way, and the truth, and the life (John 14:6).

St. catherine represents the three great stages of the soul's ascent to sanctity as three steps of a bridge. In her vision of the redeemed world, Christ, the Pontiff of the New Alliance, is the bridge uniting earth to heaven, and the steps signify both the Passion consummated in His adorable body, and the acts of the soul which summons up all its faculties to follow in the footsteps of the Redeemer.

"The feet are the first step, and they signify the affection, for the affection carries the soul as the feet carry the body. These pierced feet are steps by which you can reach His side, where the secrets of His heart are manifested to you, because the soul, rising on the steps of her affection, begins to taste the love of His heart, gazing with the eye of the intellect into the open heart of My Son, and finds there a consummate and ineffable love. . . . Then the soul is filled with love, seeing herself so much loved. Having climbed the second step, the soul reaches the third, which is the mouth, where she finds peace. . . .

"On the first step, lifting her feet from the affections of earth, the soul stripped herself of vice; on the second step she clothed herself with love and virtue; and on the third step, she tasted peace." [1]

Having reached the third step, the soul tastes God, one and triune, and is drawn to a more intimate participation in the life of the Blessed Trinity.

If the Father is the "bed" in which the soul reposes with the certainty that nothing can separate her from Him, He is also the "table" which offers food, the food of the strong: the Word and His doctrine, the Eucharistic Christ and the crucified Christ thirsting to give honor to the Father through the salvation of souls; while the Holy Spirit places Himself, as it were, at the service of the soul "to minister to her His gifts and His graces."

The excellence of the mixed life, that is, a life of action springing from contemplation, is expressed here with the picturesque clarity of an allegory. And since the ideal of Dominican spirituality is attained in the mixed life, it is not strange that the life of St. Martin presents an itinerary of sanctity in accordance with the outline of St. Catherine.

His eyes and the affections of his childish and adolescent heart were drawn to the feet of the crucified Christ, and swiftly the thought of the Passion, contemplated during his nocturnal vigils and in the Eucharistic mystery, gave him the desire to mount higher.

Martin's ascent to the second step can be identified with the gift of himself perfected through his religious profession. On the second step the gaze of the soul seeks to penetrate the secrets of the heart of God, and in its desire to plumb more and more profoundly the depths of that abyss of charity, the soul is purified and fortified through the exercise of all the virtues.

It is impossible to determine the moment at which Martin reached the third step. There is no clear line of separation between the second and third steps. The soul that perseveres in contemplating the love of the Word finds itself, almost without realizing it, in the peace of union with Him. It is probable that Martin reached the summit very early, and pitched his tent and remained there for many years of his life.

This is the impression we receive when, as we search for some indication of his having reached the "third step," we see that those who lived with him did not consider the manifestations proper to this highest grade to be transitory or extraordinary in Martin's life, but something habitual.

The first sign of union is peace. Martin's contemporaries attested that he was immersed in peace, he radiated peace, a peace undisturbed by either insults or praise. He deflected insults heaped upon him in the beginning by accepting them gladly, convinced that he received only his just due. And when people began to honor him and call him a saint, he was not impressed and repeated with the Master: "Why dost thou call me good? No one is good, but only God" (Matt. 19:17).

His peace was based on his trust in the goodness of God, on his certitude of the benevolence of that will to which he had surrendered his own will and his whole being—"I know in whom I have believed"—and the certainty that the love of his own heart would always be met by a corresponding love. It was the peace of a repose in the arms of the Father.

Martin did not give himself airs, he never posed. But the joy with which such trust and certainty filled his heart was apparent to all. Those who knew him were certain that he "was completely in God, and God in him." [2]

His prayer was completely pervaded by this peace. Tender colloquies filled the hours that he passed at the foot of the tabernacle and before the Queen of the Holy Rosary, "the most sweet contemplation of God and His Most Holy Mother"; colloquies carried on with simplicity of heart, in complete understanding; unhurried colloquies, never shadowed by a fear of interruption, for he knew they could continue at all times, in the midst of all occupations, in the secret of his heart. "No matter what he was doing, he found in whatever he did the highest subjects of celestial and divine contemplation, which enabled him to rise above himself. All the time he had, outside of that spent in the infirmary, was given totally to this duty and occupation, alone with God, enjoying the special privilege of not being seen by men, . . . keeping all his thoughts on God." [3]

In Martin's heart Martha and Mary never disputed, because Mary accompanied Martha always and everywhere. But when Martha had finished her work, Mary took Martin by the hand and led him to some hidden spot where he could enjoy the presence of his Lord, alone with Him. Solitude drew Martin like a magnet. It was his refuge from the curiosity of those around him, which, though pious and well-intentioned, was a bit embarrassing. They followed him, spied upon him, and he had to defend himself as best he could.

For example, since Brother Ferdinand was the chief infirmarian and had a second key to the supply room of the infirmary, Martin found it useless to lock himself in there. He put a little bell on the door so that its tinkling would warn him in time of Brother Ferdinand's arrival. But when ecstasies took the place of prayer, Martin was defenseless.

The one who saw Martin most frequently in ecstasy was perhaps young Vázquez. The first time, the night of the earthquake, Brother Michael told Vázquez when he fled to the cloister, beside himself with fear, that if he stayed with Martin he would no longer marvel at prodigies. After that first time, John saw him on many other occasions lifted above the earth to the height of a man, on his knees, his gaze fixed on the crucifix or some picture of a saint.

John was a discreet and sensible lad, and he understood perfectly that Martin was not to be disturbed at such moments. One morning Martin had fallen into ecstasy before the image of a saint whom he had the habit of invoking for his needs under the name of *San Socorro* (a name which he himself had perhaps given to the saint). John left him alone in the cell, locking the door behind him.

A little later he met a religious who was looking for Martin. "Is Brother Martin in his cell?" asked Father Osorio.

"Oh, no!" replied John, heedless of the fact he was lying. Father Osorio did not believe him. He saw that John had the key in his hand, took it without further ado, and opened the door.

John followed Father Osorio and saw Martin just as he had left him, raised above the ground in prayer in front of the image of his saint. John was downcast to think he had lied uselessly without saving his friend from annoyance.

Father Osorio looked in, to the right and the left, but saw no one, and he too was a little disturbed that he had not trusted John Vázquez' word. "I wonder where he can be!" he muttered as he gave the key back to John.[4]

Francis de la Torre, the other privileged friend who could

come and go freely in Martin's cell, also had the good fortune of seeing him in ecstasy several times. But other times it was due to extraordinary and unforeseen circumstances that someone came upon Martin at such moments.

One day a young boy came running into the monastery of the Holy Rosary completely out of breath. His name was Nicholas de Peñasola. Later he would be a priest in the Order of St. Augustine, but for the moment he was only an urchin trying to escape punishment. He had fled from his own home for fear of being punished by his parents after some childish prank, and he came to seek asylum at Holy Rosary.

Nicholas came to the monastery almost every day, either to see certain of his relatives who were religious there or to visit Martin, who always gave him bread and figs or raisins. Nicholas was so well known that no one paid any attention to him. Thinking only of hiding from those who were pursuing him to punish him, he went through the porter's gate at full speed, slipped into the chapter room, and hid himself in the choir stalls.

He stayed there a short while, panting and crouching down under the stalls. When he was a little calmer, he cautiously peered above the level of the stalls. He was almost certain his parents had lost the trail. It would be better to stay there and wait a bit. When their momentary anger had cooled down, he could go back home.

Meanwhile, Martin was in the same chapter room, in ecstatic levitation, raised more than twelve feet from the ground to the height of the crucifix, high on the rear wall.

The lad began to look around for a way to pass the hours without undue boredom. Suddenly he saw Martin, and was so terrified at seeing him suspended in mid-air, that he forgot everything else and fled.[5]

Sanctity certainly does not consist in ecstasies, but truly mystical ecstasy is one of the signs of the union of the soul with God. "Often the body is raised from the ground," says St. Catherine, quoting Christ's words to her, "because the union of the soul with Me is more perfect than the union between the soul and the body." [6] It is a kind of miracle that a man can continue to live when God allows the soul to feel the irresistible power of His attractions. No creature could survive the experience if God did not "encircle it with strength."

Patience, strength and perseverance are the fruits gathered on the third step of peace, the fruits on the table bearing the food of souls. Martin gathered them by handfuls.

The voice of the Lord said continuously to Martin, as it did to the weary prophet under the shadow of the juniper: "Take and eat; there is still a long journey ahead." And with the enthusiasm of an athlete running a race, Martin set out on the way of the doctrine of the Incarnate Word, into a life that was an imitation of His.

No matter what he did, Martin kept the divine example before his eyes. If he visited or tended the sick, he reflected that when the Lord came to earth to visit and heal weak humanity, His compassion for the sick was so great that He placed His omnipotence at their service to heal them. In the evening, when he began to pray, he recalled the nights Jesus passed in prayer with His Father, and prolonged his colloquy with God until the day dawned. He justified his long fasts by citing the example of the Savior, and all his mortifications were an attempt to share in some degree in the passion of Christ.

When someone insulted him, Martin remained silent, thinking that the pupil should imitate the example of the Master, "who mounted the cross to teach a doctrine founded in truth." And he remained at the foot of the cross "to learn . . . in the lowliness of true humility, because the proud cannot learn." [7]

He studied the whole life of our Lord, not by purely speculative abstractions, but with the desire of reaching practical conclusions for a rule of life. Looking at the life of our Lord in this light, all His teaching and example were coordinated in a simple synthesis: charity. Even the wisdom of the Word had found no better way of expressing His love of the Father than by loving men and giving Himself for their salvation. So there could be no other road for Martin.

When this point had been settled, all the rest followed: patience with the sick, untiring work in the service of his brethren and the poor, heroic constancy in forgetting himself in the service of others, and that complete generosity which placed at the service of others not only his physical resources but also the most jealously guarded reserves of the spirit.

That is the real proof of constancy and strength, of that "strength beyond strength" which the soul receives when it reaches the heights. "These do not hide their virtues timorously . . . and if there is need of them for the service of their neighbor, they do not hide their virtues out of fear, but use them valiantly." [8]

Martin had to make a strong effort every time anyone came to seek his advice. His own natural tastes urged him towards the hidden and obscure life which seemed to be the normal one of a humble lay brother. His spontaneous reaction was to answer, "Why do you want to mock a poor mulatto?" and then he would flee for refuge near the cross. But it was there, at the foot of the cross, that he was forced to turn back to his neighbor to fulfill the demands of spiritual charity. "The gifts I have given thee," the Lord seemed to say to him, "were not given so that thou couldst keep them for thyself, as a miser does, but that thou might fraternally share them with thy neighbor."

And Martin had to resign himself to accepting the role of

a general counselor. Naturally, the first who had recourse to him were his own brethren, and among them, the young first of all. Almost everything is said that can be said about the esteem his own brethren had for him when we note that the master of novices heartily approved of Martin's visits to the novitiate and allowed him to speak freely with the novices, either in groups or individually. And if a novice asked Martin to adopt him as a son, promising to look upon him as a father, the master of novices had no objection. Masters of novices are usually wise people, and facts proved that the master of the monastery of Holy Rosary had been right, because the young who chose Martin as their model and guide were always among the best religious. Many good and gifted religious, masters of theology and even bishops, were numbered among Martin's "sons."

It is also noteworthy that Martin's counsel was followed at the time of elections in the monastery, when interests and personal preferences render men less disposed to be guided by others. If things were not going well, and if there was discord which prevented reaching an agreement, or if a coalition was formed on some basis other than that of virtue, Martin entered the thick of the fray like an angel of peace and turned the discord and unworthy alliances into serene concord. With the freedom of one who speaks without passion and without personal interest, he went to the candidates who were an obstacle to perfect understanding and advised them to withdraw. With holy frankness he would say to one, "You are not suited to that office," and to another, "You are not yet mature enough." And all accepted his judgment, and what is more admirable, no one felt wounded or embittered. According to Father Velasco Carabantes, all were "happy and peaceful, loving each other in the Lord, each one consoling himself with the advice of such a great man, and rejoicing that the will of God should be done in them." [9]

In the field of spiritual charity, as in that of material aid, Martin's activity was not limited to the monastery. People were drawn to him by the fame of his sanctity as much as by physical hunger. There were a number who came regularly, like Captain John de Ronda, "for the consolation he received for his heart and his own profit," and returned to his home filled with a fervent desire to love and serve God and to avoid all that might offend Him.

Martin did not distribute sweetmeats to those who came to ask him for guidance in the spiritual life, but the solid and substantial bread of the great truths of the faith, and in particular the fundamental truths of death, judgment, heaven and hell. He found men capable of assimilating his teaching, for the group of his followers was large. However, those who asked advice of Martin were not preoccupied solely with spiritual matters. Father John de Barbazán asserted that "superiors sought his counsel because of his prudence; learned men, because of his doctrine; spiritual men, because of his prayer; the afflicted, because of the consolation he gave them, for he had a remedy for all ills." [10]

And by "superiors" was meant all the authorities, the "most important persons of all ranks in this Republic." The list began with the Count of Chinchón, viceroy of the King, who came to the monastery without formality at unexpected moments, or if he really could not leave his residence, sent a message asking Martin to come to his palace. It went down through all the ranks of the civil authorities and up through all the ranks of the ecclesiastical authorities, ending with the Most Reverend Felician de Vega, vicar general of the diocese of Lima, later bishop of La Paz, and finally archbishop of

Mexico City. Felician was a highly cultured man and a jurist, but he often consulted the mulatto brother "to reassure himself in the exercise of his ecclesiastical and judicial powers." [11]

With such a following, those who asked Martin's advice must have proposed difficult and delicate cases. But all who came, knew by experience that they never regretted having followed his advice.

Being a "remedy for all ills" did not mean that Martin's words were without particular efficacy for a specific kind of ill. His words were especially efficacious for the evil of discord. No discord or enmity could resist Martin's peacemaking efforts. For that reason he was especially sought after to restore peace. He seemed to have the gift of creating peace around him.

It was really a gift more than a virtue: the gift of counsel, which perfected the virtue of prudence and opened his eyes on the present as well as the future for the good of his neighbor. In the bounty of God one gift does not cost more than another, and the Holy Spirit, who "gives His gifts and graces" on the "table" of union with the Father, was pleased to give them without limit to Brother Martin.

One day the governor, John de Figueroa, came to see Martin. He was one of the most faithful visitors to his cell. He invariably came every Monday to bring Mass stipends to Martin, but he came many other times as well, because in everything regarding his soul he followed the directives Martin gave him.

John de Figueroa entered with his usual joyous air. He was always a welcome guest. He had no personal worries. The sums he gave to the poor had not diminished his patrimony, but were a blessing which had increased his wealth to such a point that at that moment he had at his disposal an income of twenty-three thousand pesos, without counting the more than two hundred thousand pesos he had saved as a reserve. The greeting Martin gave him was strange and much different from the usual one. Without preamble, Martin gravely said to him, "You must prepare yourself for difficulties!"

Overcome with surprise and shock, the governor was so startled that he did not even have the courage to ask for an explanation, and left, deeply disturbed. When he was outside the monastery, he reflected on Martin's strange words and peculiar way of acting, and a little hope sprang up in his heart. Perhaps he had not understood Martin correctly. But he was ashamed to go back and question him. So he went to visit Louise de Soto Melgarejo, a holy woman who was gifted, according to popular belief, with the spirit of prophecy.

Poor John de Figueroa! Louise greeted him at the door with Martin's very words.

The confirmation of the sentence grieved him even more, and before many days had passed, the undeniable proof of the prophecy arrived. Disaster followed upon disaster. His reputation was attacked by calumny; his health, which up to that moment had been excellent, began to decline; and even the patrimony which seemed so secure began to diminish appreciably. They were trials which God sends to those He loves in order to purify them and make them more worthy of Himself.

Martin watched over his spiritual son to sustain him during this difficult period. One day he called on him, because he feared the burden might be too heavy for his shoulders, and said to him, "Be at peace, things will not always be like this, and you will not be reduced to beggary. You will keep as much of your patrimony as you had when you arrived in Lima, and even a little more!"

All this happened in 1638, the year before Martin's death. In 1660 John de Figueroa attested that things had turned out exactly as Martin had foretold.[12]

The virtue of prudence, the gift of counsel and the spirit of prophecy combined to make Martin an ideal advisor. The virtue and the gifts contributed towards what St. Catherine called "the light of discretion," which is the power to discern what is best for each soul in conformity with the plan of God for each soul. This light is indispensable for those who must give counsel. Anyone who does not possess it will try to model everyone on his own pattern; "with the same weight that he weighs, he will try to weigh everyone," and will reduce the almost infinite variety of the spiritual world to the monotony of his own personal standard.[13]

There was none of that in Martin. He did not seek to have all follow his path. If the path was good for him, it did not follow that it was equally good for others. If he had chosen the most humble position, it was not a valid reason for everyone else to hasten to do likewise. Brother Ferdinand had entered the Order as a lay brother and had remained a lay brother for a number of years. But now he aspired to join the ranks of the clerics and finally receive sacred orders. Why dissuade him? Brother Ferdinand was a rather restless person and perhaps not perfectly well balanced; the unvarying balance of Martin seemed to have been provided to aid him. Ferdinand lived thirteen or fourteen years longer than Martin, and died in 1662. In 1619, during Martin's lifetime, Ferdinand was on the threshold of the other life, and Martin saved him. And it was well he did, because of all the testimony given during the Process, that of Ferdinand de Aragonés, his companion in the infirmary for so many years, was one of the richest in details.

In 1619 the doctors had given up all hope for Brother Ferdinand. He had received the last sacraments, including extreme unction, and the community was waiting to be called at any moment to the bedside of the dying man. Around midnight

Martin arrived, took his pulse, and asked him if the pain in his side were very severe.

"It is so severe that I can barely breathe," replied Brother Ferdinand in a weak voice.

"It occurs to me that we could try a certain remedy," Martin said. Taking a long bandage, he wound it around the chest of the sick man, now and then slipping some clover leaves between the folds of the bandage. Whatever the head infirmarian thought of this remedy, at least the community was able to sleep in peace the whole night without being called to his bedside. In the morning the sacristan took down the clappers he had prepared near the door of Brother Ferdinand's cell to summon the community. They were no longer needed because Ferdinand had fallen asleep after Martin's treatment and awoke in the morning free of pain. He arose and went about his normal routine.

Almost joking, Martin had whispered to him as he bound him up, "Don't pay any attention to what the doctors said. You'll probably die some time or other, but not of this illness."

A few years later Brother Ferdinand had another attack of the same disease, so painful that he almost regretted not having departed for the next world when he had suffered from the the same illness in the monastery with his brethren and surrounded by every care. Now he was traveling alone in a desert valley on the road between Arequipa and Lima, without a doctor, without a priest, without a house where he could ask for shelter. And the pain in his side increased to such a point that he was helpless.

Since no help was to be had from earth, he begged help from heaven, praying with all the fervor of his heart to St. Dominic and St. Francis to help him in his desperate situation. He was still praying when a young Franciscan, passing by on his mule, stopped and gave Brother Ferdinand the comfort of the sacraments. Then, while he continued to pray with his eyes closed, asking to be allowed to live and to serve God, it seemed to him that he saw St. Dominic, who said to him, "My son, you will not die, but take heed to mend your ways and serve God better."

When he opened his eyes, he found he could walk and happily resumed his journey to Lima. When he reached the monastery, he went to the cell of the prior to ask his blessing. On his way there, he saw the door of the infirmary supply room open and put his head in to tell Martin about his adventures. Without giving him time to speak, Martin said, "You had two good protectors and should be grateful to our Patriarch. But be sure to do what you promised him."

After such an experience it is inconceivable that Brother Ferdinand did not try to mend his ways and serve God better. But later that did not prevent his falling into difficulties with his superior and succumbing to melancholy because of it. So many other times he had thought that the life of a priest would be a solution for his difficulties, but was it not a little too late?

"Come, come, courage. Fourteen years from now you won't have to think any more about these things!" said Martin, who could not bear to see people sad.

"True, because fourteen years from now I'll be dead," responded Brother Ferdinand, more lugubrious than ever.

Instead, fourteen years later Father Ferdinand ascended to the altar, overcome with joy and emotion.[14]

One day Martin was discussing spiritual matters with a rather elderly Father, one of those naturally rigid and intransigent men, but gifted nevertheless with great goodness of heart and virtue. They were talking about regular observance of the rule and Christian perfection when a young religious passed by, wearing a shining new pair of shoes which fitted him perfectly and were a little too elegant. They were not the kind of shoes normally worn in a monastery.

The old priest was shocked by the sight of that pair of shoes just at the moment they were talking with such fervor of perfection and religious observance.

"What do you say of the light-mindedness of that young religious?" he asked his companion.

Martin did not like to pass judgment on others. If he had to give an opinion, he looked for the good side.

"No, no," he replied at once, "it is not a question of light-mindedness. The great providence of God permits this deviation so that sinners may be brought back to Him. You know, Father, there are people so accustomed to an easy life and to pleasures that they are frightened when one even mentions austerity to them. Let us imagine now that a man like that, whose life is quite disordered, comes here to confess his sins. . . . Do you think your austere appearance and those shoes as big as boats that you are wearing would inspire trust in his heart? Not at all! But if he saw that young priest with his beautiful little shoes, he might think, 'Now there is one who will understand me!' And he would go to confession, and then the grace of God would do the rest." [15]

The good priest accepted the lesson, and laughed heartily with Martin.

CHAPTER

⊱ 15 ⊰

He who believes in Me, the works that I do
he also shall do (John 14:12).

AT THE AGE OF SEVENTEEN Brother Louis Gutiérrez was preparing for his religious profession in the Dominican monastery
of St. Mary Magdalen. During recreation on one of the days
of carnival, he noticed another novice absent-mindedly holding a piece of fruit in his hand.

Brother Louis wanted to play a trick. He quietly drew near
the other novice and tried to snatch away the fruit. He meant
only to joke, to take the fruit and then return it. But in the
excitement of the scuffle, he closed his hand over the fruit and
the knife the other novice was holding and slashed his fourth
and fifth fingers deeply.

Frightened more by the prospect of an eventual rebuke
from the master of novices than by the cut, and convinced
that since the wound was so fresh the only thing necessary was
to stop the flow of blood, Brother Louis bound up his fingers
tightly with the first piece of cloth he found and waited for
the two cuts to heal.

He left the bandage on for three days. On the third day a
fever, throbbing pain in the fingers, and a pain that paralyzed
his arms, forced him to take off the bandage to see how his
fingers were getting along. He saw a swollen hand, inflamed
and peacock-blue, from which the fourth finger hung inert,
for the nerves had been cut.

By this time Brother Louis was under no illusion and realized that this was no joking matter. He recalled that during

the days of vacation Martin was accustomed to come to the monastery of the Magdalen to perform penance, and he started to look for him. He found him in a cell and knocked at the door.

"What is it?" called a voice from within, without the least trace of annoyance, and immediately the door opened. Martin saw a weeping novice who showed him the finger dangling from his hand in which gangrene had perhaps already set in. One glance was enough for Martin to make an exact diagnosis. There was no time to be lost. Without any pious exaggeration, Martin began by encouraging the patient. "Don't be afraid, little one! Your cut is a nasty one, and it is dangerous, too, but God will heal you." He led Louis out to the garden, near the laundry. He looked for an herb, the herb of Santa María, cut off two leaves, crushed them between two stones, applied the pulp to the wounds, and spread it over the hand to cover all the inflamed part, making the sign of the cross over it.

Brother Louis regretted having acted too quickly the first time, and he was now inclined to exaggerate in the other sense. He would have preferred to see Martin use some surgical instrument to be sure that the treatment was efficacious. When Martin finished smearing the crushed herb on his hand, Louis could not resist asking, "Is that all?"

"Yes, that is all," Martin answered serenely. "Go back to your novitiate in peace."

Still mistrustful, the young novice looked at his hand. The swelling was already beginning to go down, and his arm no longer pained him with every movement.

The next morning Brother Louis was astonished to see that not only had the inflammation vanished, but the cut nerves were obviously rejoined in some fashion or other, because he had regained full use of his finger.

For several minutes Louis flexed his fourth finger and rejoiced over the recovered use of it. It was such a joy to be able to move his fingers, hand and arm without pain. He would have been tempted to believe the whole experience of the past few days was a bad dream if the scars of the two cuts were not visible on the last two fingers of his hand.

And the scars remained, for in 1660 Louis, then a priest, showed them in relating the facts during the Process. The marvel had taken place around 1630.[1]

In healing Brother Louis, Martin worked as he usually did. As Father Gonsalvo García de Guzmán described it: "Brother Martin applied an ordinary remedy to the wound, and making a sign of the cross over it, without any other remedy, after a few days the wound was healed."[2]

Martin did not neglect the "ordinary remedies." He never forgot he was a doctor and that he had spent many hours during his youth studying remedies and the properties of medicinal herbs. When he was treating a patient, he was first of all a doctor. It would not have seemed right to him to dispense with his skills and ask for a miracle where none was necessary.

One time, for example, someone who suffered from poor digestion and insomnia apparently wished to obtain an astonishing cure. He locked Martin in to force him to stay with him until he was healed. Martin certainly laughed to himself over this dramatic action, and suggested the remedy counseled by ordinary good sense, a remedy anyone could have suggested if the oppressive summer climate of Peru were taken into consideration. "Put your bed between the door and the window, where you will get more air." Brother John de Vargas, who had expected something astounding and almost miraculous, had the good sense, however, to follow the simple, logical advice. And the restful sleep he enjoyed that night improved his digestion and persuaded him to follow the prescription the following nights as well.³

The case of Brother Andrew Martínez was altogether different, being one of the rare cases in which Martin had recourse to a remedy that was bizarre, to say the least. Andrew had just made his vows when he fell ill of tertian fever. After the fever had dragged on for a considerable length of time, he realized that his lungs were affected. He gave up all hope of recovery and fell into a state of melancholy.

One day Martin saw him in this discouraged state of mind and had compassion on him. He told Brother Andrew to take courage and advised him to take a good bath that very night in the pool in the center of the novitiate cloister.

Brother Andrew laughed at the idea. Martin must have been joking to suggest such a thing to anyone who was so weak he could barely stand on his feet.

But Martin was not joking at all and repeated his advice: a good, cold bath when night had fallen was what he needed to regain his health.

This time Brother Andrew stopped laughing and took the advice seriously. Perhaps he thought, "I am going to die anyhow, so I might as well try it." Someone who learned about the plan tried to dissuade him, saying, "Are you mad? With the disease you have!"

But Andrew had made up his mind. He ate with the others that evening and when the whole community had gone to their cells, he went to his also. About ten o'clock that night he went down to the cloister, took off his habit, and plunged into the pool. The water was so cold that he lost his breath, and hastily and angrily he jumped out of the pool. But then he decided that the immersion had been too rapid to be called a bath and resolutely he plunged in again. He stayed in the water so long that he was paralyzed by the cold and could not get out alone. Happily a lay brother passed by who fished him out, and finding him completely benumbed, dried him off, wrapped him in wool, and put him to bed, trying to warm him as best he could with blankets and hot ashes in a brazier.

Hardly had the good lay brother finished wrapping him up in the covers when Brother Andrew fell asleep and slept soundly until morning. When he awoke, he found he was cured.[4]

Martin did not abuse this type of strange remedy. He preferred ordinary remedies, or those which, even if at first glance they did not seem capable of improving the situation, at least would not make it worse. Martin used his remedies and asked God to make them efficacious as he made the sign of the cross over the affected part, but even in this prayer and this sign of the cross there was nothing dramatic. Martin invoked God's aid in utter simplicity, just as anyone with as much faith as a grain of mustard seed would invoke His help for any act whatsoever. But the Gospel says that this minimum of faith is sufficient to make the forces of nature obedient to a degree even exceeding our expectations.

In Martin's case, God was always ready to hear his prayers, to give without measure, to fulfill his simple requests with divine generosity. Truly, the Spirit of Love was almost at the orders of this humble brother "to minister different graces and gifts." And Martin could not prevent God's being generous. Even had he been able to do so, he would not have wished it, because the generosity of divine goodness helped his suffering brothers in Christ. And so Martin, with complete simplicity, drew upon the source of infinite wealth.

"I saw it done this way in France, in the hospitals of Bayonne," Martin said one time, to dispel the doubts of his colleagues in the infirmary about the efficacy of some treatment still new in Lima.[5]

Martin made the remark with the same simplicity with which he would have spoken of having learned it in the school of Marcel de Rivero, without realizing that his affirmation, for those who had known him a long time and knew he had never been away from Lima, was equivalent to a proof of his ability to travel from one place to another and exert his power in many places at once. This power, too, he had received practically without measure.

Martin had received extraordinary gifts, but he did not use them at his whim or fancy. Every displacement to a place near or far—whether it was a question of going to teach Christian doctrine to the children of the Far East, to restore peace in a family at the gates of Lima, to bring aid to a Christian fallen into the hands of the Moslems in Morocco, or to learn the latest discoveries in medicine in a hospital in France—every miraculous displacement through the gift of agility or his projected power sprang, as did all his actions from charity.

One night Martin left the monastery, all of whose doors were locked, and went to Lima. He entered the hospital of St. Ann and went to the bed of a dying Indian. No one had told him the Indian was dying without baptism. He began the conversation with some general questions, but swiftly came to the point that interested him most. "Are you baptized?"

The Indian was so gravely ill that he answered with difficulty, but no long discussion was needed for him and Martin to understand each other. In a few minutes Martin sent for the hospital chaplain, who baptized the Indian. The Indian died, and his soul, fragrant with newly received grace, left the body worn out by so much privation and suffering, and went to its eternal reward.

Martin returned to the monastery, entering as he had gone out, through the barred and locked doors.[6]

Since the care of the sick was Martin's principal occupation, it was natural that the Holy Spirit should bestow His gifts in a special manner to help him in this work. "To help the sick in their needs and afflictions, he penetrated the thickest walls, and the locked doors of the cells, and entered the most secret rooms of the novitiate at forbidden hours, having learned by divine revelation what the sick needed and suffered," said Father Christopher de Toro, who reinforced his testimony with a personal experience.

Father Christopher, like Brother Andrew, had just finished his novitiate when he had need of Martin, but for a disease different from that which was cured by a cold bath. Christopher had just been professed when he developed a severe toothache. He bore it for several days, then decided to have the tooth extracted. He went to a lay brother in the infirmary, who was a specialist in extractions, though he was a bit rough about it, so rough that in pulling the tooth he tore the gums and the tooth socket and caused a hemorrhage that could not be stopped.

After a week of hemorrhages, no food, and nights passed in such pain that he could not sleep, Brother Christopher was at the end of his strength and fainted frequently. What was worse, he began to lose all hope of being healed and he succumbed to discouragement.

A little hope revived, however, when he remembered that in addition to the poor brother who extracted teeth, Martin was also in the infirmary. He thought that if he still had any chance of being cured, it lay in the hands of the saintly infirmarian, and he obtained permission from the master of students for Martin to come to see him.

Martin entered the cell of Brother Christopher. He found him in tears, suffering intensely. Martin began by giving him two little taps, or caresses, on the painful cheek and an encouraging, "Calm down, my boy, don't worry. With the help of God this won't amount to anything."

Martin took some dry thread and put it into the socket of the tooth. The blood ceased to flow and the intense pain vanished.

Brother Christopher felt as if he had been reborn. He enjoyed his meal that evening, and the moment he put his head on his pillow, he peacefully fell asleep.

But at one o'clock in the morning he awoke with a start. The pain had come back, more severe than ever. The return of the suffering after several hours of relief renewed all the painful sensations of the preceding days, including an almost invincible feeling of discouragement.

Brother Christopher lifted his head from the pillow, which seemed to cause an intolerable agony, and sat up in his bed weeping. For the moment it was all he could do. Even if had called for help, no one would have answered at that hour of the morning because it was the hour of Matins and the whole community was in choir. Even the religious who shared his cell had gone to Matins.

As he wept, he thought of Martin, who had given him such relief a short time before. If only Martin could be with him!

And there was Martin, at his bedside, smiling over his discouragement, tapping him affectionately again on the sore cheek, and repeating what he had said the first time. "Come, lad, don't grieve so, this is nothing at all!"

Martin removed the bandage and the intact threads from the tooth socket. The threads were so intact and dry that the young religious was forced to conclude that "he had put them there to conceal the fact that the healing was the result of the contact of his hand." And this time the pain was quieted for good.[7]

In caring for his sick, Martin had at his disposal, on the one hand, his medical knowledge, his experience, a will which carried him through an unceasing, unwearying and intelligent activity; and on the other hand, he had the gifts he had received because of his high degree of sanctity. He drew upon all these resources in accordance with the needs that arose, without ever neglecting natural means, and without losing his sense of balance because of the abundance and wealth of the gifts over which he was given control. "His left hand weighed as much as his right" [8] could be said of his simple way of employing the natural and the supernatural without ever seeming to be a miraculous healer, without assuming false airs, without even letting any difference be seen between the work done by the left hand and that done by the right. If anything, as Christopher de Toro testified, Martin preferred that the work of the left hand be seen, for it seemed less dangerous to him to be esteemed as a doctor than to be considered a saint.

But he did not always succeed. Sometimes the impatience of a patient, sometimes providential circumstances rendered his precautions useless. What had happened to Martin in the last year of his life during the illness of Archbishop Felician de la Vega had already happened, the year before, in the case of Father Louis de Guadalupe. The facts were related during the Process by Father John de Barbazán, who had played an important role in the affair.

About three o'clock one morning Father John was awakened by a loud knocking at the door of his cell. It was a Negro who begged him to go at once to administer the last sacraments to Father Louis, who was dying. Without wasting a minute, Father John rushed to the bedside of the sick man. He found him speechless and barely breathing, so he had to give him absolution without being able to hear his confession.

Martin arrived, carrying a brazier filled with hot embers. As usual, he greeted the sick man with an invitation to praise God. Then he sprinkled wine on the brazier and, drawing near the bed and pulling back the covers, he asked Father Louis to show him where the pain was so that he could apply heat to it.

The only reply Father Louis could make was to take Martin's hand and press it firmly on the painful spot. The immediate relief afforded him by the touch of Martin's hand allowed him to speak, and he exclaimed, "Blessed be God and this good servant of God! The pain is gone, and there is no need of the hot embers!"

Martin was overcome with confusion because of what his own hand had rashly done, and after a moment of silence, with his eyes on the ground, he burst out protesting against Father Louis' words. "Is this the way you make fun of a poor mulatto?"

Without another word he left abruptly and went off to ring the morning bell.[9]

Sometimes the Giver of gifts and graces acted without warning Martin. Francis Ortiz was among the disciples who visited Martin's cell. He was "a man of such good life," according to Father de Saldaña, "that he was considered and venerated as a saint." Francis suffered from severe headaches. One morning, while he was in the church of the Holy Rosary to assist at Mass and receive Holy Communion, such a severe headache began that as soon as the Mass was over he fled to Martin's cell in search of help. He found Martin in the supply room.

"I'm at my wits' ends," he said as he entered. "I feel as if my head were in an iron vise."

"Come, come, don't be upset," replied Martin in his gentle, encouraging voice, sit down here. Perhaps you need something to eat. It is merely a question of weakness. Wait for me here; I'll be right back with a bit of something for you!" And he went out.

Francis Ortiz, left alone with a head which felt as if it were filled with lead, felt he must do something better than sit on a chair. Noticing Martin's bed, he lay down on it on his side, putting one side of his head on the hard bolster which served Martin as a pillow. The mere contact was enough to free that side of his head from the pain.

Meanwhile Martin had come back with a bowl of soup and invited him to eat. "One moment," said Francis Ortiz, "is this your bolster?"

"It is ours, brother," Martin replied.

"Then I understand," cried Francis, and following his line of reasoning said to himself, "If this pillow could free me from the pain on one side of my head, why should it not do likewise for the other side? Let's try it."

At once he rolled over to his other side, putting his aching head on the pillow, and the pain disappeared there too, so completely that in getting up off the bed Francis found it difficult to believe he had felt so unwell a few moments before. And, holy man that he was, he thanked God first of all for having healed him, but especially for having given such an abundance of grace to His servant Martin that even objects Martin used could work miracles. Then Francis went to see the prior and related all the details of what had happened, telling them as well to many other people.[10]

Father John de Barbazán was right when he asserted that Martin was "a living instrument of the marvels of God for the health of the sick." Natural and supernatural health were the objects of Martin's ministry, with the aid of all the gifts with which divine charity had enriched him, but especially with the aid of the gift of knowing the real state of a sick man in spite of outward appearances.

"Drop this work, it is not at all urgent," Martin said one day, taking out of Brother Ferdinand's hands whatever he was doing at the moment, "and call someone at once to give the sacraments to Brother Lawrence. There is not a moment to lose!"

The doctors had given up hope for Brother Lawrence de Pareja, but since the good old brother continued to drag along even though he complained of his infirmities, Brother Ferdinand did not believe the end was near. But the priest carrying the Viaticum had not yet arrived at the door of the infirmary when Brother Lawrence died.

On the other hand, when Brother Ferdinand de Valdés had already received the last sacraments and the clappers were readied at the door of his cell to call the community for the last prayers, Martin had stated that he would not die that time. And a few days later, he was well again.[11]

One day a family from Callao, consisting of the father, mother and six children, knocked at the door of the monastery of the Holy Rosary. They had come to venerate the body of St. Rose of Lima and to ask that Servant of God to obtain the cure of one of their boys. The child had been carried to the church in a litter. A seventh son, Brother Vincent, was in the monastery of the Holy Rosary, and the prior granted him the privilege of showing the body of the Saint to his parents. But the mother was not satisfied.

"Call Brother Martin for me," she said to her son.

Martin came, and the mother begged him, "Ask God to restore the health of my son who is ill!"

"I will do that willingly," said Martin with his usual gracious manner, filled with compassion for the grief of the mother. "But I must warn you that this son and four others will die very shortly, and only the youngest will be left to you. It is the will of God."

That was precisely what happened, and the surviving son, Peter Quijano Ceballos, testified to it.[12]

Martin was sent for one day that he might visit and comfort a young wife who was about to give birth to a child and was filled with apprehension. Martin went to see her, accompanied by Father Francis de la Cruz, and told the young mother not to be afraid, that the baby would be born without any difficulty, but that later the child would cause her much grief. Marcel de Rivero, who survived Martin, saw the son of this woman contract a marriage which was displeasing to his parents and, bit by bit, cause his family's ruin.[13]

From the case cited above as well as from numerous others, we know that Martin sometimes visited the sick outside the monastery and helped them by his natural and supernatural gifts. The Dominican tertiary, Louise de Santa María, after a miraculous cure foretold by Martin, entered the Second Order Dominican convent dedicated to St. Catherine of Siena. Frances Vélez Michel, whom Martin visited because of their long standing friendship (they were of the same age and born in the same quarter of the city), secured a piece of his habit which she applied to her body until she was freed of pain.[14]

But it is logical that the greater part of the extraordinary events brought about by the power of God took place within the walls of the monastery of the Holy Rosary. No place else ever witnessed life given back to a dead man through Martin's instrumentality. We owe the story of this event to Brother Ferdinand de Aragonés. He had participated in every detail of the event, and many years later he remembered it and the resulting excitement.

Brother Thomas lay ill in one of the cells of the infirmary.

He was an old lay brother who had worked humbly and hard for many years in the monastery of the Holy Rosary. All during his life he had been an outstanding example of every virtue, and now he was fading away gently, almost imperceptibly. He had already been anointed.

Martin often visited Brother Thomas. In addition to being fond of him because they had worked together for such a long time, he felt it a sacred duty to alleviate the last sufferings of a man whose life of dedication to the Order had been so exemplary.

Since Martin could not watch over him constantly, as was now necessary, he assigned a young Spanish assistant to Brother Thomas' cell so that he could take care of the sick man day and night.

One morning the young Spaniard heated the soup and egg, which were invariably Brother Thomas' breakfast. He helped Thomas eat, put everything in the room in order, and then left the cell for a while. When he returned, Brother Thomas was dead.

Terror stricken, the lad ran in search of Brother Martin and found him in the supply room with Brother Ferdinand. They went at once to Brother Thomas' cell. The old brother was already cold.

Martin said that the signal must be given with the clappers to call the community for the recitation of the prayers which are said when the soul leaves the body. While the community was assembling, he and Brother Ferdinand closed the door and prepared to lay out the body. Ferdinand went to get a clean habit and prepare a table on which to lay the dead man, and Martin began to pray before the crucifix.

Some secret was certainly revealed to Martin during his prayer, because when he rose from his knees, instead of preparing Brother Thomas' body for burial, he put his mouth close to his ear and called him by name: "Brother Thomas!"

Thomas responded with a faint sigh.

"Look, Brother Ferdinand, he is alive!" cried Martin to Ferdinand.

"It doesn't seem so to me," replied Ferdinand. And again Martin called, "Brother Thomas!"

This time Thomas moved his lips and tongue a little, sighed again, and seemed to yawn.

"Brother Thomas!" Martin called loudly for the third and last time, and the face of the corpse assumed a living color.

"Don't you see that he is alive?" asked Martin, covering up Brother Thomas again. And Ferdinand exclaimed, "How powerful is God who gives life to the dead!"

Martin opened the door of the cell and told the community waiting outside that they could go away in peace because Brother Thomas had regained his senses.

"A fine thing!" commented Brother Ferdinand coming to the door. "Brother Martin says he has regained his senses, when actually he has come back to this world from the next!"

But Brother Thomas did not seem to have made up his mind to remain on earth. He lay immobile on his bed, his eyes staring fixedly. Martin had the yolks of three fresh eggs brought to him. When Brother Ferdinand went up to the bed with the three egg yolks, he saw a flash of understanding in the lifeless eyes.

With the adeptness acquired over the many years they had taken care of the sick, Ferdinand and Martin fed the old brother and succeeded in getting him to swallow the egg yolks. Little by little Brother Thomas regained consciousness. Martin left the cell only when the return of his faculties was complete and certain.[15]

It was astounding to see the power of God employing Martin as a docile and adaptable instrument to work a prodigy as amazing as that of recalling a dead man to life. But perhaps the condescension of divine wisdom is even more wonderful and touching when it suggested to Martin a simple means of opening a soul embittered by suffering to the influence of grace, by revealing to him the secret desire of a heart, although that desire was only for . . . a salad of capers!

The story of the capers came about this way. Father Peter de Montesdoca had an infected leg. The infection was so far advanced that amputation was discussed. One can easily understand that the prospect did not please Father Peter. As surgery was practiced in the seventeenth century, the amputation of a leg involved atrocious pain during the operation, and death often followed shortly thereafter.

The day before that fixed for the operation, Father Peter lay in his cell, tormented by gloomy thoughts. It is not surprising that when he saw a brother infirmarian entering with his dinner, he greeted him with words that would have been rude under any circumstances, but were less so to this particular brother infirmarian who rejoiced in humiliations. The fact that the infirmarian who brought Father Peter his dinner was called Martin de Porres almost effaced the rudeness of the greeting he received upon entering the cell. It was common knowledge that the sick could relieve their tensions by insulting him any time they seemed to feel the need of it.

Paying no attention to the welcome Father Peter gave him, Martin uncovered the dish he had brought and presented to the sick man the most appetizing salad of capers ever seen in Lima.

Father Peter's eyes opened wide. "But, little father," he said, radically changing his tone of voice and manner, "is this my dinner? Who gave you the idea of this salad of capers?"

The yearning for a salad of capers exactly like the one he now saw before him had tormented the sick man for the last twenty-four hours. Food was revolting to him, and the only flavor he could think of as bearable or pleasing was the fresh, tart taste of capers. But how had Martin known that? Father Peter had not said a word about it to anyone.

Seated on his bed, Father Peter reflected and looked at his salad of capers instead of eating it. If Martin had been able to divine his secret wish, that meant that the goodness of God was taking such good care of him that even this little consolation was provided for him. And while the Supreme Majesty condescended to grant his smallest wish, he, absorbed in his own troubles, had greeted Martin roughly and rudely at the very moment that Martin was bringing him such a precious gift!

Emotion and repentance softened Father Peter's heart, which up to that moment had been frozen by the thought of his imminent misfortune. He begged Martin's forgiveness and thanked him for the gift. Suddenly hope flashed into his mind. "Brother Martin, would you mind looking at my leg? You know that it is to be amputated tomorrow."

Martin leaned over and gently began to unwind the bandage, taking great care not to jar the leg. He knew what the end of the affair would be, but after the preceding events he could not refuse Father Peter's request.

He freed the leg of the bandage and gently put his hand on it. Nothing else.

The leg was healed.[16]

In 1634 torrential rains caused a terrifying rise in the waters of the Rimac River. In various localities around Lima the river overflowed, causing serious damage. When the crest of the flood reached Lima, one of the buildings in greatest danger was a church dedicated to our Lady. Since there were furnishings of great value in the church, the citizens of the city strove to save the treasure.

When they were about to begin the salvage work, Martin arrived. He picked up three large pebbles and, after having invoked the Most Holy Trinity, he placed one pebble at the water's edge. He threw the second into the muddy water a short distance from the water's edge. He threw the third into the very center of the current. Then he fell on his knees to pray. Those who had come to empty the church of its treasures followed his example and in a short time saw that the flood was subsiding. A little while later the river had regained its normal bed.

Filled with enthusiasm and still a little under the influence of their initial amazement, the people decided to express their gratitude by building a new church in a safer location. But Martin dissuaded them, assuring them that the waters of the Rimac would never destroy the church of *Nuestra Señora de las Cabezas.*

And time has proved that Martin was right.[17]

CHAPTER

≻ 16 ≺

The path of the just, as a shining light, goeth forwards and increaseth even to perfect day (Prov. 4:18).

THE FIRST OF JANUARY, 1639, found Martin in his sixtieth year. The first of January, 1640, he would no longer be on earth.

The first months of 1639 marked no change in Martin's life. But as summer came on, Felician de Vega, bishop of La Paz, Bolivia, was made archbishop of Mexico City. He interrupted his trip to his new see with a visit at Lima, a stop that could have been the last one of his life if the healing powers of Martin's hands had not been employed in time to cure him of the pneumonia which had stricken him during his journey.

That event almost brought about a remarkable change in Martin's life. The archbishop, happy about his cure and delighted to have found his old advisor again, asked the Father Provincial to let him take Martin with him to Mexico. Since it would have been difficult to say no to an archbishop, the Father Provincial said yes, but he did it with a heavy heart, not only because he personally would regret Martin's leaving, but also because he knew all the friars would be grieved by it.

Martin, on the other hand, was happy when he learned of his superior's decision. Life in Lima was becoming too burdensome for him. He was too well known. There were too many people who treated him as if he were an oracle. It's all very well to give advice—it was an act of charity and he did it willingly—but it should not go too far. And the people of Lima were going too far. Weren't they getting the bad habit of calling him "holy Brother Martin?" [1]

In Mexico he would be unknown, and he could hope to live there in his beloved obscurity, hiding his insignificant self behind the splendor of the archbishop and his court. When he returned to the monastery after healing Archbishop Felician, a brother asked him if it would not have been better to stay in the palace of His Excellency the archbishop. The reply he gave then was a proof of his fidelity to the choice of the more humble part. That reply was still valid, even after the will of his superior assigned him to the palace of the archbishop. There, more than ever, Martin would have preserved the humility characteristic of his whole life.

But the trip to Mexico, according to Brother Francis de Santa Fe, pleased Martin because he hoped it might be a first step towards Japan, a land sanctified by the blood of so many Dominican martyrs, a land of hope for Martin.[2]

For the moment, however, the departure did not have to be considered, since His Excellency the archbishop intended to stay a few months more in Lima before resuming his journey.

Martin carried on his ordinary life without thinking about the morrow. One day the other religious were amazed to see him wearing a new habit. In the forty-five years since Martin had entered the monastery of the Holy Rosary, no one had ever seen him in a new habit.

"What's happened?" Father John de Barbazán asked him. This new habit on Martin gave him a strange feeling of uneasiness, it seemed like a false note. But, after all, Martin had to prepare for the departure for Mexico, and certainly he could not accompany the archbishop clad in his usual ragged attire.

Martin divined Father John's thought and laughed. "This is the habit I am to be buried in," he replied very simply.

Father John did not laugh. He too was Martin's faithful disciple, and strove to walk in the light of that humble, simple, luminous life. Now it seemed to him that in an instant everything was plunged into darkness. He himself was to leave in a few days, but he had hoped to find Martin at Holy Rosary upon his return, since he would not, perhaps, have to stay permanently with the archbishop of Mexico. And now he must renounce even this faint hope.

But when Father Barbazán went to bid him good-bye, Martin said to him, "We will see each other soon, because you will not be absent from Lima very long."

Father Barbazán answered, "I cannot possibly return before the end of the year, because the superiors are sending me to Cuzco to teach theology." And he set out on his journey.

Shortly after, some unforeseen circumstance forced him to

return, and his second departure must have been deferred for several months or cancelled entirely, because when Martin died, Father Barbazán was still in Lima and was in the monastery of the Holy Rosary.[3]

Martin also said something about his imminent death to John de Figueroa. The latter asked him to pray for his soul when the moment came for him to die, and Martin answered quietly, "I shall die first." [4]

A few days after Martin had put on the new habit, he removed it and took to his bed. He fell ill with a violent fever and severe pains in his whole body, especially in his head. Autumn had arrived, and every year at that season Martin had to fight against a recurrence of quartan fever, but this was not an ordinary attack. He knew it and said so from the first, because the Holy Spirit, who all during Martin's long medical career had frequently revealed to him the outcome of the illnesses of his patients, revealed to him the end of his own illness.

The very day on which the fever struck him, Martin told his brethren clearly that this would be his last illness, and the friars, alarmed at the thought of losing their dear Martin, at once called Doctor Navarro, one of the physicians for the monastery.

We have no record of Doctor Navarro's diagnosis, but we do know that he ordered the application of a poultice made with the blood of freshly killed young roosters to relieve Martin's headaches. With a calm gesture Martin restrained those who were hastening to carry out the prescription, saying it was a pity to kill the poor animals to concoct a useless remedy. And even Doctor Navarro admitted that there was nothing to be done.[5]

That was Martin's last act of love for animals. And as in his love for all created things, so also in everything else, Martin in death was what he had been in life. His whole life had been a preparation for death. Now that death was near, there was nothing to change. He did not change anything, but concentrated all his energy on being faithful to the end, while his physical forces began to desert him.

When the fever attacked him, he lay down on his usual bed of boards, in his worn sackcloth robe. The authority of the prior forced him to change to a real bed and to exchange the sackcloth robe for a tunic of ordinary cloth. Martin obeyed, docile as a child. But the tunic which should have been a relief became such a torment that he begged the superior to let him put the sackcloth on again.[6]

When that permission was granted, Martin asked for nothing else. The fever consumed him, the sudden variations in his temperature wore down his bodily resistance. All his members pained him, and his head seemed on the point of bursting. He abandoned his body to the torments of the disease without a complaint, so that he could continue to unite his sufferings passively to those of the passion of Jesus, now that his weakness prevented his doing so in a more active form.

His expression did not change. He was as serene and calm as always. But his eyes and his smile took on a softer and more profound light. The onlookers felt the presence of something great and holy in that poor body worn out by labor and suffering, something that made the bed of the dying religious a center of strong attraction.

Now that approaching death meant the end of all desire, what a little thing his whole life seemed to him! How brief his sixty years seemed, viewed at the end! And the labors which had filled those years seemed very inconsequential, now that it was time to draw the line and sum them up. So he used the presence of his brethren around him to make reparation for what seemed to him to have been lacking. He accused himself of having wasted his life, of having been careless in the service of God. He begged all of them to forgive him for the bad example he had given, and to pray for him. They could not restrain their tears. They were torn between their admiration for such great humility and their own knowledge of his heroic virtues, between the memory of all the good they had received from him and their sorrow over the loss facing them. They were filled with compassion for the sufferings of the brother who had always had the heart of a father for everyone.

Two or three days before he died, Martin asked Brother Anthony Gutiérrez, who had been assigned to him as infirmarian, "Why are you weeping, little angel?" The fact that he was already almost beyond all the formalities of this world gave Martin the right to speak with this simple familiarity.

Brother Anthony struggled for words in the midst of the tears which filled and refilled his eyes. "I weep because Your Reverence (and the formula of respect came spontaneously from his heart) told me you would die, and that it is the will of God that you should die of this illness. Since you must die, I weep, for you are my father and my whole good!"

Martin looked at him with a glance filled with affection. Then he said to him in a very sober and gentle tone of voice, "Don't weep, Brother, because perhaps I will be more useful there than here." [7]

Martin's absolute confidence in divine mercy and the merits of the Passion made him speak in that fashion. Even though his life seemed empty to him, his trust was boundless in the goodness of the Savior who would take him to heaven with Him.

The news of his illness spread throughout the city and his friends outside the monastery, no less saddened than the religious, came to Holy Rosary to see him again, to ask his advice once more. He was at the point of death, but anyone who had not known him before would have believed he was well, seeing him calmly sitting up in bed, without a complaint, without any other thought than that of exhorting his listeners to do good.[8] But for those who knew him, seeing Martin confined to his bed was a certain sign that his life was at an end.

One of the most faithful visitors was Francis Ortiz. Each time he entered the room, Martin begged him to pray for him, and Francis willingly agreed to do so. One evening he could not bring himself to leave, and when the Fathers who were staying with the sick brother insisted that he should leave and take some rest, Francis thought, "This could be the last night of his life, and so I want to bid him farewell." Turning back to the bed where Martin was lying on his side, with his face to the wall, Francis leaned over and kissed Martin on the neck. Martin's reponse was to raise his arm and press Francis' head against his own with such force and for so long a time that Francis was dripping with perspiration, while he became aware of a perfume he had never smelled before, more fragrant than the sweetest flowers.[9]

The news also reached the ears of the enemy of all good, who made a last effort to conquer one who for sixty years had defeated him. Invisible, he drew near the bed, too, and studied the lay of the land to see which would be the best point from which to launch his attack. It would have to be a strong assault with tried and sure weapons against such well-guarded strength. The devil could find nothing better than his old battlehorse and began to wave phantasms of pride before the dying man's mind.

"Now you've won," he said to Martin. "You have spurned all obstacles beneath your feet; you're a saint! You can cease beating your breast; now is the moment of triumph!"

Martin at once recognized the false voice of the father of all lies and repulsed him by redoubling his acts of humility. But the prize was too important to be renounced so easily. The enemy persisted, concentrating all his forces like a battering ram on one point. If he could force a breech there, everything else would fall. He persisted with the monotony of a drop of water falling on a stone, of a hammer beating on an anvil. He hoped Martin would finally give in, out of sheer weariness.

The anguish of the struggle was visible on Martin's face. In suspense, the brethren watched and prayed. Suddenly one of them said, "Brother Martin, don't argue with the demon, who can make white seem black, and black seem white, with his sophisms and quibbling."

Martin opened his eyes and with a slightly mischievous smile answered the Father who had spoken to him, "Have no fear that the demon will waste his sophisms on any one who is not a theologian. He is too proud to use them against a poor mulatto!" [10]

Thrown off balance by the irony, the devil had to give up for the moment and leave the terrain to Another much more powerful than himself.

The viceroy came to the monastery to see his friend and counselor. The religious accompanied him to the cell and went to the door to announce the visitor, but there was no response. Martin was in ecstasy. The viceroy, a true gentleman, begged the Fathers not to disturb Martin, and he waited outside the room for more than a quarter of an hour, talking with the superiors and other religious about their dear Brother Martin's virtues.

When the ecstasy was over, the Count of Chinchón entered and knelt down near the bed. Taking Martin's hand and kissing it, he asked him to beg God's blessing on the land of which he was the ruler. Always a good teacher, Martin replied that he would willingly pray for him and for the State when he arrived in the presence of the Eternal King, but the viceroy must offer prayers and good works to obtain the divine blessing.

The illustrious visitor left the monastery, and when the religious had accompanied him to the door with all due honor, the Father Prior went back to Martin and rebuked him harshly for having made the viceroy wait so long outside his door. It was a strange reproof, since the ecstasy prevented Martin's realizing what was going on around him. But Father Saldaña knew with whom he was talking and what he wanted to learn. As usual, Martin listened to the rebuke without replying. The prior then commanded him in virtue of obedience to state why he had made the viceroy wait.

On one side of the room there was a small altar on which the Blessed Sacrament was reserved so that all would be ready when the moment came to give Viaticum to the dying man. Martin waved his hand towards the altar and said, "Near that altar there was the Most Holy Virgin Mary, my patron and advocate, and my father St. Dominic with St. Vincent Ferrer and many other saints and angels, and I was so occupied with those holy visitors that I could not receive any other at that moment." [11]

Death was very near, and Martin knew it. He asked to receive the last sacraments. Once more he renewed his general confession and begged everyone's forgiveness for his bad example, as he had already done so many times since he fell ill. Then he received Viaticum and extreme unction.

The struggle went on. Every new access of fever was preceded by chills that shook his whole body with an agony that bathed him in cold sweat. All his members seemed pierced by knives of pain. But even now, no word of complaint escaped him.[12]

The enemy returned again. He appeared under strange and

horrible forms. Since the appeal to pride had not succeeded, he would try to overwhelm Martin's soul with terror and despair. And Martin continued to clasp the crucifix and keep his eyes fixed on the sacred wounds, source of mercy and of hope.[13]

Father Francis de Paredes was near Martin's bed at that moment. He sensed the struggle going on in Martin's soul and suggested that he invoke St. Dominic. Martin replied, "It would be useless to ask him to come. He is already here with St. Vincent Ferrer."

St. Dominic could not neglect a son who for three-quarters of his life had worked with such love and such humility in his Order. The conquest of the enemy was definitive this time.

From then on, Martin remained immersed in deep peace in spite of the attacks of fever. Father Francis watched over him attentively because each attack could be the last, and the community must be called in time. Twice he started to give the signal, and twice Martin held him back. When for the third time he asked if the moment had not come to call the community, Martin gave his consent with a nod of his head.[14]

At the sound of the clappers, from every corner of the big monastery everyone came to the cell of the dying brother: old priests, young students, novices, lay brothers, lay helpers—all the great family of Holy Rosary rushed towards the cell where Martin had entered into his last agony. The first to arrive crowded around the bed, but many were outside the cell, their eyes fixed on the door and their hearts beating in suspense. Many wept, kneeling around the bed or standing, crowded against the walls of the cell. There was no one there who did not have his own particular motive for grieving over the death of the humble brother; no one who had not received some service from him, some word of encouragement or some good example, not to mention those who had been healed, or whose vocation Martin had saved in a moment of doubt; those who had received favors in exchange for insults; those who had been witnesses of his penances or ecstasies or miracles; those who had entrusted themselves to him as a guide on the path to spiritual perfection.

Martin gazed steadily at an old priest, who wept like a baby at the foot of his bed. John de Barbazán, caught behind the barrier of the other friars, was overwhelmed with the desire to see the face of the "judge of his heart." He slipped slowly along the wall and managed to reach the head of the bed. Just seeing Martin made him weep. Martin was already almost rigid, but Father John's intense desire to have Martin look at him a last time made him ask an almost impossible thing. Martin heard his prayer, and recovering for a moment the power to move his neck, he turned his face towards him and smiled. Father John pulled a clean handkerchief out of his sleeve and dried the sweat of the death agony from the face of the dying man. Henceforward he preserved that handkerchief as a treasure.[15]

The prayers for the dying were ended. Martin lovingly continued to kiss the crucifix which he could still hold in his hands, while his brethren sang the *Salve Regina,* as is the custom of the Dominicans at the bedside of the dying. Then the Father Prior intoned the *Credo.* The entire community responded in unison, and the chant filled the cell and spread outside it. Those around the bed chanted with softer voices to diminish the vibration in the restricted space; those in the corridor chanted with full voices. The melody invaded the cloisters, and in the newly fallen night it mounted up towards the stars shining in the sky.

Martin listened to the choir of his brothers, and the chant filled him with bliss. The unmistakable timbre of those virile voices, fused in a harmony that was strong without harshness, sweet without affectation, revived the memory of the most beautiful moments of his life. For years that same sound of the monastic chant had come to his ears. During his nocturnal vigils it had come to him from the choir at the back of the church, when the psalms of Matins were chanted, a little muffled by the distance. He had heard it, full and triumphant, during the chanted Masses of solemn feasts, like an echo of the rejoicing of his own heart in the expectancy of the Eucharistic union. His own voice had joined that chant every evening after Compline, when the Queen of Mercy was honored in the singing of the *Salve Regina*.

But that chant of the *Credo!* Was it not his triumphal chant, the poem of his ideal, of his whole life?

Yes, Martin had believed in the heavenly Father, he had believed that His divine paternity would accept the tiny child rejected by his natural father, and had thrown himself into His omnipotent and loving arms.

He had believed in the goodness and the beauty of all things made by God: heaven and earth and all things contained within the sphere of the universe, down to the least among the living creatures.

He had believed in the reality of the invisible world of the spirit. He had understood that that world surpasses the visible world in variety, in beauty and in perfection. And he had preferred that invisible world to all the natural satisfactions creatures here below can offer.

He had believed in the Son, light and revelation of the impenetrable light of the Father; in the Word, who being life and truth, made Himself the way for us. And he had followed Him along His way. Following Him, he had absorbed the doctrine of love which sums up and contains all the laws. He had understood the work of the Spirit of Love in the restoration of man from servitude to liberty.

And he had believed in and had entrusted himself to that new Mother's heart, revealed to him by the mystery of the Incarnation; that most pure and holy temple of the union of the only-begotten Son of God with human nature, with all humanity, without exception of race or color or time or place, from which, like a bride, he received, together with His name, the title of his new nobility: "that we should be called, and should be the sons of God" (I John 3:1).

The choir chanted now with softer voices, and the friars were all on their knees, adoring in their hearts the mystery proclaimed by the words: ET HOMO FACTUS EST.

Martin let the crucifix drop on his breast and closed his eyes as if he had fallen asleep.[16]

CHAPTER

➤ 17 ◄

When thou shalt pour out thy soul to the hungry
and shalt satisfy the afflicted soul, then shall thy light
rise up in darkness, and thy darkness shall be
as the noonday (Isa. 58:10).

IT WAS ABOUT nine o'clock at night, November 3, 1639, when, without a tremor, without a sound, Martin's soul left the body which had been such a docile and heroic instrument of virtue, and entered the kingdom of eternal happiness.[1]

The chant died away on the lips of the friars. Their eyes were fixed on that face on which the involuntary contractions of pain had given way in an instant to an expression of peace, a peace which sweetly spread to all hearts and calmed their tears.

There was a moment of silence, while Archbishop Felician de Vega traced the sign of the cross over his friend. Then Father Saldaña began the prayers which are recited when the soul has just left the body. He invited all the saints of heaven and all the angels of the Lord to meet the soul of Martin, to accompany it and present it before the throne of the Most High.

The friars answered the prayers, following their brother in their thoughts on his awesome journey. When they recited the Psalm *"In exitu Israel de Aegypto,"* they felt they should rejoice rather than weep. Martin was freed of exile, had crossed the sea dry-shod, and had reached the shore of the true homeland.

When the last *"Amen"* had been said, the archbishop tried to say a word of consolation to the community, but emotion choked him. All he could say was, "Brethren, let us learn from Brother Martin how to die. This is the most difficult and most important lesson." [2]

Then he left to return to his palace. The prior and the other friars left the cell. Three or four religious remained to wash and clothe the corpse.

The viceroy's physician, Balthazar Carrasco de Orozco, had taken care of Martin in the last days of his illness, more as a friend than a doctor, because he soon realized that there was nothing to be done. He was present at the moment Martin died and certified that he was dead. This nobleman lived across from the bell tower of the church of the Holy Rosary. Many times he had awakened before dawn and had heard the sound of the blows Martin was inflicting upon himself or receiving from the hands of another in the room under the bell tower. [3]

The religious who were preparing to clothe Martin's body

knew of his penances. But when they removed the sackcloth robe, the frayed hair shirt and the huge iron chain drawn around his waist—all of which Martin had continued to wear even during his last illness—they were astounded and overcome with emotion to see the number of scars and open wounds on the body. It was incredible that a human being had been able to live and to work from morning to night in that condition.

Looking through the few possessions of the dead brother for the articles necessary to clothe him, the infirmarian found the new habit which had been such a surprise to all of them several weeks before. Father Barbazán remembered and he repeated Martin's words, "This is the habit I am to be buried in." [4]

They dressed him in the new habit of heavy cloth and were ready to carry his body into the church, when they were drawn to the infirmary by piercing cries.

It was Father John de Vargas, who was suffering so intensely that he could not repress his cries. For several days periodic attacks of severe pain had kept him in bed, and at the moment he was having another seizure.

The friars, who had just left Martin's cell, said to Father John, "Invoke Martin de Porres, whose loss we all feel so keenly!"

Hardly had Father John invoked Martin's name, when the pains vanished, and after a good night's sleep he found himself completely cured. [5]

Martin had not abandoned his own!

Consoled by this thought, the religious carried the body into the church. They arranged it with loving care on the catafalque Martin had lain down so many times for his brief nap, and lit the candles on each side. The pilasters and arches of the naves were lost in darkness. In the tiny circle of light created by the candles, the friars kept vigil and prayed the psalter. Perhaps some simply meditated.

In the light of the funeral candles, so many events in the life of the humble brother took on a new meaning. And if John de Barbazán, recalling all Martin had done in the monastery and outside of it, went on repeating with deep melancholy, "This void can never be filled," others thought that death could never write *"finis"* to the end of a life like his. God would reveal the virtues of His humble and good servant to the world.

Absorbed by these thoughts, Father Cyprian de Medina went up to the catafalque and touched the body. He was surprised and vexed to find it already stiff and rigid. But he was not discouraged by this untoward event, and in the presence of the most august Fathers of the monastery who formed the guard of honor, he protested aloud, almost crying out to his holy friend, "But what's this? So stiff and rigid? Brother, don't you know that as soon as day breaks the whole city will come to see you and praise God in you? Ask God to make your body flexible, for you know we would render Him infinite thanks for that!"

From the height of his beatitude Martin doubtless smiled at the impetuosity of his friend and asked God to give him the consolation he prayed for with such fervor. A few moments later the body became flexible; the face lost all its rigidity and resumed its natural expression.

Father Cyprian was overjoyed by the answer to his prayer, which he regarded as a confirmation of his opinion of Martin as a saint and his hope to see him publicly glorified. He lifted the body to a sitting position on the catafalque and arranged it so that it seemed alive.[6]

In spite of the fact it was night, the news of Martin's death spread outside the monastery. It was not yet four in the morning when people began to gather in front of the church and press against the doors. When the sacristan opened the doors, a veritable river of humanity rushed in, invaded the nave and crowded behind the friars forming a square around the catafalque. The first arrivals stared, stupefied to find that Martin in death was so much like Martin as they had known him in life. He seemed asleep. What amazed them more, and held them as if bewitched, was the fragrance which emanated from the body, a strange and indefinable perfume, like a mixture of most delicately scented flowers. The fragrance penetrated the soul with a sense of joy and filled the whole church.

People continued to come like an immense sea, wave upon wave. They walked with their eyes fixed on the spot towards which everyone was converging, urged on by the desire to see better, to touch what no one hesitated to call the body of a saint, drawn by its perfume.

During the Office and the Mass, the people respected the free space around which the authorities had taken their place. The latter had come spontaneously to render honor to the brother who had labored so much for all the citizens of Lima, great and small.

When the Office and Mass were ended, the crowd rushed to the catafalque, all trying to touch it. Their hands were filled with rosaries and other objects of devotion. They tried to touch the body, which still seemed to be alive. They would not go away emptyhanded, but carried away something that had been in contact with the holy Brother, something that could be considered a souvenir or relic.

Martin had to be clothed more than once because the people had torn his habit to shreds in spite of the prohibition of those on guard. It was not only the unimportant and ignorant who were avid for relics. With the same care that Father John de Barbazán exercised in jealously preserving as a great treasure the handkerchief he had used to wipe the sweat of the death agony from Martin's face, Peter de Ortega, bishop-elect of Cuzco and a professor at the Royal University of Lima, carefully preserved a small piece of cloth with which he had performed the same pious office.[7]

Like a tide, the throng ebbed and flowed. Little by little the first arrivals, pushed forward by those who came after them, edged their way towards the exit. Once outside, they incited others to come by recounting their reactions to what they had seen.

The throng crossing the central nave became more intense. It no longer consisted of individuals but of little groups carrying the sick and invalids. It seems that many of the sick and invalid were able to return to their homes on foot after having touched the body of Brother Martin.

This lasted until evening. When darkness fell, the friars took counsel and agreed they had been fortunate to save the body of their holy brother from the assaults of that crowd, and they decided to bury him without further delay.

The cortege was formed, and a cordon of religious and friends of the monastery protected the body from the crowd. Four of Martin's most intimate friends carried the catafalque: the viceroy, the archbishop of Mexico, the bishop of Cuzco, and John de Peñafiel, judge of the Royal Court. The chapter of the cathedral, superiors of many monasteries, lay dignitaries and military officers accompanied the body. Father Gaspar de Saldaña, the prior, officiated and recited the last prayers over the tomb of the dearest of his sons. His office entitled him to that privilege and he would not have ceded it to anyone.

The cortege filed under the arches and descended into the crypt under the chapter room where the religious were buried. It did not seem fitting to place the remains of a man so far above the ordinary in the area reserved for the lay brothers. Martin was buried among the priests, in a new niche near one in which another lay brother was buried, Brother Michael de Santo Domingo, also judged worthy of this honor because of his holy life.

When the tomb was closed and all had left for their homes, Archbishop Felician de Vega expressed his thoughts about the events of the last twenty-four hours, saying, "Yes, this is the way saints should be honored." [8]

CHAPTER

⊱ 18 ⊰

And the Lord will give thee rest continually
and will fill thy soul with brightness and deliver thy bones;
and thou shalt be like a watered garden
and like a fountain of water whose waters
shall not fail (Isa. 58:11).

MARTIN DID NOT REMAIN LONG in the new tomb beside Brother Michael. His body was hidden from the eyes of his brothers, but his spirit continued to live in their midst. As before, Martin watched over his own, ready to help them at any moment in any need.

The first to realize it was Father John de Vargas, at the very moment that Martin's soul left his body and entered into heavenly glory.

Two days later, Brother Anthony Gutiérrez, Martin's infirmarian during his last illness, fell ill with the same fever that had carried Martin to his grave. The fever was so violent that within a short time Anthony was at death's door. On the sixth day the doctor declared, "The only thing left to do is to give him the last sacraments." But it was impossible to administer the sacraments to the patient while he raved like a madman in the delirium caused by the fever, and that saddened his brethren even more than the possibility that he might die at the early age of twenty-three.

A small altar was set up near his bed and the Blessed Sacrament was placed upon it. Night fell. The sick man grew somewhat calmer and seemed to be sleeping. Suddenly he opened his eyes and said, "Don't worry; this time I shall not die."

"That's wonderful, but how do you know it?" asked the infirmarians, merely to have something to say, for they thought that Brother Anthony was still delirious.

"Brother Martin told me. He was here, beside my bed," answered the sick brother. "He came into the room with the Blessed Virgin Mary and our father St. Dominic and St. Catherine, virgin and martyr. The others stayed near the altar, but Brother Martin came to my bed and said, 'This visit will cure you.'"

Then Brother Anthony closed his eyes and slept peacefully all through the night. In the morning he was completely well again and asked for his breakfast.[1]

While Brother Anthony had been caring for Brother Martin during his last illness, the master of students had said to him, "If Martin dies, take the black wooden cross which he wears next to his body and keep it with great reverence."

Brother Anthony obeyed gladly, and without waiting for death to come, he took advantage of a moment in which Martin was dozing to cut the cord on which the cross hung from Martin's neck and to take possession of it. The slight movement caused Martin to wake up. Brother Anthony was caught with his "pious theft" in his hands. He reddened with embarrassment and asked Martin's pardon, saying, "Your

Reverence told me you were going to die, and to have a memento of you, I took this cross." Martin let him do so and closed his eyes again without a word. For the moment, Anthony put a cord through the ring of the little cross and placed it around his neck, as Martin had done.

But Brother Anthony had a difficult time defending his treasure against those who wished to take it from him. His tenacity and skill in keeping it were extraordinary when we think that even the prior of the monastery, Father Gaspar de Saldaña, was among those who wanted the little cross.

Several years later, after his ordination, Anthony was traveling and discovered he no longer had Brother Martin's little cross. He wrote to the monastery, asking that his cell be searched, to see if by chance the cross had been left there. It could not be found. When he returned to Lima, Brother Anthony searched for it in vain. One day he was passing by the meadow in front of the church of Our Lady of Guadalupe where, six months before, he had noticed for the first time that the cross was missing. Suddenly he saw it on the edge of a track dug in the road by the wheels of the wagons and the hoofs of the mules constantly passing that way with provisions for the nearby city.

Between the end of 1642 and the beginning of 1643, Father Cyprian de Medina returned from Spain, where he had been taking care of the affairs of his Province as delegate to a General Chapter of the Dominican Order. Almost immediately upon his arrival he developed an illness which caused acute pain in his arms and legs "so that it seemed to him they were being pierced with needles." Sleep was impossible in this torment, nor could he take even a mouthful of food. As a result, at the end of three or four days Father Cyprian's condition was extremely grave.

A consultation was held. The most renowned doctors of

Lima came, and though they could not agree what treatment should be used, they were at least unanimous in declaring that the sickness was mortal. And having pronounced sentence on Father Cyprian, they left.

But Father Cyprian's brethren refused to give up hope. He had always been such a good and exemplary religious that they could not resign themselves to the prospect of losing him so suddenly. They remembered how fond Martin had been of him and they suggested that he invoke Martin's aid. Father Gaspar de Saldaña did even more. He sent him the rosary which Martin had worn around his neck.

Father Cyprian followed their advice and with deep reverence and joy took his friend's rosary and put it around his own neck. At approximately nine o'clock that night such an attack seized him that all he could do was cry out while he writhed in spasms of pain. Several religious were with him and tried in vain to give him some relief. Suddenly Father Cyprian saw a lay brother standing calmly at the foot of his bed in the midst of all the excitement. His hands were joined in the sleeves of his habit, and his head was a little bowed. It was the habitual modest attitude and smile Father Cyprian knew so well.

Father Cyprian recognized Martin and spoke to him without a moment's hesitation, with the same brusque frankness with which he had rebuked him years ago for not taking care of him when he was gravely ill and, more recently, for letting his body grow rigid the night of his death.

"Brother Martin, what has become of your love for me? Have you forgotten me? Now that you are enjoying the vision of God in eternal glory, you think only of your own happiness and you let me suffer without helping me! You know very well that they say I won't live until morning."

Undisturbed by the outburst, Martin looked fixedly into

Father Cyprian's eyes. Then he smiled faintly, shaking his head.

"You will not die of this illness."

The infirmarians saw Father Cyprian talking to himself and thought the pain had driven him to delirium. But immediately he grew calm, closed his eyes, and fell asleep.

At six o'clock the next morning the doctors arrived and were surprised to find their patient, not dead as they had expected, but so much improved that he was almost well. They drew a little blood, just to claim that they, too, had done something. But without any further treatment, Father Medina was able to leave his bed "free of pain and well . . . to the admiration of the whole monastery."

The "whole monastery" disregarded the last-minute treatment of the doctors and recognized the work of their holy Brother Martin in the recovery and thanked God and Martin. Father Cyprian naturally told how Martin had appeared to him at the height of the crisis, and how in an instant he had freed him of the unrelenting pain he had suffered for so many days.[2]

Another cure under similar conditions was that of Brother Nicholas de Guadalupe. For four months Nicholas had been tormented by lumbago. Because of the constant pain "he could not rest, could not sleep either day or night, and passed entire nights without being able to close his eyes." Not knowing what to do to be cured, one night when he was suffering more than usual he began to invoke Martin and asked him to pray for him, reminding Martin of their old friendship. The prayer was barely uttered when sleep overcame him, and in the morning when he awoke he discovered he was as free of the pain and as rested as if he had never suffered the torments of lumbago. This happened about 1653, fourteen years after Martin's death.[3]

Naturally the news of these happenings spread beyond the walls of the monastery and comforted the people of Lima, who saw in them the confirmation of the fame of Lima's great and humble son.

However, just as he had done during his life, Martin did not confine himself to healing only the sick of his own monastery. A child six years old, Francis de Ribera, was ill in Lima. Apparently he was at the point of death. He lay in his bed, motionless, his pulse so faint it could no longer be felt, his eyes closed as if they would never open again. At the mere invocation of Martin's name, his parents saw the little corpse return to life, and in a short time the house was again filled with little Francis' happy shouts and games.[4]

In a similar manner, Elizabeth Ortiz de Torres was healed instantly of the neuralgia which had tormented her for many days. "You helped me while you were on earth," she said to Martin as she looked affectionately at a rude picture which ingenuously attempted to reproduce Martin de Porres' lineaments. "Through your prayers God vouchsafed to cure me when my life was despaired of. Now that you are in heaven, do not abandon me, but hear my humble petition for relief."[5]

One of Martin's old tunics was brought to Elizabeth de Astorga who was suffering from a violent fever. When the tunic was spread on her bed, the fever left her instantly.[6]

These and other remarkable events helped keep alive the memory of Martin's holy life and the confidence in his power of intercession with God. They also brought many of the faithful to the church of the Holy Rosary, which was the spot nearest the tomb those outside the monastery could reach. The tomb was inaccessible, since it was within the cloister. But it would not always be thus. Martin had foretold it. He was talking one day with his friend John de Figueroa, who had revealed a plan to him. John intended to contribute to the cost of a chapel in the church of the Mercedarians and thus acquire the right of burial for himself and his family in that chapel. Martin approved and encouraged his friend to contribute such generous alms for the embellishment of the Mercedarian's church.

"But as to your burial," he added, "don't be concerned about that, because you will not be buried there. You and I are to be buried here." And he pointed to the floor of the room in which they were talking, which was the supply room of the infirmary.

Later, when the Dominicans began to seek some way of satisfying the desire of the devout to visit the tomb of their holy brother, the spot best adapted for the location of his body seemed to be the supply room where Martin had worked so long, where he had taken care of the sick and counseled so many as their spiritual guide.

The room could easily be transformed into a chapel, and the cost of the work would be relatively modest. Naturally, when Father Saldaña tried to find a place for this "modest" figure in the budget of the monastery, he realized at once it was impossible and thought, "We need a benefactor." He mentally reviewed the list of Martin's most intimate friends and seemed to see one face, that of John de Figueroa, emerge clearly out of a formless and nameless crowd.

Losing no time, Father Saldaña tucked this wonderful project under his arm and went to visit John de Figueroa. He offered him the possibility of contributing to the cost of the new chapel as a way of acquiring the right of burial there for himself and his family in the crypt to be constructed under the pavement of the future chapel. Father Saldaña knew nothing of Martin's prediction, but John de Figueroa recalled it instantly and enthusiastically agreed to the proposition. The work was begun and the chapel was soon ready.[7]

The exhumation and recognition of Martin's body was carried out in March, 1664, twenty-four years and four months after his death.

Late at night, in order to avoid all publicity, Father John de Barbazán, then vicar general of the Dominican Province of St. John the Baptist of Peru, Father Francis de Oviedo, acting vicar of the community at Holy Rosary, and three lay brothers gathered in the chapter room. The three lay brothers were Bartholomew del Rosario, Thomas Marín and Lauren de los Santos.

Brother Thomas, who was the assistant sacristan of the monastery, had asked the provincial for the honor of disinterring the bones. He began to dig. It was hard work, for the grave was deep. But finally the body came to light, almost intact, with the bones still covered by the muscular tissue and held together by the ligaments. Since it was entire, Brother Thomas thought he could lift the body in his arms as one would lift the body of a living person. He took it around the waist, but the bones came apart in his hands revealing the freshness of the muscular tissue covering them.

As soon as the holy body came to light, a most sweet perfume like that of rose petals invaded the chapter room, and an immense joy filled the hearts of those present. It was a repetition of the scene enacted when the humble grave in which St. Dominic had wished his body to be deposited, "under the feet of his brothers," was opened by Blessed Jordan of Saxony, and those in attendance felt they were not opening a tomb but a chest of precious perfumed essences. Once more Martin proved himself to be a true son of his father, Dominic.[8]

Brother Thomas realized that his initial method was too brusque and he extracted the body from the grave with great care. Father Oviedo arranged it on the catafalque with deep love and reverence. Repeated contact with Martin's body left his hands impregnated with the delightful perfume of dried rose petals. Even after he had washed his hands many times, the perfume was so strong that the day after the exhumation the friars who had not been present could still smell the perfume on his hands.

When he had taken the cranium out of the grave, Brother Thomas found a little lump of earth in his hands which had adhered to some part of the body. He broke it apart with his fingers, and fresh blood came out of it.

The following morning the friars made preparations for the private translation of the corpse and the obsequies. Father Barbazán took every possible precaution to avoid calling attention to the ceremonies and gave explicit orders that everything should be done quietly, without any publicity. No one was invited, and it was forbidden to give any information about the event to anyone outside the monastery. But, as had happened the day after Martin's death, day had just dawned when people began to fill the church, and not only the ordinary citizens, but all the authorities up to and including the viceroy.

When the obsequies were ended, all the "great ones" of Lima began to contest for the honor of carrying the casket containing the precious relics. His Excellency the viceroy of Lima, took the post of honor among the bearers, without any discussion or fear of rivalry. But the others contested for the honor of carrying the casket or at least getting as near as possible to the source of that exquisite perfume, putting forward their titles of nobility, of high office, or of age.

When the cortege began to move, the religious appointed by Father Oviedo to form a cordon around it were not sufficient to hold back those who wished at all cost to touch the catafalque with their rosaries or other objects of devotion. Step by step the procession wedged through the crowd and reached the chapel. And even when the casket was lowered into the crypt and a stone covered the opening, the fragrance of rose petals remained in the air, and all hearts were filled with a sense of quiet joy and great confidence in Martin's sanctity.[9]

"No outward signs of devotion can be rendered to Martin because the Church has not yet passed judgment on his life," the friars warned, but the people continued to kneel down on the stone over the crypt and to invoke Martin as the saints are invoked.

Little by little the crowd thinned out. His Excellency the viceroy, the chief of the department of justice, the lords of the royal commission, the members of the cathedral chapter, the noble knights, the religious of every order represented in Lima—one after the other they left. And Martin's brothers, the Dominicans of Holy Rosary, went to their cells, worn out after the hard day. The little chapel was empty.

But Martin was not alone. The inseparable companion of his whole life was in the little chapel with him. From the wall over the altar a huge crucifix looked down on the stone closing the tomb, as if Christ on the cross were musing over the moment to raise that stone and show by means of the humble friar who had believed in Him, the fulfillment of His words: "He who believes in Me, even if he die, shall live" (John 11:25).

➤ 19 ◄

*Eye has not seen nor ear heard, nor has it entered
into the heart of man, what things God has prepared
for those who love him* (I Cor. 2:9).

"THIS IS THE WAY saints should be honored," said Felician
de la Vega, archbishop of Mexico City, on the evening of
November 4, 1639, after the body of Martin de Porres, accompanied by all the authorities of the city of Lima, had been
solemnly transferred from the church of the Holy Rosary to
the crypt under the chapter room.

In March of 1664, when Martin's remains were removed
from the first tomb and reburied in the former supply room
of the infirmary, which had been transformed into the little
chapel of the Most Holy Crucifix, the twenty-four intervening
years had served only to confirm the conviction of the people
of Lima that Martin was worthy to be called a saint and to
receive public veneration.

The translation of his body was like a puff of wind on glow-
ing embers. It revived devotion and confidence in Martin, and
all the more so, since new miracles flowered from the opening
of the old tomb. Even the earth from the grave worked miracles.

Among the many who learned from personal experience
the power of that blessed earth was a Negro named John
Criollo. He had been suffering for some time from a persistent fever. In spite of countless remedies, the fever never
left him. Although the doctors had not frankly expressed their

opinion, John Criollo had a deadly fear of ending as a consumptive. One day in March of 1664, Brother Lauren de los Santos came to visit him.

"How are you?" asked Brother Lauren.

"What can you expect? I still have the fever. This is going to end badly."

"Listen," said Brother Lauren, "I have brought you a good remedy, a little earth from the tomb of Brother Martin de Porres. Just yesterday we carried his body from the old tomb to the new one, and I helped exhume his body. A little of his blessed flesh remained attached to my fingers, with a perfume I cannot describe. Take this bit of earth with a little water and ask Martin to obtain health for you from God if it is for the good of your soul."

John readily consented. Praying as hard as he could to Martin, he drank the mixture and instantly his temperature returned to normal. The doctor kept him under observation a few days more, then said he could get out of bed, confident that he was cured.[1]

If it had been possible to proclaim Martin a saint by popular vote, there is no doubt he would have been given the title the day after his death. When Archbishop de la Vega called him a saint, he expressed everyone's opinion. But the voice of the people is not the last word in questions of sanctity, even if it comes from authoritative lips. The Church must speak officially. So Martin's brethren and the citizens of Lima began to request the judgment of the Church.

The Dominican Order was not slow to recognize Martin's virtues officially. A solemn encomium on his life and works was pronounced in the Provincial Chapter held in Lima in 1641, two years after his death. Information about his life spread rapidly throughout South America and swiftly crossed the ocean to the Old World. The first biography of Brother

Martin appeared in Valencia in 1647, and another in Rome in 1658.

But when the question arose of asking the Holy See to introduce Martin's cause, it was the King of Spain, Philip IV, who took up his pen to request the honors of the altar for the little mulatto brother.

"Most Holy Father," the King wrote on December 17, 1659, "I am writing to my ambassador, Louis de Guzmán Ponce de León, asking him to place before Your Holiness the concurrent reasons for which we hope Your Holiness will send the remissorial letters for the beatification of Brother Martin de Porres of the Order of St. Dominic. I am told that in his virtuous and exemplary life, together with extraordinary miracles and the spirit of prophecy, other very remarkable events occurred, and I beg Your Holiness to give full credence to what he will propose about this matter, and to order that whatever is necessary should be done in the case without delay, according to the grace he will receive from Your Holiness. . . ."²

A year and a half later, on June 20, 1661, at the request of the viceroy of Peru, the King of Spain sent a second petition to the Holy Father to obtain the decree for the introduction of the cause of the beatification of the Servant of God, Brother Martin de Porres of the Province of Peru, urging as one of the motives for the action the great comfort the exaltation of his virtues would bring to the faithful of that Province. Under the same date and with the same purpose, the King also wrote to Louis Ponce de León, commanding him to take the matter actively in hand.³

The Holy Father had received letter after letter in 1660. Letters came from the archbishop of Lima, the chapter of the cathedral, the religious orders having monasteries or convents in Lima, the University of St. Mark. Each letter, in its own way and with flourishes of style and varieties of writing, praised Martin's extraordinary virtues and asked that the Apostolic Process be opened.[4]

In 1660 Peter de Villagómez, archbishop of Lima, opened the Ordinary Process concerning the sanctity of life of Martin de Porres, his practice of virtue, and the miracles attributed to his intercession. Twenty years after his death, many were still alive who had lived with Martin, collaborated in his works or benefited from his charity.

The first to present himself as a witness was John de Figueroa, the generous contributor to Martin's charitable works, who had once heard Martin predict that he would suffer poverty and would have the privilege of lying in a tomb beside his holy friend.

He was followed by the Dominicans, Cyprian de Medina, now a bishop, but once the ugly, stunted novice; Gaspar de Saldaña, the prior who had forced Martin to reveal his nocturnal penances and had witnessed his death while the friars chanted the *Credo;* Ferdinand de Aragonés, Martin's colleague in the infirmary; and Francis Velasco Carabantes, who owed his life and his perseverance in his vocation to Martin.

Then came Francis de la Torre, who had shared Martin's room and had been present during the assaults of the demon; the other captain of the guard, John de Guarnido, who knew every corner of the monastery of the Holy Rosary because he had been a student there; and John Vázquez, whom Martin had so often told not to broadcast right and left what he saw when he was with Martin. John could not be convinced otherwise, now that Martin was dead. He could not bring himself to give his testimony until Martin had appeared to him, walked with him for a while, and exhorted him to speak out frankly.[5]

And many, many more, religious and lay, men and women,

came to testify, including Martin's niece, Catherine de Porres, the wife of Nicholas Beltrán.

When the notary, Francis Blanco, had taken the sixty-fourth deposition, which was that of Martin's niece, he rose from his bench and asked another notary to take his place so that he might also serve as a witness. His colleague, Ignatius Pujadas, took his place, and Francis Blanco gave his deposition. Stating he had not known Martin during his life, he told of something which had happened to him several days after the opening of the Process.

The Dominican archbishop of Santa Fe, John de Arguinao, was passing through Lima. Out of respect for his dignity, the notary was to call upon him to take his testimony. But on June 27, the day before the appointment, Francis Blanco could not walk. Some time before that, a thorn had pierced one of his toes. When it was removed, a festering wound remained, which healed after a few days. Up to that point there was nothing serious about the incident. With the aid of a cane Francis continued to go to work, limping along in a pair of old shoes. But the sore had just healed when a second thorn pierced the exact spot where the first had entered, resulting in a much more malignant infection and an enormous swelling of the foot and leg. To no avail, Francis tried on all the old shoes he found in his attic. He had to be content to limp about at home, shoeless, hopping as best he could from one room to another on his good foot because it was impossible to put the other one on the ground.

In that condition how could be possibly cover the considerable distance between his home and the archbishop's palace? On the other hand, it was unthinkable to ask such an important personage to come to his house, nor could he ask the archbishop to delay his departure. It distressed the notary greatly to be deprived of the testimony of such an important witness who had lived in the monastery of the Holy Rosary when Martin was there.

Francis Blanco turned to Martin. He had already heard enough about him to realize that he was precisely the person who could help him. "You see what a state I'm in," Francis said to Martin the evening of June 27, when he went to bed, worn out with hopping from one chair to another. "I can't stand on my foot, and tomorrow I must go to the other end of Lima to take the archbishop's testimony. You know how important that testimony is for the cause of your beatification. Ask our Lord, among all the other favors and graces He has given to so many people through your intercession, to grant you this grace for me, too, even though I am such a great sinner."

Francis pulled the covers over himself, taking care not to touch his throbbing foot, and fell asleep at once.

In the morning he woke up cured and had no need of old shoes when he went to see the archbishop of Santa Fe.[6]

Thus, to the sixty-four depositions taken by Francis Blanco, two others were added: his own, and that of Joan de Ortega, who had extracted the first and second thorns from his foot. There were in all, therefore, sixty-six depositions. Sixty-six depositions but not sixty-six witnesses, for some came back a second time to complete their depositions with details they had forgotten the first time.

Joan de Ortega's deposition ended the first inquiry on July 12, 1660. The Process had opened on June 16.

In December of 1664, after the translation of Martin's remains, Francis Blanco took up his pen again to record the depositions of another eleven witnesses. The testimony this time concerned mainly the translation of Martin's remains and the graces received through his intercession.

The year 1664 saw in its turn other petitions sent to the Holy See for the introduction of the cause of Martin's beatification: from King Philip IV (March 30); from the viceroy of Peru (November 17), who still saw in his mind's eye the crowd coming to the church of the Holy Rosary the day of the translation of Martin's body; from Peter de Villagómez, archbishop of Lima; from the metropolitan chapter; from the University of St. Mark; from the communities of religious such as the Knights Hospitallers, Augustinians, Friars Minor, Mercedarians, Dominicans and Jesuits, all of them still almost inebriated by the exquisite fragance of roses given off by Martin's relics.[7]

After a searching inquiry by the Sacred Congregation of Rites into the acts of the Ordinary Process, the favor was finally granted four years later in a relation given by Cardinal Vidoni in the Ordinary Congregation of June 21, 1668.[8]

On December 10, 1668, the Supreme Pontiff, Pope Clement IX, signed the decree for the introduction of the cause of beatification and canonization of Martin de Porres.[9]

The following year the commission charged with carrying out the Apostolic Process was named and the famous remissorial letters were sent. But they were hardly out of the port of Genoa when they went to the bottom of the sea with the ship carrying them. Nevertheless, the box in which they were enclosed was recovered intact from the water.

Things should have moved along swiftly then, but another nine years went by before the remissorial letters arrived in Lima and the work began.[10] When they finally arrived on October 26, 1678, the citizens of Lima, who had waited so many years, went mad with joy. An eye-witness report of the first solemn day, Thursday, October 27, was transcribed in the Process of 1678 by the notary, Peter del Arco:

By order of the most illustrious and most reverend Melchior Lignan y Cisnero, our Lord Archbishop of Lima, of the Council of our Lord King, the Viceroy, Governor, and Captain General of the Kingdom and Provinces of Peru, Tierra Firma and Chile . . . , Doctor Joseph de Lara Galán left the palace of the archbishop, accompanied by me, the present public and apostolic notary, and by all the members of the ecclesiastical tribunal, priests and laymen; by the Very Reverend Father Gaspar de Saldaña, Prior of the monastery of Our Lady of the Rosary of this city and Vicar Provincial of this Province of St. John the Baptist of Peru of the Order of Preachers; by the Very Reverend Fathers of the same Order; and thus accompanied by many secular priests, knights of the said city, and by the greater part of the people commonly called in America *pardos* (mulattoes), all clad in festal clothing, all manifesting the joy they felt at seeing the day arrive on which the work of the cause of the beatification and canonization of the Venerable Servant of God, Brother Martin de Porres, was to begin by apostolic authority. . . . And from the said palace of the archbishop they passed before the royal palace and from there to the house of the governor and ruler of the said city, and in every section there was a crier; and from there they passed through many of the principal streets of the same city, and at the crossing of the said streets there was a crier, preceding the said passage with drums and cornets, trumpets and other similar musical instruments to bring to the attention of all the said city the apostolic letters ordering that the apostolic authorities should be informed of the life, virtues, death and miracles of the Venerable Servant of God, Brother Martin de Porres. . . . And the number of men and women of all stations and qualities gathered in the streets was the greatest I have ever seen in my life in this city, and many of the streets where the procession passed were covered with fragrant herbs and flowers, which showed the jubilation and joy of the people of the said city over the event which they were celebrating. And . . . the night of that day, the great square of the said city was filled with fireworks, as were the towers of the churches, royal palace, the palace of the archbishop, and the houses of the ecclesiastical and secular authorities; and from the tower of the church of our Lady of the Holy Rosary there was the same display of fireworks as in the public square, with firecrackers and rockets, and other illuminating displays, the whole being accompanied by a general ringing of bells which began at eleven o'clock of the same day and continued until nine o'clock at night, at which hour the fireworks and celebration ended.[11]

The following morning, Friday, October 28, the feast of the Apostles Simon and Jude, a solemn Mass was sung in the cathedral. The archbishop-viceroy was present with all the authorities of the city, the academic body of the university, representatives of the religious and military orders, and a dense crowd of men and women of every social rank.

Father Gaspar de Saldaña preached, and "at the Offertory of the said solemn Mass," Peter del Arco writes, "the said archbishop-viceroy gave me two envelopes, one larger than the other, which it seems contained the said apostolic letters, and having received and held them above my head, I mounted into the pulpit, and having adored the Most Holy Sacrament and bowed to the said archbishop-viceroy, and to the lords of the royal council, and to the ecclesiastical and secular authorities and to the rest of the gathering, in a clear and loud voice I read the address on the larger envelope, and having finished that, I read the address on the other envelope in the same manner, leaving them sealed, and in the condition which the said archbishop-viceroy had given them to me, and as soon as I had descended from the pulpit I consigned them, in accordance with the command of His Excellency . . . , to the Father Francis del Arco, praesentatus, preacher general . . . postulator of this cause, whose representative I was for the said ceremony; and I affirm to have done all this, and many people thus rendered thanks to God that this day so earnestly desired had arrived, in which the question of the beatification and canonization of the said Venerable Servant of God, Brother Martin de Porres, is being taken up with the apostolic authorities, some of the people having known him during his life, and others having heard of his heroic virtues, praiseworthy life, and astounding miracles." [12]

It was natural that the people thanked God for the dawn of the longed-for day. But it was only the first glimmer of daybreak. The full day in which the complex mechanism of the Process would start work in earnest was still far off. When Peter del Arco came down from the pulpit and gave the two envelopes to the proper authority, difficulties at once began to arise. One of the designated judges had been appointed to the bishopric of Tucamán and had to leave; another was blind and deaf. Forty days were spent in deciding whether these two judges should refuse the appointment, in finding substitutes for them, in checking the titles of each judge. Not until December 6 was the renowned "larger envelope," which contained the decree of the introduction of the cause, opened and read by the same notary, Peter del Arco, in the presence of the archbishop-viceroy and all the authorities, "word for word, in a loud, clear and intelligible voice." [13]

Another obstacle arose. For some strange reason the remissorial letters gave the year of Martin's birth as 1589, in the city of Guamanga. The mistake was to be cleared up in the first hearing by the first witness, but two and a half months went by before the interrogations began.

The first hearing took place on February 20, 1679, in the chapel of the adoration of the Magi in the cathedral. The first witness was Father Anthony de Morales, O.P., bishop-elect of Concepción, Chile. Although Father Morales was more than sixty years old, he could not have based his rectification of Martin's birth date on personal memories because 1679 was the centenary of Martin's birth. But Father Morales had

had the good fortune of coming upon the very document which ended all discussion of the question: the baptismal register of the parish church of St. Sebastian in Lima. There had been discussions about the matter, and Father Anthony, who had shared in them from the time he entered the Order, was always perplexed about it. Martin was then fully mature and so much esteemed by his brethren that many of them wished to claim him as a native of their own city. And thus some said he was from Cuzco, others from Guamanga. Martin did not bother to rectify the error; in his opinion such useless questions did not merit even one word of discussion.

Father Anthony had lived ten years with Martin at the Holy Rosary monastery, from 1623 to 1633. Then his superiors had sent him elsewhere to preach, teach and assume various responsibilities. But in 1661 he was once more in Lima. The master general of the Order had assigned him the task of organizing the celebration for the beatification of Rose of Lima. Father Anthony wanted to see the official registration of Rose's baptism at the church of St. Sebastian and he found it without difficulty by running through the pages of the baptismal register for the year 1585. Then, as he aimlessly leafed backwards through the register, his eye fell on the name of Martin de Porres. Neither those from Cuzco nor those from Guamanga could boast any longer of being from Brother Martin's birthplace. Rose of Lima had vindicated the right to that honor for herself and her city.[14]

During the first Process, Francis Blanco had been able to record the testimony at the accelerated rhythm of five or six witnesses a day. The second Process went more slowly, and the witnesses who succeeded Father Morales appeared at intervals of two or three weeks, or whatever number of days were necessary to answer questions on the more than eighty points of the interrogation.

It is not remarkable that the Process, for which the testimony of one hundred sixty-four witnesses was taken, lasted almost eight years. It ended in 1686, and when the acts of the Process were enclosed in a rich container and placed on the main altar of the cathedral, a solemn *Te Deum* was chanted and the archbishop preached a eulogy of Martin. Then the gilded case with the acts of the Process was carried in triumph to the church of the Holy Rosary while the population once more enthusiastically poured out into the streets and filled the church. The case was then put on board a ship about to set sail for the Old World. But like the ship that had set sail from Genoa with the remissorial letters, this one went down, too, and the result of the patient and exacting work of eight years' investigation was at the bottom of the sea.

Fortunately, a second authenticated copy had been conserved at Lima. Pope Innocent XII issued an authorization to make a copy of it and to send it to the Sacred Congregation of Rites. The second copy arrived in Rome without any untoward incidents, but another three-quarters of a century went by before the heroism of Martin's virtues was approved. Pope Clement XIII signed the decree on February 27, 1763.[15]

That was a decisive step forward, but still more was needed. Among the many miracles worked by Martin after his death, two had to be officially recognized by the pontifical authority. The two miracles chosen for official approval were astounding ones.

Elvira Moriano of Lima was the first case. Elvira had prepared a home remedy and placed it on the window sill to cool in the night air. When she arose the next morning, she went to take it in, but the earthenware jug slipped from her hands, fell to the floor and broke. One of the pieces rebounded into her eye with such force that it pierced the cornea. The crystalline lens came out of the wound with all the surrounding fluids, and the eyeball was left flaccid and empty.

Elvira thought she would die of the pain and began to scream. Her neighbors came and called a surgeon, Peter de Urdanibia, one of the most skillful in the city. This kind-hearted doctor felt deep compassion for the poor woman. How could he tell her the truth?

"Is there any hope that my eye can be healed?" asked Elvira Moriano.

The doctor replied, "God is your only hope, because your eye is completely empty, and only God can re-create the organs of our bodies. I will do all I can so that the damage will not grow worse. But if you have faith in any saint, pray to him with all your heart."

The surgeon spoke like the honest man he was, and like an honest man he used whatever remedies he had at his command.

Meanwhile the news of the accident spread about the city and reached the monastery of the Holy Rosary, where Elvira's son was a novice. The Father Master, Jerome de Toledo, pitied the novice's mother, and sent her a relic consisting of a small fragment of the bones of Martin de Porres, explaining what it was and exhorting her to put it on the wounded eye with faith.

With great confidence, Elvira applied the relic to the empty eyeball. The tormenting pain died down and a delightful drowsiness overcame her. She slept until the following morning and as soon as she awoke, she touched the wounded eye. The cavity was filled. She leaped from her bed and ran to the mirror. The eye was well and as perfect as if it had never been injured.

Elvira's neighbors heard her cries and ran to her home, but

this time she had screamed because she was almost insane with joy. The doctor also came, and being an honest man, praised God and His saints.[16]

The other miracle came about as follows. A thorough house-cleaning was under way in the home of Agnes Vidal. In order to polish the floor in the main salon, the servants had piled up all the chairs against the iron railing on the balcony. Among those occupied in polishing the floor was a Negro slave who had a baby a little more than two years old with her. The name of the slave is unknown, but the baby was called Melchior Varanda.

Melchior had nothing to keep him occupied while his mother was working, and he trotted back and forth without anyone paying any attention to him. He went out on the balcony and discovered the barrier of chairs. At first he was annoyed. How could he see what was going on in the street with that wall of chairs in his way? But then he decided that all he had to do was climb up on them to see better. So, using a stool as a ladder, he hoisted himself up on a chair. All was going well.

Melchior was contented and happy because he felt as big as the adults, and he could lean over the iron railing and wave at all the passersby. How amusing it was for someone who always had to look up at people, to watch them from a point so far above their heads. Melchior went on leaning over the railing and rejoicing over his accomplishment, until he leaned over too far and fell into the street, a drop of eighteen feet. His head struck the pavement first. His mother and the other servants heard the noise and ran down into the street. Melchior's skull was split open, he was bleeding from the eyes, ears, nose and mouth. He no longer seemed to be breathing. No, he was alive, because his temperature was mounting madly. His left arm moved convulsively.

The doctor, Peter de Utrilia, came at once and instantly admitted that he was powerless in the face of such a desperate situation. He could give only one piece of advice: pray to Martin de Porres. The poor mother could not utter a word, but her employer was at her side. Agnes Vidal went in search of a picture of the Servant of God and placed it on the child's wounded head saying, "Saint Porres! Saint of my soul, my friend, heal this baby for me!"

Martin smiled down from heaven. How happy he was to see this noble Spanish lady so stricken because of the grief of the child of a poor Negro slave.

Three hours later, little Melchior jumped up from the bed where he had been laid, as healthy and bright-eyed as he had been before his fall. And neither then nor at any time afterwards did Melchior Varanda show any signs or consequences of the fracture.

When Doctor Peter de Utrilia returned to see him, he found him playing and running about with all the thousand winning ways of babies of his age. Peter left the house of Agnes Vidal to recount the miraculous case, and his testimony had all the more weight because of his indisputable competence as a doctor.[17]

The two miracles were approved by Pope Gregory XVI on March 19, 1836. Four and a half months later, on July 31, the decree was signed wherein it was judged safe to proceed to the beatification.

And finally, on October 29, 1837, in the splendor of the Vatican Basilica, Martin de Porres was solemnly raised to the honors of the altar a week after John Massias, his brother in the Order and his most intimate friend, had been given the same honor.

After successfully reaching this long desired point, Martin's cause seemed destined to rest inactive for an indefinite period.

Decade succeeded decade without the completion of the necessary steps to reach the point of his canonization.

Only in 1926, at the request of the Very Reverend Louis G. Fanfani, O.P., who was at that time postulator general of the Dominican Order, and in response to numerous petitions received from ecclesiastical and lay authorities, did Pope Pius XI appoint a commission to resume the cause.

Ten years later, the Dominican master general, the Most Reverend Martin Stanislaus Gillet, addressed a circular letter to the entire Order, exhorting Dominicans to promote devotion to Blessed Martin and to hasten by prayer and the gathering of testimony the moment in which his canonization would add a new and splendid flower to the garland of St. Dominic.[18]

A markedly enthusiastic response to the request of the master general came from St. Joseph's Province in the United States, which took charge of the movement. For more than half a century, Martin had been winning the hearts of the North Americans. An Italian priest, Father Felix Barotti, had introduced Martin to the United States. In 1866 he was sent to evangelize the Negroes of that country and he erected a chapel in Washington for his little flock and dedicated it to Blessed Martin. In a few years the chapel became too small and a church was built. Since a church cannot normally be dedicated to a blessed, the one built for the Negroes of Washington was dedicated to St. Augustine. But the seed sown by Father Barotti had taken root and it flourished at the end of the nineteenth century under the care of Monsignor John E. Burke, the great apostle of the Negroes and a Dominican tertiary.

Monsignor Burke saw in Martin a powerful ally and became an ardent promoter of devotion to the holy Negro, aided by the Dominican Sisters of Sparkill, New York, to whom he had entrusted one of his schools for Negroes, St. Benedict's

Home, in 1886. The first articles in North America on the life and virtues of Martin de Porres appeared in the school's periodical, the *St. Benedict's Home Journal*.

That was the point of departure for a movement which today has acquired national importance. Monsignor Burke guided it in two directions: propaganda and devotion. Thus, while he wrote articles for the *Journal*, he also composed a prayer to Blessed Martin for which he obtained an indulgence of 100 days from Pope Leo XIII.

That was in 1894. Five years before, in 1889, the first life of Martin de Porres in English was published in New York. It was a translation from the Italian, with a preface by the future Cardinal Vaughan.

After Martin's cause was reopened, Father McGlynn and Father Georges, Dominicans of St. Joseph's Province, contributed to making him better known with their biographies and numerous articles in the Dominican magazine, *The Torch*. And when the Blessed Martin Guild was founded by Father Edward L. Hughes, O.P., editor of *The Torch*, the diffusion of prayer leaflets and brochures mounted into the hundreds of thousands.

In 1936 the Dominican Sisters of the Perpetual Rosary of Union City, New Jersey, became zealous promoters of devotion to Blessed Martin by means of novenas and triduums in their Blue Chapel, under the promotion of Father Hughes. The most notable result of these efforts was the permission granted by the Holy See to various dioceses in the United States to render public veneration to Blessed Martin, even outside of the churches and chapels of the Dominican Order.[19]

In contrast to this consoling progress in the field of devotion to Blessed Martin, it was somewhat disconcerting to learn of the failure of the three Apostolic Processes on cases of remarkable healing which, nevertheless, were not recognized as miraculous. These occurred in the dioceses of Cajamarca, Peru (1928); Detroit, Michigan (1941); and the Transvaal in Africa (1948).

Then suddenly, as happens for all things too long awaited, between March and April of 1962, the news spread abroad that the canonization of Martin de Porres was near and certain because two of the many extraordinary cases of healing attributed to his intercession had been declared by doctors to be beyond any natural explanation and had been recognized by the ecclesiastical authorities as authentic miracles.

Fourteen years had passed since the first miracle. It had taken place in Asunción, Paraguay, where Dorothy Caballero Escalante, a widow who bore with ease the weight of her eighty-seven years and enjoyed excellent health, had fallen ill on September 8, 1948, with a serious intestinal malfunction. The doctors' diagnosis of an intestinal obstruction was confirmed by X-ray. The only possible remedy was an operation, but surgical intervention was excluded by the patient's general condition, which was complicated by a heart attack and the inevitable progress of the intestinal obstruction. A week later Dorothy Calallero Escalante's life hung by a thread.

Her daughter lived in Buenos Aires and was notified of the mother's illness. She at once prepared to go to her mother's side as quickly as possible. But on the evening of September 14, before she started out, she began to pray to Martin de Porres, asking him to save her mother's life. She prayed while she hurriedly prepared her valise; she prayed on the way from her home to the airport; she continued to pray during the flight.

And certainly she was still praying the next morning when, with a fast beating heart, she knocked at the door of a house in Asunción. But her prayer was transformed into the jubilation of thanksgiving when she learned that Dorothy Caballero

Escalante had been instantly and completely cured at dawn of the same day.

She was so completely restored to health that she lived several years more and celebrated her ninetieth birthday in good health. She did not, however, attain the century mark and so did not have the consolation of being present at the supreme glorification of the Saint who had helped her.

The other person cured by a miracle did have that joy. He was a child four and a half years old. On the evening of August 25, 1956, at Tenerife in the Canary Islands, Anthony Cabrera Pérez was perhaps dreaming of scaling the most inaccessible heights while he tried to climb up a wall under construction. But when a block of cement weighing about seventy pounds broke loose and rolled on his left foot, he was recalled to harsh reality. When the cement block was lifted off his foot, it was found to be terribly mangled. The child had suffered, as the doctors said later, bone and vascular lesions of an ischemic type. And as if that were not enough, very shortly thereafter the toes developed moist gangrene, followed by a general toxic state.

Four doctors of St. Eulalia's Hospital in Tenerife held a consultation because of Anthony's serious condition and agreed that it was necessary to amputate the limb to save the child's life. Over a period of seven days they had futilely tried every possible remedy to combat the gangrene, and there was no time to be lost.

But on September 1 a friend of the family arrived from Madrid and tried to comfort Anthony's parents with the thought of the power which surpasses the limits of medical science and the resources of nature. He gave the mother a picture of Blessed Martin, saying to her, "Pray to him, ask him to save the child for you."

With her whole heart the woman clung to this thread of hope, and while she repeatedly passed the picture over the injured foot of her child, she continued to pray until late that evening at the bedside with her husband and the superior of the hospital.

During the night something marvelous happened. The ischemia and the gangrene disappeared, the blood began to circulate again in the foot. Life had returned to dead tissues!

These two cases of miraculous cures were discussed and approved by the medical college of the Sacred Congregation of Rites on January 11 and October 18, 1961. On February 13, 1962, they were presented to the preparatory meeting of the theological consultors, and were definitely approved by the General Congregation of March 20, over which Pope John XXIII personally presided.

It was only during the first two weeks of April that the date of the canonization, May 6, was made public. Feverish activity began at once to organize pilgrimages and to secure good places, or at least some place, for the ceremony in St. Peter's. For years there had not been such a demand for tickets to a Vatican ceremony.

One is tempted to wonder how many pilgrimages there would have been had more advance notice been given, since so many were organized in the brief space of time available. They came from all parts of the world: from Europe and Asia and Africa; from South America, Martin's native land; and from North America, the land that had adopted him as its own.

And so, on the morning of May 6, the Vatican Basilica welcomed one of the most varied and exuberant throngs its ample naves had ever held, a crowd of about forty thousand persons. Once more, men of all colors from all the corners of the earth, in costumes of every nation and every social rank, stood side by side under the majestic arches of St. Peter's. There, even the most extreme contrasts are not jarring, for in their Father's house all men are simply brothers.

Before this throng, in the throbbing silence which followed the polyphony of the *Veni Creator,* the voice of Pope John XXIII was raised to proclaim the sanctity of Martin de Porres and the virtues which made him worthy of the supreme honor of canonization. His Holiness linked Martin's glorification with the fifth centenary of the canonization of Catherine of Siena. The celebration of her anniversary of canonization had culminated a few days before, with the unveiling of a monument honoring the great Dominican, placed beside Castel Sant'Angelo and facing St. Peter's. The Holy Father did not hesitate to set the figure of the humble brother of Lima beside that of the great saint of Siena.

From his niche in St. Peter's, where his statue was framed by a festal scintillation of lights, St. Dominic seemed to listen and to rejoice over the association of the two saints, pointing out to his sons scattered throughout the basilica and crowded in front of him in the tribune of the postulation, the identical key of the spirituality of the two saints, so different in other aspects—his spirituality, which had become the soul of their souls.

Indifferent to the restless, vivacious activity of photographers and journalists behind and above them, the members of the diplomatic corps listened to the words of the Holy Father in their tribune at the foot of the statue of the patriarch of the Friars Preachers. And around the papal throne, backed by hangings glimmering with gold, thirty-eight cardinals clad in splendid purple listened to the pope. They stretched in a double line along the center of the apse from Bernini's "Glory" to the altar of the Confession. From the tribunes erected against the main pillars, from the areas of the cross nave and central nave, all the attention of the immense throng was likewise concentrated on that voice, on the Latin as serene and luminous as the dome of Michelangelo, which proclaimed the long awaited message.

The Mass followed, a solemn Papal Mass with all the ceremonies characteristic of a canonization: the chant of the Epistle and Gospel in Latin and in Greek to attest the unity of the Church in the multiplicity of her rites; the procession of the offerings of candles and flowers, bread and wine, and cages of twittering birds, led by the highest authorities of the Order of St. Dominic and ending with two young Negro Dominicans, thrilled by the privilege of mounting the steps to the papal throne; the blaring of the silver trumpets; the cortege leaving the church, with the Pope smiling and blessing the crowd from the height of his *sedia gestatoria,* in full view of all.

Then the throng poured out on St. Peter's Square between the embracing arms of the colonnade, and all eyes turned towards a well-known window of the Apostolic Palace. Would the Holy Father still have the strength to recite the *Angelus* with his children, after a ceremony that had lasted nearly four hours?

Yes; at midday the window opened and against a dark background a white figure appeared, tiny in the distance. The kindly eyes of the pope looked again at that magnificent assembly of diverse people united for the glorification of the humble brother of Lima, of that "mulatto dog," as Martin would have said. Joy must have made the pope's fatigue vanish. His voice was full and vibrant, and he spoke of joy and festivity. What a feast day for Peru, which witnessed the glorification of one of its sons! What a feast day for Italy, which saw so many pilgrims gathered together on its soil to honor the new saint! But after all, what do feast days on earth amount to? Only in heaven shall we be able to grasp what sanctity means in its fullest sense. For in heaven, "what rejoicing, my children, what rejoicing!"

Against the clear blue of the Roman sky, the statues of the saints on the colonnade of St. Peter's Square seemed almost to come alive, as if to symbolize the rejoicing of the blessed in heaven. The flags and banners hanging from the central windows of the Vatican Basilica waved in the breeze, and the brilliant noonday light brought them to full beauty, turning them into a crown surrounding the tapestry which portrayed the heavenly glory of St. Martin de Porres.

CHAPTER

≻ 20 ≺

Then shall thy light break forth as the morning, and thy health shall speedily arise, and thy justice shall go before thy face, and the glory of the Lord shall gather thee up (Isa. 58:8).

St. Martin's posthumous career seems to move at an extraordinarily slow pace when compared with that of many saints of recent years. In some cases, members of the family have been present to address their praises and prayers to a saint on the day of his canonization. In one case—that of St. Maria Goretti—the saint's own mother had that privilege.

But for Martin de Porres, long intervals of time separate the various steps required to reach the honors of the altar.

Thirty years elapsed between his death and the signing of the decree for the introduction of the cause; ten years between the signing of the decree, its arrival in Lima, and the actual beginning of the Apostolic Process; eighty-five years from the beginning of the Process to the proclamation of the heroism of his virtues; seventy-four years elapsed between that proclamation and his beatification; in all, two centuries from his death to his beatification.

For ninety years after the beatification, the Sacred Congregation of Rites suspended all activity in the cause of Martin de Porres, and even when the cause was reopened in 1926, thirty-six more years went by until the date of his canonization was reached. In all, the space of three hundred and twenty-three years divided his death and his canonization.

One is inclined to ask why all this delay? In God's plan, nothing happens by chance. If the divine Sower drops the seed into the furrow and "sleeps at night while the seed sprouts," the night of God can be more or less long, but His rising is a sign of the dawn of the day in which the ripened fruit is ready to be harvested.

Certainly Martin's body, placed in the sepulcher as the seed is planted in the earth, did not remain inert. Even the earth that came in contact with his body became a healing and revivifying agent. But above all, Martin's spirit remained, living and working among his own.

Even today, Martin still lives in his own land. I felt that one evening when I met an old Peruvian lady in Rome. With the charm that we find in those who are trying to speak a language not their own, she talked to me of her distant land.

At one point I asked her, "Did you ever hear of Blessed Martin de Porres?"

Her face lit up. "Fray Martín!"

It was as if I had mentioned the dearest member of her family. But her tone of voice also carried a note of great amazement. Was that a question that needed to be asked?

Everyone in Peru knew "Fray Martín." And she continued to talk about him, not as someone who belongs to history and nothing more, but as a person with whom one has daily, affectionate contacts. She told me of one reason, among many others, why she loved Martin so much. It was nothing astounding, only one of those little trifles, one of those delicate attentions between friends.

One of her nephews was a student parachutist. He was a little uneasy the day he was to make his first jump. If he at least had with him a little holy picture! But now he could not get one. "Oh Fray Martín!"

He glanced down on the floor of the cockpit of the plane, and a little picture of the Sacred Heart of Jesus met his eyes, fallen from who knows where. With the image of the Sacred Heart of Jesus, he jumped tranquilly and he gently floated down to the earth under the light cupola of his parachute, cradled by the breeze.

Any one who consults the archives of St. Martin's Guild in New York or the Blessed Martin Society in Chicago will find abundant material for a sketch of the more modern Martin. These associations were founded by Father E. L. Hughes, O.P., the first in 1935 and the second in 1941. They resemble the *Sociedad y Hermandad del Beato Martín de Porres,* founded by Father D. Iriarte, O.P., in Lima. From all parts of the United States come testimonies of graces attributed to the intercession of Brother Martin. A perusal of the letters in those files demonstrates the stupendous capacity of Martin de Porres to adapt himself to the life of our time, and one sees him exercising not only his old skill as a healer of souls and bodies, but other skills he would never have imagined he would one day possess, such as making electrical equipment and radios work, or refueling in mid-flight planes whose supply of fuel has been exhausted. Learning he has these "skills" peculiar to our modern life increases our confidence in him and our affection for him.

Perhaps precisely because of the holy ease with which he adapts himself to the needs of life today, Martin has conquered the hearts of the North Americans and has become a citizen of the United States, without renouncing one iota of his native rights in South America.

Nevertheless, this is only one aspect of St. Martin. It is perhaps the most popular aspect, but also the least profound. The master general of the Order saw the importance of his cause in quite another light when he wrote to the Dominican provincial of New York, the Very Reverend Terence S. McDermott, O.P., to express his satisfaction with the intelligent activity carried on and encouraged by the Dominicans of the United States. The master general expressed the hope that such generous efforts would be crowned by the consolation of seeing the name of such a worthy son of St. Dominic added to the list of saints. "That day," wrote the Most Reverend Martin Stanislaus Gillet on June 11, 1936, "will add new splendor to our holy Order by the exaltation of one of the greatest of her sons. But it will also be a day of special triumph for the entire Catholic Church, for it will be yet another proof that her all-embracing charity transcends the barriers of race and class." [1]

Peacemaker among diverse races; that is what St. Martin is, principally, for the people of North America.

There is a propaganda stamp which, between the words, "Blessed Martin—Peacemaker," shows a picture of Martin with his open arms encircling two young men, one white and one colored, who are shaking hands.

If he did only this, St. Martin would have accomplished a great deal. The presence in the United States of thirteen million Negroes constitutes a serious problem and a vast field for the laborers of the Gospel. While this multitude strives to secure social rights equal to those of the whites, it has not yet displayed much interest in the true faith. Not even one-fiftieth of the Negroes in the United States belong to the Catholic Church.

Martin's image, raised above this disorientated race, has two missions: to break down the prejudice of the whites, showing them by the example of the high state of perfection he attained that God makes no distinction between races or people but offers all men of good will the grace of the dignity of divine adoption, and to point out to the Negroes that the Catholic Church, the depository of the treasures of the Redemption, is the only institution capable of securing for their race, degraded and humiliated through the centuries, that true nobility common to all men who can call themselves, and are, sons of God.

Although the racial problems of the New World are at the moment so acute and so far from a satisfactory solution, they diminish before the greater ones of the Old World, where many colored peoples are confronted with entirely new problems and responsibilities as a consequence of their recently acquired independence.

It can be understood how His Eminence Cardinal Rugambwa could say on the day after the canonization that "especially because of the particular needs of our own times, we thank God for St. Martin's providential mission during the course of his life and during the twentieth century." His Eminence synthesized this mission by pointing out to men the fundamental truth of love:

Even in Martin's time, when the races of the Occident were penetrating the Americas, and then in the following centuries which saw their penetration into Africa . . . , it was necessary to remind Christians of the great truth our Lord extolled so often: the brotherhood of men under the paternity of God. "A new commandment I give you, that you love one another: that as I have loved you, you also love one another" (John 13:34). It was necessary to remind Christians that the fundamental law of fraternal love cannot tolerate any difference between men, since Christ recognizes no such differences, and so there must be no difference based on race, on riches, on social position. . . .

God in His wisdom and goodness raised up a man whose own life was to make him an apostle of this truth. . . .

Let us admire now the work of God in preparing His chosen servant for this task. Martin de Porres was of mixed blood, Spanish on his father's side and African on his mother's side. Thus, in his own person he was a link joining together the different races. . . .

In Lima there were very sharp distinctions between different races, but . . . certainly in Martin's eyes, everyone was a brother.[2]

To regard every man as a brother. Is that not the only, true solution to every racial and social problem? Thus, as early as January 10, 1945, in response to the petition of the Peruvian episcopate, the Sovereign Pontiff, Pope Pius XII, proclaimed Martin de Porres the patron of social justice in the Republic of Peru.[3]

This, then, will be St. Martin's mission throughout the centuries: to bring about peace between white men and colored men, to bring about peace between men of different social classes, showing by his example how the fundamental law of charity should be carried into practice.

It is a great and necessary mission, for never has social justice been so discussed as in our own time, but in no other era has society's inability to find a just solution been so apparent. Often the remedy applied does not cure the material suffering, and it increases the spiritual suffering by sowing hate. Perhaps this is because anyone who treats social questions today cannot ignore that tinge of hate with which the Marxist theories have colored such questions, even if fighting against it is the only recognition he gives to that tinge of hate. It is difficult to avoid the contagion of those theories.

It is possible to take a stand against certain ideas and then, in the process of fighting them, adopt the same methods as those who profess those ideas. Hatred thus succeeds in finding a place even in the field of charity. It is the old story of the bad seed sown with the good.

As one modern writer has stated: "Catholic youth is losing its sense of charity. It is strange that the maturation of the social conscience, in the tormented, disorderly, yet almost sublime struggle of our day, has almost reached the point where 'charity' has come to include the deprecated 'paternalism' of the Marxist idea.

"While the Orient offers to the minds of our youth this contribution to the confusion of ideas, the Occident contributes in the other sense with its 'woe to the vanquished' to be applied to life's defeats. . . .

"From the level of charity, which is the consequence of the spiritual level and is nourished by it, action for greater justice on the social level springs naturally and legitimately, as does that on the political level." [4]

As we have seen, Martin was a pioneer in the field of social action, and an exceptional organizer. But not only the originality and the vastness of his work make him an example for those who dedicate themselves to social work; it is likewise his way of working that makes him a model.

"There are very few on earth who know how to love as Christ loved," wrote Father Voillaume to his Little Brothers of Jesus after he had meditated near the relics of St. Martin, on the altar of the Peruvian saints in the church of the Holy

Rosary in Lima, together with those of St. Rose and Blessed John Massias. "Some pretend they know how to do it, but their love is often deformed by a beginning of hate, by a haughty piety or a false sweetness which serves to avoid the exacting demands of justice." Almost interpreting a desire of Martin de Porres, he asked for those who would become apostles, "not a counterfeit of love, not even the piety of a strong man, not even a love troubled by revolt or hate for the oppressors of the poor. No, but . . . the strength and the sweetness of a love which can come only from the heart of Christ Jesus." [5]

Now that the authority of the Church has raised him so high that he can serve as a standard-bearer for all the forces of Christ here on earth, Martin has a message reserved by providence for us of the twentieth century.

And what will the little mulatto brother teach, if not what it means to love with a "love which can come only from the heart of Christ Jesus?"

Martin will not deliver impressive discourses. He will speak to us through the example he gave during his life. He will take us by the hand and lead us to the feet of his great Friend, Christ crucified, so that we may understand what charity is and how much it can do.

He will say nothing new to us. He will recall things we have heard many times, but which are so simple that we forget them immediately, or live as if we had forgotten them.

Martin will remind us, first of all, that charity is indispensable if we wish to be Christians, because it is the only sign God has given us by which we may be known as His followers.

He will say, too, that it is the only efficacious means to heal the world. It was the means our Lord and Savior Jesus Christ used, so that He could say, "I have conquered the world."

Then Martin will make us see that charity and hate are

incompatible, and that we are deluding ourselves if we think we are signed with the sign of the followers of Christ while we allow hate, under any disguise, to insinuate itself into our soul, which is the sanctuary of divine love.

And he will insist that authentic charity does not consist purely and simply in giving. One could speak with the tongues of angels and men and be only as sounding brass and tinkling cymbal, and even distribute all one's possessions to the poor, without sharing in the banquet of charity.

Martin will make us see all this in the book in which he himself read it, leading men to the feet of the crucified Christ, who communicated the secrets of His heart to him, raising him up to the point of ecstasy.

But in His turn, the Master will send us to the faithful disciple who succeeded so perfectly in carrying out the mandate of love. He will tell us to do as he did, who did good without making any distinction between the oppressed and the oppressors, who repaid injuries with benefits, and could not endure the thought—he who was so willing to be insulted—that the most insolent among his neighbors might think his love and benevolence had diminished as a result of their insults.

The Master will make us understand that it is possible for us in the twentieth century, even as it was possible for Martin de Porres in the seventeenth, to find the solution to every social or individual problem in perfect charity, in that supernatural charity which becomes a principle of action after it has been developed by contemplation.

Happy the day, then, that witnessed the supreme glorification of the Saint of charity. The divine Sower jealously preserved the fruit of the plant that sprouted three centuries ago in the earth of Peru, but the Vicar of the Lord of the harvest has opened the door of the granary, while all over a world devastated by hate the furrows lie open, hungry for the seed.

If we know how to accept that seed "with a good and perfect heart," swept clear of thorns and stones, a new springtime will flower in the valley of our exile, and the fields of the Lord will be filled with good grain, the fruit of the seed which germinates after a long sleep and sprouts to multiply itself. "First the stalk, then the ear, then the grain in the full ear."

BIBLIOGRAPHY

Official Documents

Processus ordinaria auctoritate fabricatus super Sanctitate Vitae, Virtutibus heroicis et Miraculis; Manuscript of the Archives of the Order of Friars Preachers, Santa Sabina, Rome, segn. X. 2404 of fol. 629 with two series of numbering: cc. 1–542: *Processus* 1660; cc. 1087: *Processus* 1664.

Positio super Dubio an constet de fama sanctitatis in genere, ita ut deveniendum sit ad Inquisitionem specialem (Romae: 1669); Archives of the Postulation O.P., M. 15. I.

Beatificationis et Canonizationis Servi Dei Fratris Martini de Porres, Laici Ordinis S. Dominici, Processus Limanus in specie, auctoritate Apostolica constructus (a. 1678–1712); 9 manuscript volumes of the Archives of the Order of Friars Preachers, Santa Sabina, Rome, X. 2406–14.

Actus authentici, varia documenta foliaque adversaria de virtutibus, miraculis, et cultu; Mss. et typ. ed.; Archives of the Postulation O.P., X. 2405.

Responsio ad Novas Animadversiones R.P.D. Fidei Promotoris super Dubio an constet de Virtutibus ecc. (Romae: 1742); Archives of the Postulation O.P., M. 15. III.

Novissimae Animadversiones cum Responsionibus super Dubio an constet de Virtutibus ecc. (Romae: 1762); Archives of the Postulation O.P., M. 15. IV.

Proceso de Beatificación de fray Martín de Porres (Palencia: 1960).

Canonizationis Beati Martini de Porres Positio super Miraculis (Rome: 1962).

Acta Gregorii XVI, Vol. 2, pp. 217–19 (Romae: 1901).

Analecta S.O. FF. Praedicatorum, Vol. 17, pp. 651–53.

Acta Capitulorum Generalium O.P., Vol. VII, VIII, IX.

QUETIF-ECHARD, *Scriptores O.P.,* t. II, p. 989.

Biographies

DE MEDINA, Bernardo, *Vida prodigiosa del venerable siervo de Dios Fr. Martín de Porras* (Lima: 1673; Madrid: 1675). This life, the first biography of St. Martin, was reproduced by the Bollandists in *Acta Sanctorum,* Nov. 5.

MARCHESE, Domenico Maria, *Sacro Diario Domenicano,* t. VI, pp. 6–24. (Napoli: 1681).

MELENDEZ, Juan, *Tesoros verdaderos de las Yndias en la Historia de la gran Provincia de San Juan Bautista del Perú de el Orden de Predicadores,* t. III, pp. 201–346 (Roma: 1682).

ANONYMOUS, *Prodigiosa e ammirabile Vita del gran Servo di Dio Fr. Martino Porres, Terziario Professo dell'Ordine del glorioso Patriarca S. Domenico* (Palermo: 1696).

DE LIMA, Manuel, *Agiologio Dominico*, t. IV, pp. 297–317 (Lisbona: 1712).
PONSI, Domenico, *Ristretto della vita, virtù e miracoli del ven. Servo di Dio Fr. Martino Porres* (Roma: 1732).
ANONYMOUS, *Compendio de la prodigiosa vida del Venerable Siervo de Dios Fr. Martín de Porres, Natural de Lima, Religioso Donado Profeso de la Orden de Predicadores, Sacado de los Autores los RR. PP. MM. Fray Jayme, Barón y Fran Juan Meléndez de la misma Orden* (Barcelona: 1799).
ANONYMOUS, *Vita del B. Martino de Porres, Terziario Professo dell'Ordine de' Predicatori nella Provincia di S. Giovanni Battista del Perù* (Roma: 1837).
VENTURA, Gioacchino, *I disegni della Divina Misericordia sopra le Americhe* (Panegyric of Blessed Martin delivered during the triduum for the beatification in the Church of Santa Maria sopra Minerva) (Rome: 1838).
VALDEZ, José Manuel, *Vida admirable del Bienaventurado Martín de Porres natural de Lima y Donado Profeso del Convento del Rosario del Orden de Predicadores de esta ciudad* (Lima: 1863), 26th ed. (Lima: 1945).
HERBERT, Lady, *The Life of Blessed Martin de Porres* (New York: 1889).
VALDIZAN, Hermilio, *Martín de Porres Cirujano* (Roma: 1913).
OSENDE, Victorino, *Vida Sobrenatural del Beato Martín de Porres* (Lima: 1917).
CEPEDA, Felix A., *Vida del B. Fray Martín de Porres, sacada de "Flores de América"* (San Antonio, Texas: 1921).
MARTINDALE, C. C., *Blessed Martin de Porres—The Life of an American Negro* (St. Louis: 1924).
IRIARTE, Domingo, *Vida prodigiosa del gran Taumaturgo Peruano B. Martín de Porres* (Lima: 1926).
A DOMINICAN FATHER, *Blessed Martin Porres, O.P.* (Dublin: 1930).
FUMET, Stanislas, *Le Bienheureux Martin de Porrès, serviteur prodigieux des Frères Prêcheurs* (Paris: 1933).
GEORGES, Norbet, *Meet Brother Martin!* (New York: 1935).
KEARNS, J. C., *The Life of Blessed Martin de Porres, saintly American Negro and Patron of Social Justice* (New York: 1937).
TORNERO, José, *El Bienaventurado fr. Martín de Porres, Dominico Peruano, Apostol de la Justicia Social* (Caracas: 1938).
GRILLET, Martino, *Il B. Martino de Porres, Confessore Domenicano* (Italian translation of a Dominican religious of the monastery of Bibbiena) (Roma: 1940).
WINDEATT, Mary Fabian, *Lad of Lima* (New York: 1941).
GRANGER, Arthur M., *Vie du Bienheureux Martin de Porrès* (St. Hyacinthe, Québec: 1945).
DOHERTY, Eddie, *Martin* (New York: 1948).
BEDOYA VILLACORTA, Antolín, *Fray Martín de Porres y su apostolado hipocrático* (Lima: 1949).
GAFFNEY, Henry, *Blessed Martin, Wonder-Worker* (Tralee, Ireland: 1949).
GARCIA FIGAR, Antonio, *Biografía breve del Beato Martín de Porres* (Madrid: 1952).
DOHERTY, Eddie, *Blessed Martin de Porres* (St. Paul, Minnesota: 1953).

VAN DE VYVERE, *De Gelukzalige Martinus de Porres. Uit, het fransch vertaald. Dominicaansch Missiewerk* (Groot Regijnhof, 52, Sint Amandsberg).

BEDOYA VILLACORTA, Antolín, *Martín de Porres y los Congresos panamericanos de Farmacia* (Lima: 1954).

VARGAS UGARTE, Rubén, *El Beato Martín de Porres,* 2nd ed. (Palencia: 1955).

SUAREZ, Juan J., *El mulato de la escoba,* 2nd ed. (Buenos Aires: 1956).

MINGOTE, Angel A., LAPAYESE, E., SANCHEZ SILVA, J. M., *Fray Escoba* (Palencia: 1958).

GAINOR, Leo C., *Blessed Martin de Porres, Powerful Patron of the Sick, Infirm, Needy* (Appleton, Wisconsin: 1959).

ROMERO, Emilio, *El santo de la escoba* (Lima: 1959).

BEDOYA VILLACORTA, Antolín, *Mosaicos históricos del Siervo de Dios fray Martín de Porres* (Lima: 1959).

VELASCO, Salvador de, *Fray Martín de Porres,* 2nd ed. (Mexico: 1959).

GALDUF, Vicente, *El primer Santo negro, Martín de Porres* (Barcelona: 1961).

SANCHEZ SILVA, José M., *San Martín de Porres* (Palencia: 1962).

WILMS, Hieronymus M., *Der Heilige der Neuen Welt, Bruder Martin von Porres O.P.* (Köln: 1962).

Articles

DE GANAY, M. C., *"Les Bienheureux frères convers de l'Ordre de Saint-Dominique"* in *"La Vie Spirituelle,"* Oct., 1923.

DE GANAY, M. C., *Comment représenter les Saints Dominicains* (Autun: 1925).

JANVIER, R. P., *"La canonisation d'un noir"* in *Nouvelles Religieuses,* 1925.

McGLYNN, M. M., *"A Negro Saint for Negroes"* in *Dominicana,* Sept., 1931.

LA FARGE, John, *"Blessed Martin, Patron of Social and Interracial Justice"* in *The Catholic Mind,* Vol. XXXV, No. 23, Dec. 8, 1937.

Homenaje a Martin de Porres, special number of *Mercurio Peruano* of Lima on the occasion of the third centenary of the death of Martin de Porres; A. XIV, Vol. XXI, No. 153–154, Nov.–Dec. 1939.

Special number of *La Rosa del Perù* of Lima, published on the occasion of the third centenary of the death of Martin de Porres, A. 38, No. 12, Dec., 1939.

THE BLESSED MARTIN GUILD, *Fifteenth Anniversary Book* (articles from *The Torch,* 1945–1950 [New York: 1950]).

NOTES

CHAPTER ONE

[1] Cf. L. D. Baldwin, *The Story of the Americas*, p. 91 (New York: 1943).

[2] Cf. *ibid.*, pp. 109–10.

[3] Cf. *ibid.*, pp. 150 ss.

[4] The *Enciclopedia Universal Ilustrada Europeo-Americana*, Espasa Calpe (vol. 51, p. 587, *Rimac*) explains the derivation of the name of Lima from that of the river Rimac by the habit of the Spanish conquistadors of changing into "l" the soft "r" of the local language, even though it is possible that the word "Lima" may derive from the pronunciation of the natives of the coastal regions, being less pure than that of the natives of the mountain areas. Since the word *"rimac"* in the Quechua language means "the speaker," it could have been given to the river as a poetical way of expressing the murmuring of its waters.

According to W. H. Prescott (*The History of the Conquest of Peru*, p. 258) the river derived its name from that of a temple situated in the valley and often frequented by the Indians because of its oracles.

D. Enrique Tusquets (*Los grandes contrastes de un continente*, p. 376) disregards the generally accepted etymology and writes: "Lima was founded by Pizarro . . . and given the names of *Lima* and *City of the Kings*. He gave it the first name because of the great number of lime trees growing in the region, and the second, because he intended it, with the passage of time, to become the capital of the vast empire of the Spanish possessions in America." (*"Lima"* means fruit of the lime tree; the Peruvians call both the fruit and the tree *"lima."*)

[5] *Responsio ad Novas Animadversiones R.P.D. Fidei Promotoris super Dubio ecc.*, pp. 4-5 (Romae: 1742). All succeeding references to this source will be simply *Responsio*.

[6] Cf. H. G. Gaffney, *Blessed Martin, Wonder Worker*, pp. 12-13 (Tralee: 1949).

[7] *Responsio*, p. 5.

CHAPTER TWO

[1] Cf. Gaffney, *op. cit.*, p. 16.

[2] Cf. J. C. Kearns, *The Life of Blessed Martin de Porres*, p. 15 (New York: 1937).

[3] Cf. *Vita del B. Martino de Porres*, by an anonymous author, p. 9. (Rome: 1837).

[4] Cf. *ibid.*, p. 10.

CHAPTER THREE

[1] G. Pascoli, *La piccozza*.

[2] Letter 8.

[3] *Responsio*, (XXIV), p. 103. (Throughout the footnotes, the Roman numeral in parentheses is the number of the testimony in the *Processus*, to which the footnote refers.)

CHAPTER FOUR

[1] Letter 242.
[2] St. Catherine of Siena, Letter 201.
[3] *Responsio* (XXII), p. 74.
[4] *Responsio* (VII), pp. 26-27.
[5] *Ibid.* (IV), p. 58.
[6] *Ibid.* (IV), p. 104.
[7] The *venia* is a full-length prostration made by religious to ask pardon (as in the chapter of faults) or as an act of humility and submission (as in receiving a formal precept).
[8] *Vita del B. Martino de Porres,* anonym., p. 20.
[9] *Responsio* (VIII), p. 103; (XLIX), p. 60.
[10] *Ibid.* (VII), p. 26; (V et seq.), pp. 91-92.
[11] *Ibid.* (XXII), p. 56.
[12] *Ibid.* (VIII), p. 103.

CHAPTER FIVE

[1] "The religious state is a certain discipline or exercise for striving for perfection. But those who are instructed or trained for the attainment of some goal should follow the direction of another, and be instructed and trained according to the judgment of that person so that they may reach the aforesaid goal, like disciples under a master" (*Summa theol.,* IIa IIae, q. 186, a. 5).
[2] *Responsio* (CXV), p. 39.
[3] *Dialogue,* c. LXVI.
[4] *Responsio* (LV), p. 79.
[5] *Ibid.* (XXXV), p. 37, and (XXII), p. 79.
[6] *Ibid.* (V), p. 40; (XXIV and XLVIII), p. 78.
[7] *Ibid.* (CXV), p. 79.
[8] *Positio super Dubio an constet de fama sanctitatis in genere ecc.* (Romae: 1669), p. 6.
[9] Cf. *Responsio* (XXXII), p. 43.
[10] *Ibid.* (VI, VII, XXIII), p. 16; (LV, CXV), p. 17.
[11] Cf. *ibid.* (VI), p. 15.
[12] *Ibid.* (VII), p. 15.
[13] Cf. *ibid.* (LI, LX, LXII, XXIII, CXV), pp. 14-16.
[14] Cf. *ibid.* (XII), p. 56.
[15] *Ibid.* (CXVII), p. 17.
[16] Cf. *Dialogue,* c. LXVI.
[17] Cf. *Positio,* p. 39.
[18] *Responsio* (XII, XIII, XV, XXIII), pp. 90-91.
[19] *Positio,* p. 28.

[20] *Responsio* (XXX), pp. 36, 87; (XXII), p. 88.
[21] *Ibid.* (CVI), p. 40.
[22] *Ibid.* (XV, IX, VII, XXII), pp. 86–88; (LIII), p. 91.
[23] Cant. 3:2, 4.
[24] *Responsio* (XXIII), p. 39.
[25] Cf. *ibid.* (LIX), p. 87.
[26] *Ibid.* (XII), p. 89.
[27] Cf. *ibid.* (XLVIII), p. 98.
[28] *Ibid.* (I), p. 88.
[29] *Ibid.* (XXX), p. 36.

CHAPTER SIX

[1] *Processus ordinaria auctoritate fabricatus, super sanctitate Vitae, Virtutibus heroicis et Miraculis* (LXII), cc. 496–97 (1660).
[2] *Responsio* (V et seq.), pp. 91–96.
[3] *Ibid.* (VII), p. 96.
[4] Cf. Mark 5:1–13.
[5] Cf. *ibid.* (XLII), pp. 96–97; see also (VI and VII), p. 96.
[6] *Ibid.* (XXII), p. 100; (E), p. 99.
[7] *Ibid.* (VI), p. 24.
[8] *Ibid.* (XLIX), p. 74.
[9] Letter 217.
[10] *Beatificationis et Canonizationis Servi Dei Fratris Martini de Porres, Laici Ordinis S. Dominici, Processus Limanus in specie* (I), t. I., c. 221-b (1678).

CHAPTER SEVEN

[1] Ps. 18:6.
[2] *Positio,* p. 7.
[3] *Ibid.,* p. 9.
[4] *Responsio* (XXXV), p. 101.
[5] *Acta Tolosana,* n. 15; cf. Lacordaire, *Life of St. Dominic.*
[6] *Processus* 1660, c. 293; *Responsio* (XXXV), p. 101.
[7] *Responsio* (I), p. 102.
[8] St. Catherine of Siena, Letter 67.
[9] *Ibid.,* Letter 217.
[10] *Responsio* (XXIII) and (XLIX), p. 100.
[11] Letter 217.
[12] Phil. 2:8; cf. *Summa theol.,* IIa IIae, q. 186, aa. 1, 5.
[13] *Responsio* (I), p. 81.
[14] *Positio,* n. 10, p. 16.
[15] *Responsio* (XXIV), p. 105.
[16] Letters 84 and 85.
[17] Letters 201 and 203.
[18] *Responsio* (VII), p. 82.

[19] Such expressions, of course, are deserving of all respect because they have been conceived and used by great saints and masters of the spiritual life. Nevertheless, I consider it an abuse to place too much emphasis on the negative aspect of obedience—the renunciation of one's own will—instead of emphasizing the positive aspect, which is the seeking of the will of God in lawful authority. If the positive aspect is slighted, there is no justification for the negative aspect. Cf. *Summa theol.*, IIa IIae, q. 104, a. 1.

[20] Cf. *Summa theol.*, IIa IIae, q. 104, aa. 2, 3.

[21] *Responsio* (VII), p. 83.

[22] Letter 217.

[23] *Responsio*, p. 130 and (V), p. 85; *Positio*, p. 6.

[24] *Positio*, p. 25; *Responsio* (II), p. 83 and (VII, VIII), p. 84.

[25] *Responsio* (IX), pp. 104–5.

CHAPTER EIGHT

[1] Cf. H. Gaffney, *op. cit.*, p. 18.

[2] Ps. 15:6.

[3] *Dialogue*, CLVIII.

[4] Cf. *Summa theol.*, Ia. q. 3, a. 4.

[5] *Responsio* (II), pp. 10–11.

[6] Cf. *ibid.* (VIII), p. 11.

[7] *Ibid.* (VII), p. 11; cf. also (I–CXV), pp. 10–12.

[8] Cf. Ps. 118:99-100; Matt. 5:8.

[9] Dante, *Paradiso*, Canto XII, 99.

[10] Cf. *Summa theol.*, IIa IIae, q. 188, a. 6.

[11] Dante, *Paradiso*, Canto XXII, 42.

[12] *Responsio* (VII), p. 10.

[13] *Ibid.* (VIII to LV), pp. 12–13.

[14] *Ibid.* (XXIV), p. 13.

[15] St. Catherine of Siena, Letter 242.

[16] *Responsio* (I and VII), p. 10.

[17] *Ibid.* (I), p. 9; *Novissimae Animadversiones cum Responsionibus super Dubio ecc.*, Rome, 1762 (XXII, II, V, XLIX, LXXVII), pp. 11–14. In the passages cited, response is made to the objections raised by the Promoter of the Faith against the testimony regarding the presence of St. Martin at Lima and elsewhere at the same time.

[18] *Vita*, p. 85; cf. also Kearns, op. cit., pp. 121-22.

CHAPTER NINE

[1] John 12:24.

[2] *Responsio* (XXX, VIII, XXIV), pp. 19–20; *Positio*, p. 6.

[3] Sr. Maria della Trinitá, *Colloquio Interiore*, n. 359, p. 180, Custodia di T. S. (Gerusalemme: 1942).

[4] *Positio*, p. 30.

[5] *Responsio* (LV), p. 58.
[6] *Positio*, p. 37.
[7] *Responsio* (LIII), p. 63.
[8] *Positio*, p. 37.
[9] *Responsio* (XXIII), p. 66.
[10] *Ibid.* (VI), p. 64.
[11] *Positio*, p. 40.
[12] *Ibid.*, p. 37.
[13] *Responsio* (V), p. 61; (XLIX and LV), p. 62.
[14] *Positio*, p. 23.
[15] *Responsio* (LVII), p. 60.
[16] *Ibid.* (XXXVIII), p. 53; *Processus* 1660, c. 443.
[17] *Ibid.* (VII), p. 53.
[18] *Ibid.* (XXXVIII), p. 53.
[19] *Positio*, p. 43.
[20] *Ibid.*, p. 44.
[21] *Ibid.*, p. 45.
[22] Cf. Gaffney, *op. cit.*, p. 31.
[23] *Responsio* (XXIII), p. 28.
[24] Letter 32.
[25] *Dialogue*, c. XXX.

CHAPTER TEN

[1] *Responsio* (V), pp. 55–56, and (XXII), p. 54.
[2] *Ibid.* (VIII), pp. 46–47.
[3] Cf. *ibid.* (VII), pp. 64–65.
[4] *Ibid.* (LV), pp. 47–48; cf. Kearns, *op. cit.*, pp. 123–24.
[5] *Positio*, p. 31.
[6] *Responsio* (II), p. 111; *Positio*, p. 23.
[7] *Positio*, p. 24.
[8] *Responsio* (VII), p. 114; see also Kearns, *op. cit.*, pp. 125–26.
[9] *Ibid.* (LXI), p. 112.
[10] Dante, *Paradiso*, Canto XXX, 41.

CHAPTER ELEVEN

[1] The Spanish spelling of John's name is Macías, but in English and in Latin the name is spelled Massias.
[2] Cf. Anonymous, *Vita del B. Giovanni Massias*, pp. 1–13 (Rome: 1837); Kearns; *op. cit.*, p. 105 f.
[3] Letters 246 and 194.
[4] *Responsio* (VII), p. 88; and *Processus* 1660 (XXXI), cc. 229–30.
[5] Cf. Kearns, *op. cit.*, p. 109.
[6] Letter 250.
[7] St. Gregory, *Homil. XI in Ev.*
[8] Cf. Gaffney, *op. cit.*, p. 31.

[9] *Responsio* (XXXVI), pp. 75, 113.
[10] *Processus*, 1660 (XXXVII), cc. 293–95.
[11] Dante, *Purgatorio*, Canto XV, 56 f.

CHAPTER TWELVE

[1] *Responsio* (XII), p. 48; (VI), p. 49.
[2] *Ibid.* (XXIII), p. 50.
[3] *Ibid.* (XIX), p. 50; (LV), p. 51 and (XII), p. 48.
[4] Cf. Kearns, *op. cit.*, p. 41.
[5] *Responsio* (VII), p. 56.
[6] *Processus* 1660 (XXXI), cc. 221–22.
[7] *Responsio* (XXX et seq.), pp. 51, 52; *Processus* 1660 (XXXI), cc. 223–24.
[8] Cf. Gaffney, *op. cit.*, p. 34.
[9] Cf. Kearns, *op. cit.*, pp. 50–51.
[10] *Vita*, p. 89; cf. also Kearns, *op. cit.*, p. 123.
[11] *Responsio* (V), p. 48; (II), p. 57.
[12] Gaffney, *op. cit.*, pp. 31–32; *Responsio*, pp. 130–31.
[13] St. Catherine of Siena, Letter 226.
[14] *Responsio* (VII), p. 55.
[15] *Processus* 1660 (XXXVII), c. 301.
[16] *Responsio* (VII and XXIV), pp. 53–54.
[17] Cf. Kearns, *op. cit.*, p. 47.
[18] *Responsio* (V), p. 52.
[19] *Positio*, p. 9.
[20] *Processus* 1660 (LXIII), c. 513.
[21] *Responsio* (VII), p. 55.
[22] *Homil. III in Evang.*
[23] *Responsio* (I), p. 44.
[24] *Dialogue*, ch. VII.

CHAPTER THIRTEEN

[1] *Responsio* (VII and LIII), p. 70; (XXIV), p. 72.
[2] *Positio*, pp. 44–45.
[3] St. Catherine of Siena, *Dialogue*, ch. LXXVIII.
[4] *Responsio* (II), p. 68.
[5] *Ibid.* (XXIII), p. 72.
[6] *Ibid.* (XII), pp. 68–69.
[7] *Positio*, p. 4.
[8] *Responsio* (VII), pp. 70–71.
[9] *Ibid.* (XII), pp. 68–70.
[10] *Positio*, p. 45.
[11] *Processus* 1678 (V),t. I, cc. 536–37.
[12] E. Doherty, *Martin*, p. 98 (New York: 1948).
[13] *Processus* 1660 (XXXVII), cc. 296–97; *ibid.* (LXII), cc. 500–501.
[14] *Positio*, p. 10; *Responsio* (VIII), p. 71; (XII), pp. 68–69.

CHAPTER FOURTEEN

[1] *Dialogue,* ch. XXVI.
[2] *Responsio* (CXV), p. 32.
[3] *Ibid.* (CXV), p. 41.
[4] *Ibid.* (XXX), pp. 42–43.
[5] *Ibid.* (LI), pp. 43 and 115.
[6] *Dialogue,* ch. LXXVII.
[7] St. Catherine, Letter 216.
[8] St. Catherine of Siena, *Dialogue,* ch. LXXVII.
[9] *Responsio* (VII), p. 75.
[10] *Ibid.* (VII), p. 76.
[11] *Ibid.* (VI), p. 76.
[12] *Ibid.* (I), p. 110.
[13] St. Catherine, Letter 213.
[14] *Positio,* pp. 41–42.
[15] *Processus* 1678 (I), t. I, cc. 264–65.

CHAPTER FIFTEEN

[1] *Processus* 1660 (VIII), cc. 81–85.
[2] *Positio,* p. 14.
[3] *Processus* 1660 (X), cc. 95–96.
[4] *Positio,* p. 15.
[5] *Novissimae* (XXII), p. 11.
[6] *Responsio,* p. 132.
[7] *Ibid.* (XXII), pp. 65–66.
[8] *"Tanto gli pesa la mano manca quanto la ritta,"* a saying of St. Catherine of Siena which has become an axiom in Italy. Cf. *Dialogue,* c. *CXLI.*
[9] *Positio,* p. 33.
[10] *Ibid.,* p. 28.
[11] *Ibid.,* p. 43.
[12] *Responsio* (XVI), p. 112.
[13] *Positio,* p. 46.
[14] *Ibid.,* pp. 11–12; *Processus* 1660 (V), c. 63-b.
[15] *Positio,* pp. 42–43.
[16] *Processus* 1660 (I), cc. 24–25.
[17] Cf. Kearns, *op. cit.,* p. 136.

CHAPTER SIXTEEN

[1] *Positio,* pp. 18 and 26.
[2] *Processus* 1660 (LXIII), c. 513.
[3] *Positio,* p. 34.
[4] *Processus* 1660 (I), c. 27.
[5] *Responsio* (V), p. 110.
[6] *Ibid.,* p. 129.

[7] *Ibid.* (V), pp. 116–17.
[8] *Ibid.* (LXII), p. 116.
[9] *Ibid.* (XI), p. 116.
[10] Cf. Kearns, *op. cit.*, p. 152.
[11] *Responsio* (VII), p. 117; (XXII), p. 118.
[12] *Ibid.* (XLIX), p. 119.
[13] *Positio*, p. 32.
[14] *Ibid., loc. cit.*
[15] *Ibid.*, p. 33.
[16] *Responsio* (VII et seq.), pp. 117–19.

CHAPTER SEVENTEEN

[1] *Responsio* (VII and XXII), p. 118; (XLIX), p. 119.
[2] *Vita*, cit. p. 169.
[3] *Responsio* (XL), pp. 30, 34.
[4] *Positio*, p. 34.
[5] *Ibid.*, pp. 34–35.
[6] *Ibid.*, p. 26.
[7] *Ibid.*, p. 33.
[8] *Ibid.*, pp. 32, 36.

CHAPTER EIGHTEEN

[1] *Processus* 1660 (VIII), cc. 85–86; (LX), cc. 470–72; *Processus* 1678 (V), t. I, cc. 544–46.
[2] *Positio*, pp. 26–27; *Processus* 1660 (LXIII), c. 518.
[3] *Positio*, p. 12.
[4] *Vita*, cit. p. 185.
[5] Cf. Kearns, *op. cit.*, p. 159.
[6] *Ibid., loc. cit.*
[7] *Processus* 1660 (I), cc. 21–23; (LXIII), cc. 516–17.
[8] Martin was thus described by Cardinal Vidoni in the report of the Diocesan Process to the first preparatory congregation of July 21, 1668; cf. *Positio*, p. 7.
[9] *Positio*, pp. 19–22.

CHAPTER NINETEEN

[1] *Processus* 1664 (VII), c. 69; (XI), cc. 81–82.
[2] *Positio*, p. 47.
[3] *Ibid.*, pp. 47–49.
[4] *Ibid.*, pp. 53–69.
[5] Cf. Kearns, *op. cit.*, pp. 177–80.
[6] *Processus* 1660 (LXV), cc. 525–31.
[7] *Positio*, pp. 50–71.

[8] *Ibid.*, pp. 3 f.
[9] *Ibid.*, p. 1.
[10] Cf. Kearns, *op. cit.*, p. 175.
[11] *Processus* 1678, t. I, cc. 9–11.
[12] *Ibid.*, cc. 11–12.
[13] *Ibid.*, c. 84-b.
[14] *Ibid.* (I), c. 220.
[15] Cf. Kearn, *op. cit.*, pp. 180–82.
[16] *Vita*, pp. 190–92.
[17] *Ibid.*, pp. 192–94.
[18] Cf. Kearns, *op. cit.*, p. 209.
[19] *Ibid.*, p. 191; cf. also Gainor, *Blessed Martin de Porres*, pp. 109–12. In Spain, two outstanding workers for the cause of Martin have been Brother Benigno, a Dominican lay brother of Palencia, and Father Anthony Huguet, Dominican of Barcelona. Special recognition is also due to the Irish Dominicans.

CHAPTER TWENTY

[1] Cf. Kearns, *op. cit.*, p. 190.
[2] Discourse of His Eminence Cardinal Rugambwa during the celebrations in honor of St. Martin de Porres held in the Dominican church of Santa Maria sopra Minerva in Rome immediately after the canonization. Taken from *Missioni Domenicane*, n. 4, 1962, pp. 2–3.
[3] *Acta Apostolicae Sedis*, Ser. II, vol. XV (1948), pp. 444–45.
[4] Cf. U. Sciascia, *"Pier Giorgio Frassati a trent' anni dalla morte,"* in *Il Quotidiano*, July 3, 1955.
[5] Cf. R. Voillaume, *Come loro*, p. 410 (Rome: 1953).